CW00546155

Tom Ferris

THE IRISH NARROW GAUGE

A Pictorial History

Volume Two
The Ulster Lines

A CDR 4-6-4 tank shunts at Stanorlar in the 1930s. Len's of Sutton.

For Jonathan

Published by
Midland Publishing Limited
24 The Hollow, Earl Shilton
Leicester, LE9 7NA
England

ISBN 1-85780-017-6

Printed and bound by
Woolnough Bookbinding Limited
Irthlingborough, Northants.
NN9 5SE

Designed by
Midland Publishing
and Stephen Thompson Associates.

Typeset in
Garamond and Gill Sans.

Front cover photograph:
Though a pioneer in the use of diesel railcars, the CDR ran steam hauled excursions right up to the closure of the system in 1959. In the summer of that year, class 5 2-6-4T No.4 *Meenglas* heads such a train at Mountcharles on the line to Killybegs.
Drew Donaldson, courtesy W.T.Scott.

Title page photograph:
Londonderry & Lough Swilly Railway No.1 *J.T.Mackey,* a Black Hawthorn built 0-6-2T dating from 1882 has just arrived at Buncrana in this turn of the century view.
Charles Friel Collection.

Tom Ferris

THE IRISH NARROW GAUGE

A Pictorial History

Volume Two
The Ulster Lines

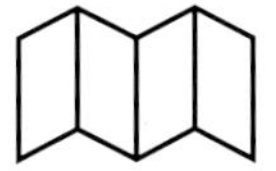

Midland Publishing
Limited

PREFACE AND ACKNOWLEDGEMENTS

As was the case with volume one of this work, a great many people have gone out of their way to be of assistance to me in the course of my research. Particular thanks are due to the photographers whose pictures appear in the pages that follow and to those who have made a point of collecting and conserving old railway photographs which might otherwise have been lost to us. Individuals who have allowed me access to their photographs or collections are: W.H.Butler, Desmond Coakham, John Edgington, Des Fitzgerald, Charles Friel, George Haire, R.C.Ludgate, Des McGlynn, Michael Pollard, Norman Johnson, J.H.Price and W.A.C.Smith. Tim Shuttleworth kindly allowed me to publish some of his own pictures and also put his considerable skills as a photographic printer, at my disposal. I must thank W.T.Scott for providing me with pictures taken by William Robb MBE and the late Drew Donaldson, both of whose collections are in his care.

I am grateful to the Deputy Keeper of the Records, Public Records Office of Northern Ireland for permission to reproduce some pictures from the Cooper collection which is in the care of the PRONI. I am also indebted to the trustees of the Ulster Folk and Transport Museum for permission to use pictures from their collection. Mark Kennedy of the Museum's Education Department was of particular assistance in obtaining information on the pictures available.

By the time this book is published the Museum's splendid new railway gallery will be open to the public at Cultra in County Down and visitors will be able to see the Museum's collections of both broad and narrow gauge locomotives and rolling stock from perspectives which were never possible in the cramped premises of the old Belfast Transport Museum, which the new building has replaced.

Special thanks are once again due to Richard Casserley for permission to use many of the superb photographs taken by his late father, H.C.Casserley, during the course of his many trips to Ireland. Another useful source of pictures from the early decades of this century was the collection of the late Ken Nunn, which is now in the care of the Locomotive Club of Great Britain. The LCGB's Graham Stacey was most helpful in obtaining pictures from this source.

Len's of Sutton were kind enough to lend me a large collection of Irish narrow gauge negatives many of which I have been able to use. Peter Kelly and Chris Milner editor and deputy editor respectively of Britain's oldest journal for the railway enthusiast, *The Railway Magazine*, allowed me to browse through their picture files and to publish some of the gems that I found there. I am most grateful for their assistance in this regard.

I wish to thank Joe Carroll of the South Donegal Railway Restoration Society for the use of some pictures in the Society's care. All of us with an affection for the Irish narrow gauge fervently hope that the SDRRS succeed in their ambitious project to rebuild part of the CDR from Ballybofey to near Donegal Town. The thought of CDR locomotives and stock once again running through Barnesmore Gap will quicken the pulse of many railway enthusiasts.

I was particularly fortunate in being able to pick the brains of Joe Curran, a son of Bernard L. Curran, the Manager and Secretary of the County Donegal from 1943 to 1966. Information from Joe cleared up a number of long standing queries which I had about the CDR and made me wish that I could have turned up other affable and articulate insiders like him, to speak for the other narrow gauge lines covered in these books.

Two Midland Publishing authors took time out from their own projects to help me with mine. In the middle of writing *Don't Knock The Southern*, George Behrend was kind enough to provide the account of his trip on the Giant's Causeway Tramway which he made before the last war, and which is published in the appropriate chapter of this book. Even as I harried him to complete his superb book, *Rails in the Isle of Man: A Colour Celebration*, to almost an impossibly tight schedule, Robert Hendry was able to find the picture that I wanted of an IMR engine in near original condition, in order that I could draw attention to the similarities between the engines produced by Beyer Peacock for the Isle of Man and those supplied to the Ballymena & Larne line in County Antrim – *see page 31*.

We have again utilised our well proven format for this two-volume work, aiming for high standards of readability coupled with photographs of high definition, and taking care to include the peripheral details, where they appear on the original illustrations. We have also made a conscious decision not to print any photographs across the fold.

We have fortunately been able to utilise good quality photographs in all but an handful of instances: the odd exceptions relate to some of the lines which were among the first to close. Priority for inclusion has, in some instances, been given to historical significance over technical perfection.

I must thank Chris Salter, my colleague at Midland Publishing and designer Steve Thompson, not just for their many hours of work in producing the book, but for their support and encouragement throughout the course of the project. Working with colleagues who have a real empathy for the subject has made the production process which has led to these books appearing, a rewarding and enjoyable one.

Last but by no means least I must put on record my thanks to my wife Elizabeth. As well as having to cope with many nights of interrupted sleep in the course of the last year, occasioned by the arrival of our third child, she has had to put up with me disappearing for long periods in the course of the gestation period which led to the birth of my narrow gauge twins. Without her help and support I would probably never have completed the books in time.

Despite the best efforts of all those who have helped me in the course of my narrow gauge odyssey to keep on the right track, the responsibility for the finished product rest with me and no blame for its inadequacies can be apportioned to any of the aforementioned persons. The final verdict rests with you, the reader, but if you derive at least a part of the enjoyment from it, that I have had in compiling it, then I think I will have done my job.

Tom Ferris
Shrewsbury, September 1993.

CONTENTS

INTRODUCTION

This, the second volume of *The Irish Narrow Gauge: A Pictorial History,* deals with those lines located within the province of Ulster. The term Ulster today is often used to refer to that part of Ireland which remains within the United Kingdom, the six counties which constitute Northern Ireland. The historic province of Ulster however has nine counties. In the partition of Ireland in the 1920s the three Ulster counties of Cavan, Donegal and Monaghan became part of the Irish Free State. This has led to the delightful anomaly of County Donegal, which includes the most northerly parts of the island of Ireland, being referred to as 'in the south'. In drawing our own boundaries between the two volumes which constitute this work, it seemed sensible to cover in volume one, those lines which became the responsibility of the Great Southern Railway on the amalgamation of the railways of the Irish Free State in 1925. This has led to our own geographical anomaly in that the last few miles of the Cavan & Leitrim Railway's main line passed through County Cavan, and thus took us prematurely into the province of Ulster.

The GSR were only interested in lines which were wholly located in the Irish Free State in 1925. By dint of the fact that the last few miles of the Londonderry & Lough Swilly Railway strayed over the border and into Northern Ireland to reach the city in its title, that concern remained independent. The County Donegal system also remained outside the clutches of the GSR. Its branch from Strabane to Derry ran entirely through Northern Ireland and the first part of its main line, from Strabane up the valley of the River Finn towards Stranorlar, ran through County Tyrone. Thus the two largest 3ft gauge systems in Ireland carried on after partition in much the same fashion as they had before, though with the complications of an international frontier crossing their tracks. The new border, as well as causing delays whilst trains and their contents were examined by Customs and Excise officials from both administrations, had the more serious longer term effect of disrupting patterns of economic activity which had built up over many years; indeed the promoters of these railways would have paid particular attention to such patterns in determining the routes their schemes would follow. This is not the appropriate forum to discuss the economic effects of the division of Ireland into two states but it is fair to say that it must have affected the fortunes of the two Donegal systems and in particular the L&LSR, as the border cut Londonderry off from that part of its natural economic hinterland which was in north Donegal.

The difficulties faced by the L&LSR may have been due to the border, but they also had much to do with the fact that it remained an independent concern and did not have the protection of the larger companies who owned Donegal's other narrow gauge system, the CDR. The Donegal Railway was taken over by the English Midland Railway and the Great Northern Railway of Ireland in the early twentieth century. The MR had acquired the Belfast &

Below: **On 20th April 1953, L&LSR 4-6-2T No.15, built by Hudswell Clarke in 1899, takes water at Newtowncunningham whilst working a goods train from Letterkenny to Derry.** R.M.Casserley.

Above: **On 3rd April 1956, railcar No.18, a 43-seater vehicle built in 1940 at a cost of £3,021, arrives at Donegal Town on the 11.20am service from Strabane. The savings that could be made by using railcars on passenger services were appreciated by the management of the CDR in the 1930s, long before most other railway operators did.** W.A.C.Smith.

Northern Counties Railway some years before and the GNR, anxious to protect its territory against incursions from a powerful English predator, came to an agreement to take over the DR jointly with the MR. A management committee was formed with its members drawn from both owning companies. This went under the name of the County Donegal Railway Joint Committee. With the support of the GNR and the MR and strong local management the CDR was a much more dynamic and enterprising concern than the L&LSR, which went into a steady decline from the 1920s onwards. As will be seen later in the book, relations between the CDR and the L&LSR were less than cordial. They were almost indifferent to each other even though on the face of it they had much in common.

Moving into Northern Ireland itself, the largest group of narrow gauge lines were those run from 1923-24 onwards by the Northern Counties Committee of the mighty London, Midland & Scottish Railway. The origins of the narrow gauge in County Antrim lay with the need to export the considerable deposits of iron ore found high in the glens. Two lines were promoted to carry this mineral, the Ballymena, Cushendall & Red Bay and the Ballymena & Larne. The boom years of the iron ore mines were in the 1870s and the trade went into decline not long after the two railways were built. These were the first 3ft gauge lines to be opened in Ireland and I have suggested in volume one that the origins of the gauge may have been due to contacts with the Isle of Man which saw its first 3ft gauge line at around the same time that those in County Antrim were proposed. The similarities between the engines which Beyer Peacock produced for the IOMR and the B&L are also very striking – *see page 31*. By the 1880s, the BC&RB and the B&L had both been absorbed by the B&NCR. The decline in the iron ore trade had left them in some difficulties. In turn they became part of the MR, when that company took control of the B&NCR, and with the grouping of Britain's railways in the 1920 they became small parts of the LMS empire.

I have dealt with the third Antrim narrow gauge line in the same chapter as the two based in Ballymena even though it had no physical connection with the others. This was the Ballycastle Railway which was built to connect the small coastal town of Ballycastle with the broad gauge line from Belfast to Londonderry, at Ballymoney. This line retained its independence up to 1924 when its unhealthy finances almost led to its closure. It was rescued by the LMS/NCC and thus was saved from the melancholy distinction of being Ireland's first 3ft gauge casualty. The line survived to become the last of the Antrim lines to have a passenger service. The heart was knocked out of these lines by closures in the 1930s but in reality the lines based around Ballymena never really found a satisfactory way of replacing their mineral traffic once that went into decline. The tourist and general traffic sought by the later owners of these lines were not sufficient to make up for the loss of the enormous tonnage of minerals carried in their early years.

The other lines dealt with in this volume were a mixed bag of independents. Two very different 3ft gauge lines were to be found in County Tyrone. The first of these was the Castlederg & Victoria Bridge Tramway. Very much the product of the Tramways Act of 1883, which encouraged the construction of cheaply built local lines such as this, it linked the small market town of Castlederg with the broad gauge GNR line from Derry to Belfast at Victoria Bridge. The track followed the public road for most of its length. Lines such as these were sitting ducks for road competition. This was reflected in the steady downward spiral of its receipts throughout the 1920s which inexorably led to its closure in 1933.

The other narrow gauge line which ran through County Tyrone also served part of County Fermanagh and had one terminus in a third county, Tynan in County Armagh. A much grander undertaking than the little C&VBT, this was the Clogher Valley Railway which meandered across mid Ulster from Tynan on the GNR line from Armagh to Clones to Maguiresbridge in County Fermanagh on the continuation of the GNR line from Clones to Enniskillen. The CVR was another product of the Tramways Act and the system that allowed local districts or baronies to be made liable for interest charges on the capital used to construct railways in underdeveloped parts of Ireland where funds to build the lines might otherwise not have been forthcoming. These baronial guarantees played a significant part in the development of Ireland's network of narrow gauge railways. At first they were applicable only to narrow gauge schemes though latterly they became available for 5ft 3in gauge branches in remote parts of the country. Many of the lines promoted in this way became millstones round the necks of the ratepayers in the districts which they served. This was certainly the case with the CVR though it did not lead to the acrimonious disputes between ratepayers representatives and directors of the railway that we saw in volume one on the Tralee & Dingle and Cavan & Leitrim lines. Perhaps the ratepayers of Tyrone and Fermanagh were more placid than their peers further south. They had good reason to complain, not just at the cost of the railway in terms of baronial subsidies, but at such things as the size of some of the stations on the line, which were rather elaborate for what was in effect, an extended roadside tramway. The directors of the CVR may have succumbed to the megalomania which was often found in the boardrooms of nineteenth century railway companies. The CVR was at the centre of several grandiose schemes to build narrow gauge lines stretching from Newry to Galway which would also have linked it to the Cavan & Leitrim line. It is probably just as well that these plans, hatched in the early years of this century did not reach maturity, coming as they did, a mere few years before the rise of the internal combustion engine began to put the Irish narrow gauge to the sword.

The first Irish 3ft gauge line to close was situated in Ulster. This was the Portstewart Tramway which was abandoned in 1926. This tramway connected the seaside town of Portstewart in County Derry with its distant broad gauge station on the B&NCR branch from Coleraine to Portrush, which was some 1½ miles away. The steam tram was replaced by buses, perhaps the first example of a practice that was to occur many times in these islands in the decades that followed. A few miles along the coast from Portstewart was another 3ft gauge line. As well as having a longer innings than the Portstewart line, the Giant's Causeway Tramway is significant as being one of the earliest examples of the application of electric traction to railways. There is a debate as to whether the Giant's Causeway line or the Volk's Electric Railway in Brighton was the first electrically operated railway to open for service in these islands. The official opening date of the VER was a short time before the Irish line, but there is some evidence to suggest that fare paying passengers were carried on the GCT before the line was officially opened. In any event the moral victory must go to the Irish line as it was a much longer and more elaborate affair than the short pleasure line along Brighton's seafront. The pioneering work of the Traill brothers who promoted the GCT deserves proper recognition, if only because of the way in which electrification has transformed the fortunes of so many railways throughout the world.

Below: **Three of the railwaymen who worked the Ballycastle branch, the last remaining narrow gauge line in County Antrim to retain a passenger service, pose in front of a 2-4-2 compound tank locomotive, at Ballymoney. The engine bears the livery of the Ulster Transport Authority, who were to close the line in 1950.** John Edgington.

The other 3ft gauge electric line in Ulster was a very interesting concern. This was the Bessbrook & Newry Tramway, which ran from the mill village of Bessbrook to the nearby port of Newry. This tramway's permanent way consisted of five rails. There were two running rails, one for electrical pick up and two additional rails outside the running rails which accommodated an ingenious method of running road vehicles on the tramway. A number of wagons were fitted with flangeless wheels which could be drawn by horses on the road. When put on the tramway their wheels ran on the lower outer rails and were kept in place by the tramway's 3ft gauge running rails. Nowadays, elaborate road/rail systems are proposed to combine the flexibility of road haulage for short journeys with the economy of rail for longer distances, I often reflect that there is nothing new under the sun and that the management of the B&N had resolved this problem in their own way many years before.

The narrow gauge railways of Ulster were a fascinating group of lines, each one different from the other and full of character. The locomotives and rolling stock of each concern were unique to that system; there was no hint of standardisation in their equipment. In their heyday motive power ranged from the mighty 4-8-0 tender locomotives of the L&LSR to the distinctive 0-4-2Ts of the CVR and the venerable electric tramcars of the Bessbrook and Giant's Causeway lines. We must not forget the pioneering diesel railcars of the CVR and the CDR, the wagons of all shapes and sizes and coaching stock ranging from the rattling four wheelers of the C&VBT to the magnificent corridor bogie carriages built by the LMS/NCC for the narrow gauge boat trains which ran between Larne and Ballymena. Those interested in railway modelling will find a wealth of prototypes illustrated in these pages which I hope may stimulate some skilled modellers to recreate parts of these lines in miniature.

The narrow gauge lines in Ulster serve to confirm the observations made in Volume One about the Irish narrow gauge in general. The 3ft gauge was adopted to save money when the line was being constructed. Though narrow gauge stock and track were lighter than their broad gauge equivalents, most lines were fully staffed and signalled so there were no real savings in those areas. The choice of a different gauge presented the problems of having to trans-ship goods from one line to the other. The very fact that the 3ft gauge was chosen meant that the line's promoters were not that confident of the levels of traffic on offer. In any case, by the time the narrow gauge network had begun to develop, most of the main centres of population had been connected by broad gauge lines which meant that the narrow gauge was left with remote and potentially unremunerative districts to serve. They were relatively safe up to the time of the Great War, but after that conflict, which did so much to develop and spread the internal combustion engine, they were in mortal danger.

The GSR in southern Ireland had little money to invest in any of its railways. There was no real attempt to apply the internal combustion engine, with all its potential savings, to its narrow gauge lines. All the lines in the south remained steam worked to the end, with the notable exception of the West Clare section, which was completely dieselised by CIE, the successor to the GSR as operator of the railways of the Irish Republic. The pattern in Ulster was somewhat different. The L&LSR was steam worked exclusively until it abandoned its railways in favour of buses and lorries. Despite being backed by the resources of the LMS, the only diesel vehicle ever to run on its 3ft gauge lines in Ulster, the one depicted on page 36, was destined for a railway in South America. In the 1930s the CVR introduced Ireland's first diesel railcar and a diesel rail lorry at the same time. Even the humble C&VBT constructed an internal combustion engined railcar in its Castlederg workshops. The great pioneer in this respect was the CDR which introduced a succession of petrol and later diesel engined railcars from the 1920s onwards. These vehicles stopped along the line wherever there was business to be had, and the good and flexible service they offered, whilst they did not ultimately save the CDR, at least kept it going until 1959 – the last narrow gauge survivor in the province of Ulster.

The narrow gauge lines of Ireland were the products of the economic and social conditions which prevailed in the late nineteenth century. They represent the aspirations of an age when the steel rail and the iron horse were the apogee of technology, when the construction of a railway was seen as the catalyst which would bring prosperity to the district it served. These conditions have so long been superseded that it is sometimes hard, from the perspective of the late twentieth century, to understand the conditions which led to many of these lines being constructed. We look back on the narrow gauge era with unashamed nostalgia and are not too concerned with the reality of a slow, bumpy journey, let us say one from Londonderry to Burtonport, which would have taken perhaps over five hours to complete and probably have left the traveller tired and dirty and with the feeling that there must be an easier way of doing things than that which they had just endured.

Thanks to the efforts of the many photographers who travelled on and recorded the narrow gauge in Ulster, we can relive at least some of the charm and the atmosphere of these lines, in the pages that follow. I was too young to experience the lines covered in these books, but having read, researched and thought about them now for a long time, I feel I know something of their character. If I have managed to convey at least a part of that in this book and its companion volume, then I think I will have achieved what I set out to do.

Above: **On 15th May 1920, Clogher Valley Railway 0-4-2T No.1 *Caledon*, enters Fivemiletown with the 12.20pm mixed train from Tynan. CVR engines ran cab first to give their drivers a better view of the road.** Ken Nunn collection.

Below: **A panorama of the CDR station in Londonderry taken from the Craigavon bridge on 24th June 1937 by H.C.Casserley. The siding in the foreground ran down to meet the mixed gauge track which was laid on the bottom deck of the bridge. This formed a tenuous link between Derry's four termini –** ***see page* 77.**

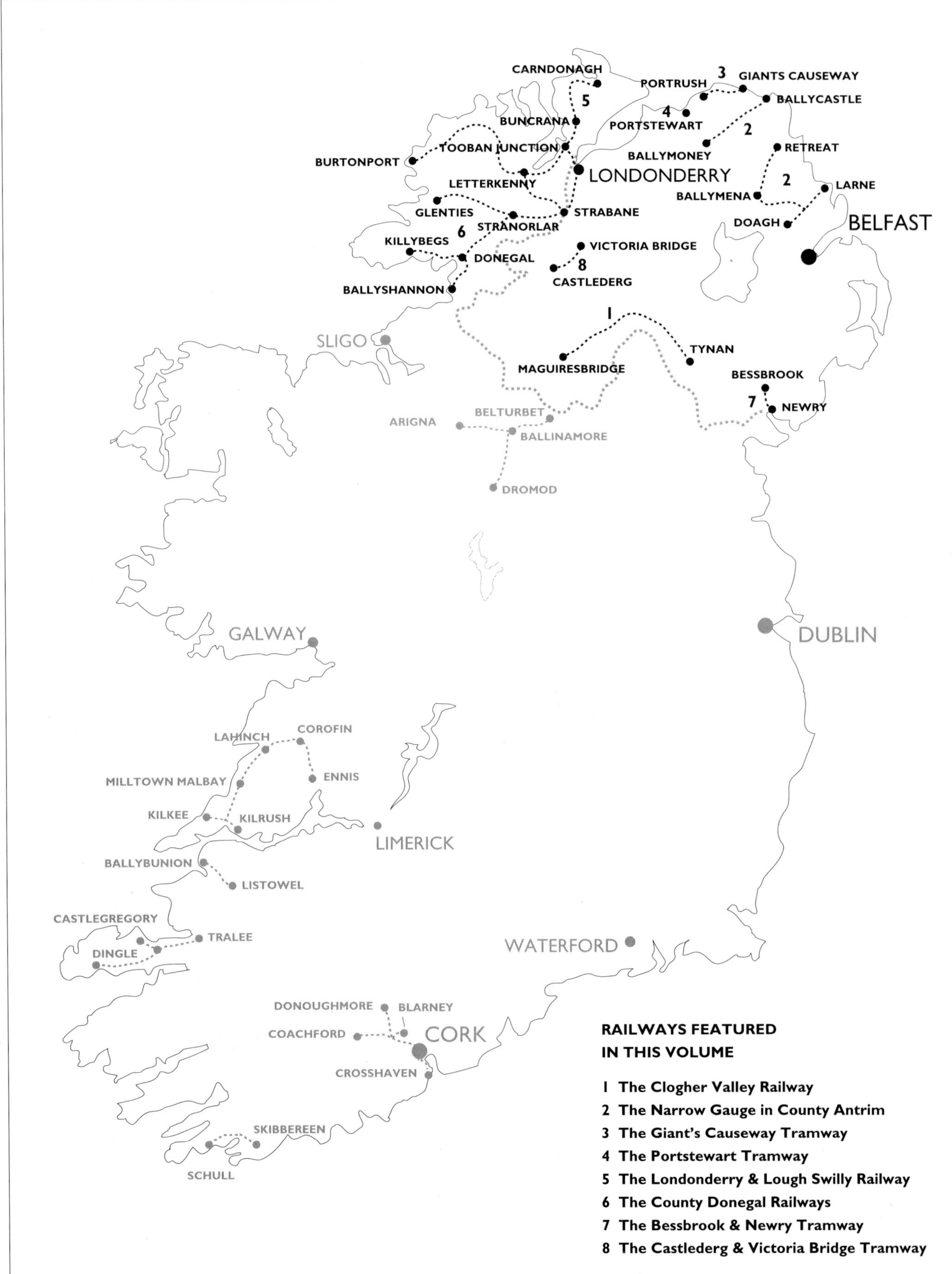
CARNDONAGH
PORTRUSH
3
GIANTS CAUSEWAY
BALLYCASTLE
5
BUNCRANA
4
PORTSTEWART
2
BURTONPORT
TOOBAN JUNCTION
BALLYMONEY
RETREAT
LONDONDERRY
LETTERKENNY
BALLYMENA
2
LARNE
GLENTIES
STRABANE
STRANORLAR
DOAGH
BELFAST
6
KILLYBEGS
VICTORIA BRIDGE
DONEGAL
8
CASTLEDERG
BALLYSHANNON
SLIGO
1
TYNAN
MAGUIRESBRIDGE
BESSBROOK
7
NEWRY
BELTURBET
ARIGNA
BALLINAMORE
DROMOD
GALWAY
DUBLIN
LAHINCH
COROFIN
ENNIS
MILLTOWN MALBAY
KILKEE
KILRUSH
LIMERICK
BALLYBUNION
LISTOWEL
CASTLEGREGORY
TRALEE
DINGLE
WATERFORD
DONOUGHMORE
BLARNEY
COACHFORD
CORK
CROSSHAVEN
SKIBBEREEN
SCHULL
RAILWAYS FEATURED
IN THIS VOLUME
1 The Clogher Valley Railway
2 The Narrow Gauge in County Antrim
3 The Giant's Causeway Tramway
4 The Portstewart Tramway
5 The Londonderry & Lough Swilly Railway
6 The County Donegal Railways
7 The Bessbrook & Newry Tramway
8 The Castlederg & Victoria Bridge Tramway

Chapter One

THE CLOGHER VALLEY RAILWAY

THE geographical expression, the Clogher Valley was not in common currency before the coming of the railway that was to serve the area. It has come to refer to a district in mid-Ulster, located mostly in County Tyrone but partly in County Fermanagh, centred on the old diocesan town of Clogher. This seems to be a rare instance of a railway defining an area rather than the other way round. Various schemes had been mooted, with varying degrees of seriousness, since the 1850s, to serve the small towns and villages of this largely agricultural district. The Tramways Act of 1883 provided a stimulus to this process. A committee was formed and a public meeting was called in Omagh in September 1883 to discuss proposals to build various lines. Two routes were discussed. Starting from Maguiresbridge on the GNR Enniskillen to Dundalk line, the railway was to go via Fivemiletown and Clogher to Ballygawley. There was disagreement as to where it should go from there. Some wanted the line to go to Dungannon on the GNR Portadown to Derry section, others that it should strike south east to Tynan on the Armagh to Clones stretch of the GNR. As often happens in Ireland, the meeting was followed by the split. The faction supporting the line to Dungannon set up a separate undertaking calling their scheme, the Tyrone Steam Tramways. This failed to get the support of the Tyrone Grand Jury and the initiative passed to the Clogher Valley Tramway and the line from Maguiresbridge to Tynan.

The capital required by the CVT for its 37 mile long line was to be £150,000. James Barton, who had worked for the recently opened Castlederg & Victoria Bridge Tramway, was appointed engineer and the company was formally incorporated in December 1883. By March 1884 the Grand Juries of Tyrone and Fermanagh had agreed to guarantee the interest on the capital and in May 1884 the Privy Council authorised the 3ft gauge line. It was the second scheme to be approved under the Tramways Act of 1883. Construction began in mid 1885 but the CVR quickly ran into financial difficulties. A finance house, Salter and Son, had undertaken to subscribe for the £70,000 worth of stock not taken up by the public. When they renegued on this arrangement the CVT almost ran out of money. Appeals to the Board of Works eventually realised a loan of £44,000 which enabled the construction of the railway to be completed. The line was inspected and approved by Major General Hutchinson in April 1887 and opened for traffic the following month.

The tramway followed the public road for much of its route though the track on the western section from Fivemiletown to Maguiresbridge was mostly on its own right of way. The headquarters of the line was at Aughnacloy where the locomotives and rolling stock were maintained. Aughnacloy also boasted a large brick built station and two spacious platforms; indeed all the main stations were built to a scale that the traffic was never likely to justify. Initially the service consisted of two through trains along the whole length of the line with a short working from Fivemiletown to Tynan in addition. In later years the number of short workings over various sections of the line increased.

In its first seven years of operation the CVT failed to make a profit. This set the pattern for a dismal financial performance throughout its entire career. The line's prospectus had painted the usual glowing picture of anticipated traffic levels, but even in its most prosperous year 1904, receipts were only £791 in excess of working expenses and in that year alone guaranteed dividends to shareholders amounted to £5,375. In the 1920s the yearly deficit on the line's current account was never less than £4,000 per annum.

The financial realities did not deter some expansion plans which verged on megalomania. In 1894 the name of the company was changed to Clogher Valley Railway. Before this, in 1891, the proposal to build the branch from Ballygawley to Dungannon resurfaced again but this was modest compared to some of the schemes mooted at the turn of the century. In 1900 the Newry, Keady & Tynan Railway was authorised by Parliament. At a cost of £173,000 this proposed to extend the 3ft gauge tracks some 28 miles eastwards beyond Tynan to join those of the Newry & Bessbrook Tramway and by using their metals thus gain access to the port of Newry. A westbound extension to the CVR was also linked to this scheme and was laid out by the engineers who had planned the NK&T. Under the title the Ulster & Connaught Light Railways, a line was to run from the CVR at Maguiresbridge to meet the Cavan & Leitrim at Bawnboy Road. The U&CLR also planned to extend the C&L and take over the Arigna mines. The cost of the scheme was estimated to be in the region of £130,000.

A year after the U&CLR got its Act of Parliament, a final flourish of narrow gauge folly was proposed in the form of a plan to extend the C&L from Dromod to Clifden in Connemara. Perhaps fortuitously all these plans perished, though had they been realised they would have elevated both the C&L and the CVR from being purely local lines into part of something much more significant. One dreads to think how long a journey from Clifden to Newry would have taken, perhaps 3ft gauge sleeping cars would have been introduced!

To work the Clogher Valley line six 0-4-2Ts were ordered from Sharp Stewart in 1885. Three of these lasted until the line's closure. These engines worked the line's traffic unaided until 1910 when a 0-4-4T was supplied by Hudswell Clarke. This engine was obviously not a great success. It was offered for sale in 1926 but attracted no takers and was finally scrapped in 1934. The next acquisition was the Atkinson Walker steam tractor which ultimately found fame as the CDR's only diesel locomotive. The last steam locomotive bought by the CVR was the ex-C&VBT 2-6-0T No.4. This was rebuilt as a 2-6-2T and lasted until the line closed.

From their acquisition in 1932 and 1933 respectively, of a diesel railcar and a rail lorry, both built by Walkers of Wigan, steam operations declined with most of the traffic being worked by the new diesels. There was usually only one steam operated mixed train daily which ran between Tynan and Fivemiletown, after the arrival of the diesels.

The CVR was located wholly within Northern Ireland. In 1922 the new government in Belfast set up a commission to look at the railways within its jurisdiction. This body recommended that the GNR take over the CVR. This the broad gauge company declined to do. The CVR carried on its independent existence with its shareholders continuing to draw upon the generosity of the ratepayers of Tyrone and Fermanagh. In 1927 another government enquiry recommended that the shareholders be bought out and a committee of management be set up appointed by Tyrone and Fermanagh County Councils.

The committee was duly established and included the redoubtable Henry Forbes of the CDR who did much to revitalise the line with more services and shorter journey times.

Most of the shareholders accepted an offer of £6 for each £10 share made by the Northern Ireland government.

Despite the improvements, road competition stiffened and as the losses continued the government refused to support the line indefinitely.

The last day of service was 31st December 1941. Some wagons went to the C&L section of the GSR and to Bord na Mona; the railcar became CDR No.10 and was eventually preserved but sadly all of the CVR steam locomotives were sold for scrap.

We will begin our survey of the CVR with an abbreviated photographic journey along the course of the line from Maguiresbridge to Tynan, calling at some of the main stations en route.

At Maguiresbridge the CVR shared the station facilities of the broad gauge GNR. As with many stations in Ireland, this was some distance from the centre of the town. The CVR had a halt at the Fair Green in Maguiresbridge itself, some half a mile from the GNR station at which No.2 *Errigal* waits for the off in 1930. Norman Johnson collection, from a photograph by Joseph Johnson.

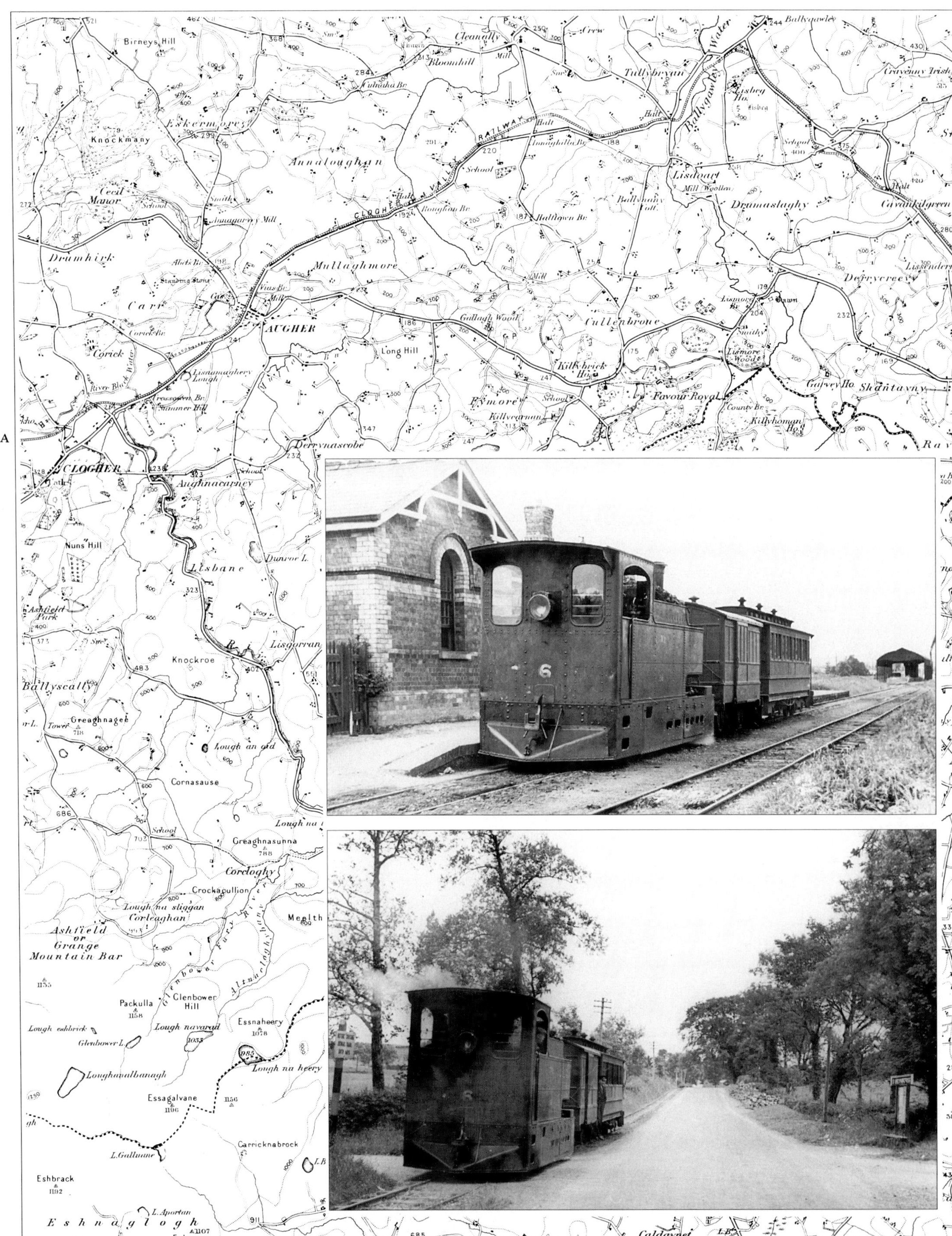

Birneys Hill
Cleanally
Bloomhill
Tullybryan
Ballygawley Water
Ballygawley
Lisbeg Ho.
Eskermore
Knockmany
RAILWAY
Halt
Annaloughan
Cecil Manor
School
CLOGHER VALLEY
Lisdoart
Drumaslaghy
Cavankilgreen
Drumhirk
Standing Stone
Mullaghmore
Derryvreevy
Carr
AUGHER
Long Hill
Gallagh Wood
Cullenbrone
Lismore Wood
Corick
Lisnamaghery Lough
Killybrick Ho.
Favour Royal
Garvey Ho.
Shantavny
Crossowen
Killyhoman Ho.
Derrynascobe
CLOGHER
Aughnacarney
Nuns Hill
Lisbane
Dunroe L.
Ashfield Park
Lisgorran
Knockroe
Ballyscally
Greaghnagee
Lough an eid
Cornasause
Greaghnasunna
Corcloghy
Crockacullion
Lough na sliggan
Corleaghan
Ashfield or Grange Mountain Bar
Packulla
Glenbower Hill
Lough navaroll
Essnaheery
Loughanalbanagh
Lough na heery
Essagalvane
L. Gallnane
Carricknabrock
Eshbrack
L. Aportan
Eshnaglogh
Eshmore
Caldaynet

A

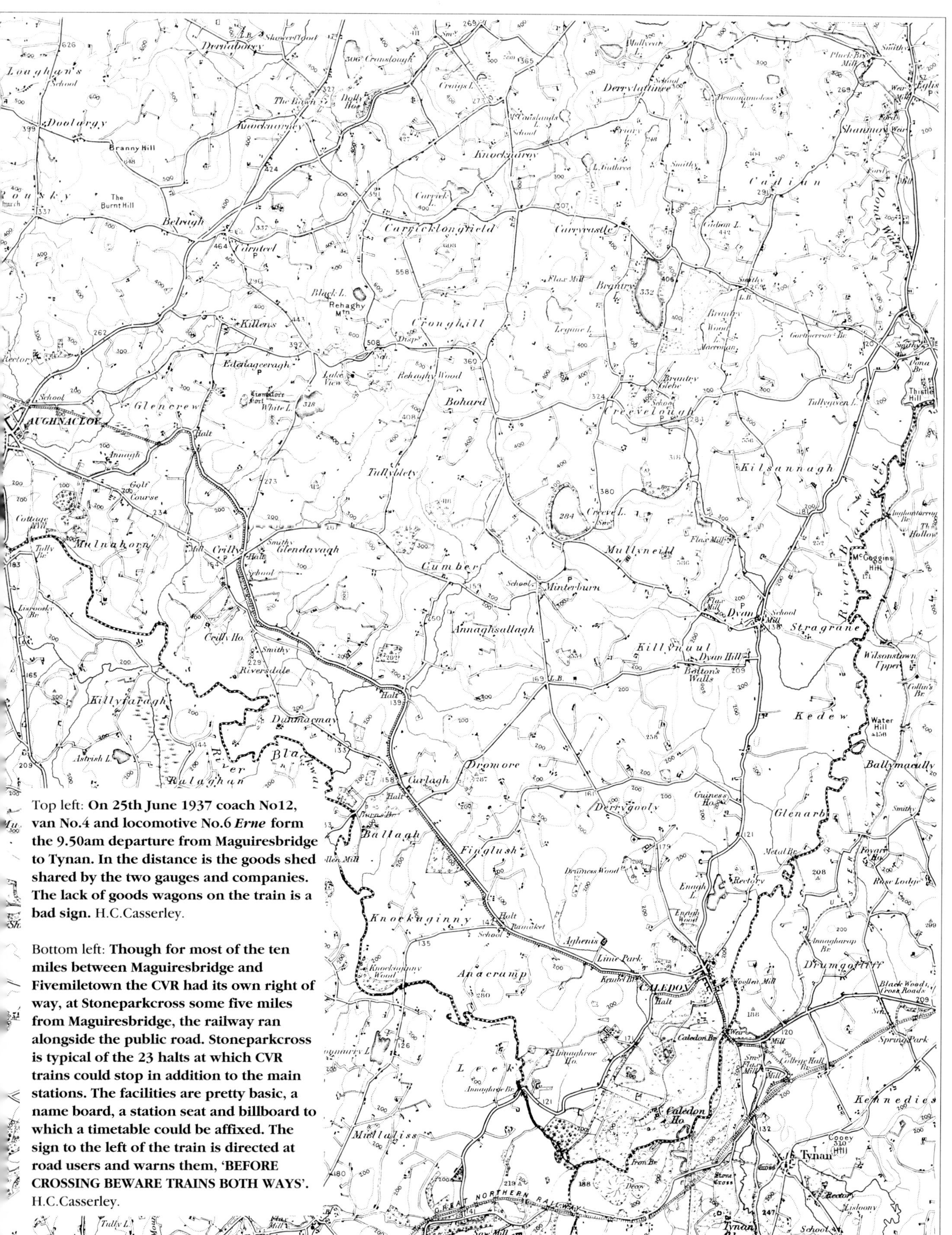

Top left: **On 25th June 1937 coach No12, van No.4 and locomotive No.6 *Erne* form the 9.50am departure from Maguiresbridge to Tynan. In the distance is the goods shed shared by the two gauges and companies. The lack of goods wagons on the train is a bad sign.** H.C.Casserley.

Bottom left: **Though for most of the ten miles between Maguiresbridge and Fivemiletown the CVR had its own right of way, at Stoneparkcross some five miles from Maguiresbridge, the railway ran alongside the public road. Stoneparkcross is typical of the 23 halts at which CVR trains could stop in addition to the main stations. The facilities are pretty basic, a name board, a station seat and billboard to which a timetable could be affixed. The sign to the left of the train is directed at road users and warns them, 'BEFORE CROSSING BEWARE TRAINS BOTH WAYS'.** H.C.Casserley.

Top left and centre left: **Fivemiletown was the second largest station on the line. Some services began or terminated here. From Maguiresbridge to just outside Fivemiletown the line had been in County Fermanagh. From here to Caledon it was in County Tyrone though for the last mile or so from there to the GNR station at Tynan, where it terminated, it entered County Armagh. The station boasted a large station house, a sizeable goods yard and a locomotive shed. The larger CVR stations were built to a scale far in excess of the traffic that the line was likely to generate.** Both H.C.Casserley, the centre left illustration courtesy *Railway Magazine.*

Bottom left and bottom right: **Fivemiletown station was located to the west of the little town. To get to it trains from the east had to pass down the centre of Main Street. The group of locals outside Bells hardware shop seem more interested in the motor car than in the approaching CVR train.** Norman Johnson collection. **In the other picture taken to the east of Main Street, the CVR's Walker railcar is pursued by what looks like a Foden lorry, on 25th June 1937.** H.C.Casserley, courtesy *Railway Magazine.*

Opposite page, top: **The town of Clogher, which gave its name to the railway and to the area which it served boasts the smallest cathedral in Ireland. The town is on a hill and was about half a mile away from the CVR station. On 25th June 1937 No.3 *Blackwater,* on the 10.45am mixed train from Tynan, crosses the diesel railcar and a van which formed the 12 noon working from Fivemiletown to Tynan.** H.C.Casserley.

Opposite page, bottom: **The village of Augher was 2½ miles beyond Clogher. The station, which is still extant, had only one platform. A creamery which adjoined the station, once a source of considerable traffic for the railway, took over the station building when the line closed.** H.C.Casserley.

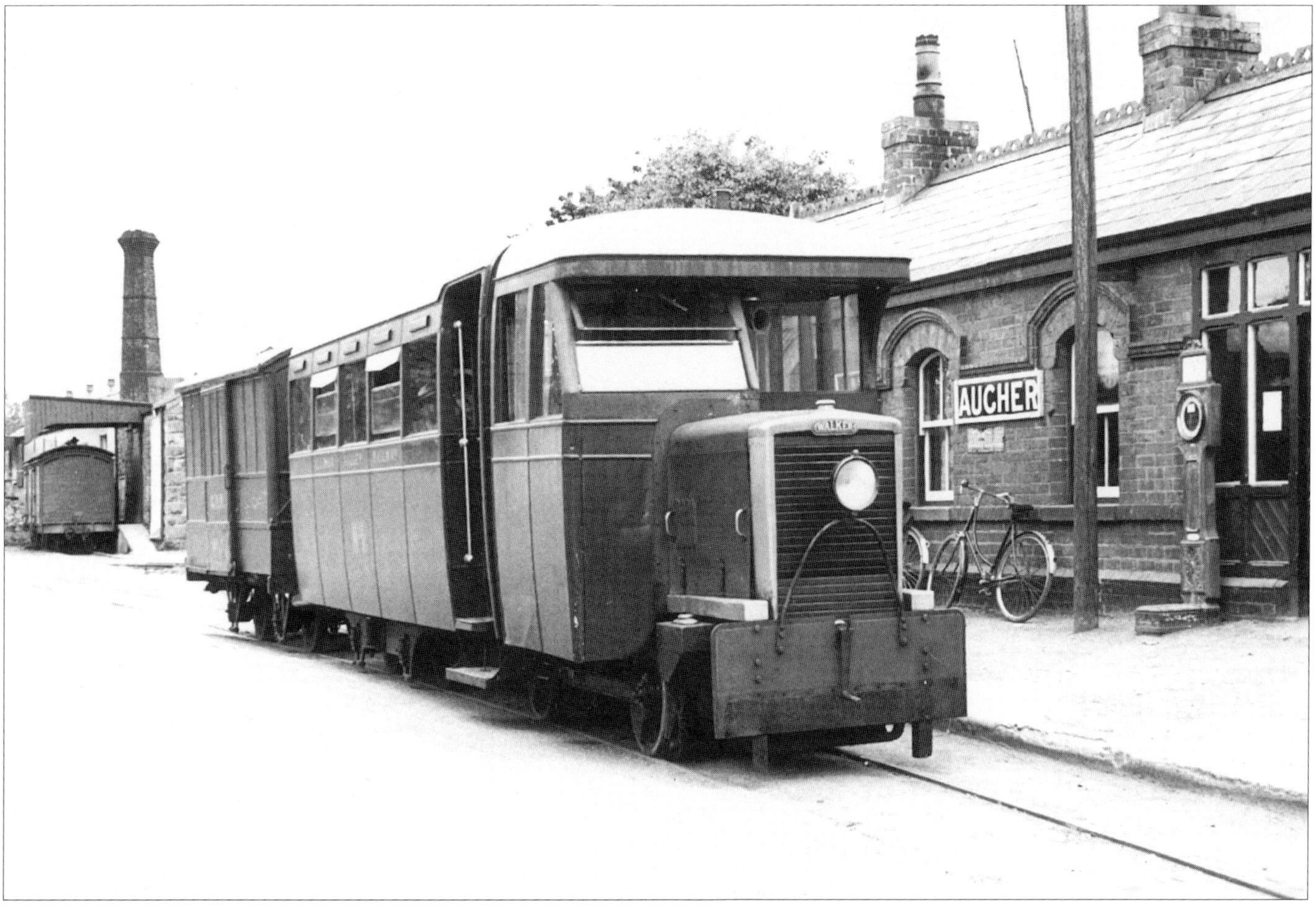

Top left: **Ballygawley was a station which seems to have rarely attracted the attention of photographers. Its two platforms were staggered and in this undated view No.6 *Erne* seems to be shunting. As on so many of the Irish narrow gauge lines, Clogher Valley trains were often mixed and much shunting took place at stations and halts along the way to attach and detach wagons. The delays that this caused made travel on these lines a leisurely business and helped to increase their vulnerability to road competition after the First World War.** Michael Pollard collection.

Top right: **Aughnacloy was the principal station on the line. The station building housed the company's offices and the locomotive and rolling stock repair shops were located here as well. The structure across the line, beside the water tank at the rear of the train, was used to deliver coal to the bunker's on top of the locomotives.** Courtesy *Railway Magazine.*

Centre left: **Tynan in County Armagh was the eastern terminus of the Clogher Valley Railway. As at the other end of the line at Maguiresbridge, the CVR shared the GNR station site. There was a small narrow gauge loco shed here and an exchange siding. By the time this picture was taken, the 10.45 am mixed train from Tynan to Fivemiletown, was the only scheduled steam working on the line. All other services were handled by the two diesels. The engine on this occasion, 24th June 1939, was No.3 *Blackwater,* delivered in 1887 and still going strong over fifty years later.** Stewart Dewesbury, courtesy *Railway Magazine.*

Bottom left: **Like all the small independent Irish narrow gauge lines, the CVR had to maintain its own workshops. Two of the original Sharp Stewart 2-4-0Ts with, in the rear, the solitary Hudswell Clarke 0-4-4T *Blessingbourne,* are outside the workshops and loco shed at Aughnacloy.** Michael Pollard collection.

Above: **In this rare view inside the works at Aughnacloy, the belts used to drive various pieces of machinery, that criss-cross the picture would give a Health and Safety Inspector of the 1990s, a seizure! The locomotive in the shops is the former C&VBT No.4, which the CVR bought when the Castlederg line closed in 1933. This was in the process of being converted from a 2-6-0T to a 2-6-2T at Aughnacloy. A bigger bunker was fitted to give the engine the coal capacity needed for the much longer runs it would be asked to undertake on its new line. The extra pair of wheels at the back were needed to carry the bunker. The presence of this engine in the works would date this picture to 1936, the year in which this work was carried out.** Courtesy *Railway Magazine.*

Above: **The six original locos were ordered from Sharp Stewart in 1885 (works numbers 3369 to 3374) and delivered in 1887 at a cost of £1,186 each. These 0-4-2Ts had driving wheels of 3ft diameter and trailing wheels of 2ft 3ins. Boiler pressure was 140lbs, their cylinders measured 13½x18ins, water capacity was 600 gallons and up to one ton of coal could be carried in bunkers on top of their tanks and boiler. The locos weighed just short of 24 tons, they ran bunker first and carried a large headlamp at that end. No.4 *Fury* was the first to be withdrawn in 1929 followed by No.1 *Caledon* in 1934 and No.5 *Colebrook* in 1936. The other three engines, No.2 *Errigal* No.3 *Blackwater* and No.6 *Erne* lasted until the line closed in 1941. No.3 *Blackwater* is seen at Maguiresbridge on 14th May 1920. The engines retained their tall chimneys and the skirts over their motions throughout their careers.** Ken Nunn collection.

Centre right: **No7 *Blessingbourne* at Aughnacloy on 18th September 1929. Ordered and delivered in 1910, this engine was built by Hudswell Clarke & Co to the design of the CVR locomotive superintendent, G.F.Akerlind. In every respect bar one this engine was the superior of its predecessors. It was longer and heavier at nearly 30 tons. Cylinders, boiler pressure, coal and water capacity were greater. It was deficient only in its ability to haul trains. After 1926 it was hardly ever used and I have been unable to find a picture of it in steam, let alone working a train. It was offered for sale in 1926 but found no takers. It was finally disposed of in 1934.** H.C.Casserley.

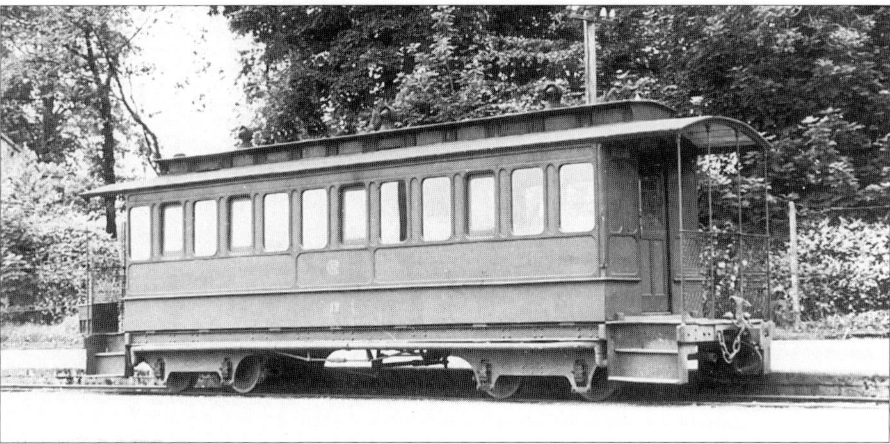

Bottom right: **All CVR passenger stock ran on bogies and had end balconies. No additions were made to the original fleet of thirteen coaches supplied by the Metropolitan Carriage and Wagon Company in 1887. No.12 seen here, was an all-3rd. When 1st class was abolished in 1928, all-3rd class coaches were upgraded and had their previously bare wooden seats upholstered.** H.C.Casserley.

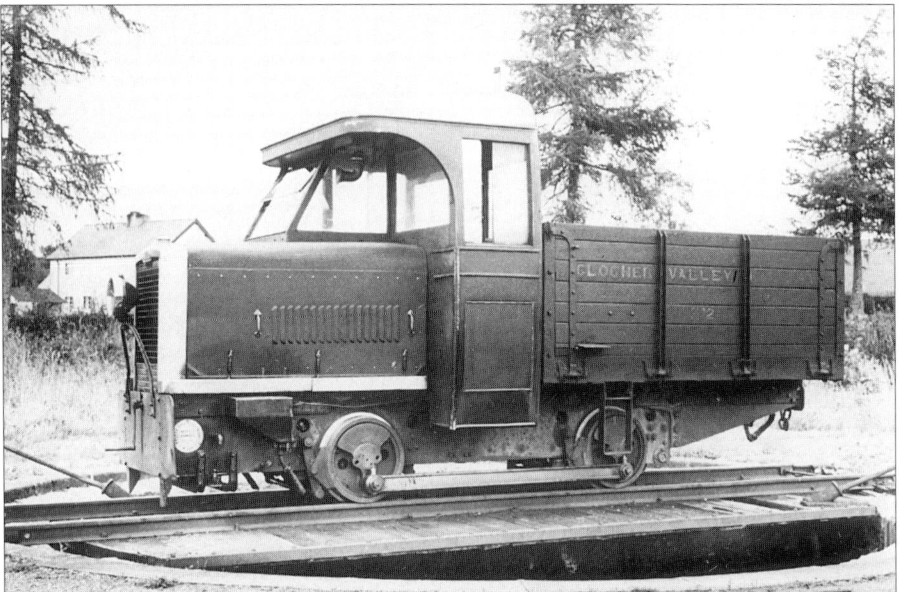

Top: **When the committee of management was set up by the County Councils of Tyrone and Fermanagh in 1928, to run the line, one of the members appointed to it was Henry Forbes, manager of the CDR. He had experience of the operation of internal combustion engined vehicles on his own line and there can be little doubt that he was behind the acquisition of the railcar and the rail lorry which much improved services on the CVR. The rail lorry was used to haul existing rolling stock. Three 3rd-Class coaches Nos 12, 15 and 17 were equipped with electric lighting to run with the two diesel vehicles. As well as the coach and van, the lorry, which carried the number 2, could haul additional goods or cattle wagons as required.**
Courtesy *Railway Magazine.*

Top right: **One vehicle acquired as part of the modernisation programme in 1928 was not a success. This was No.8, an Atkinson Walker steam tractor (Works No.114). No.8 was a vertical boilered geared steam locomotive. As built it proved to be useless and was quickly rebuilt with a bigger boiler and grate. The rebuild did not improve the machine greatly: it was still underpowered. No.8 had been supplied on a trial basis and had not been purchased by the CVR. Whilst the engine was in Ireland its builders went out of business. The machine languished at Aughnacloy until 1932 when it was sold to the CDR where it was drastically rebuilt again, this time as *Phoenix* – a diesel locomotive. This may be a works photo taken at the Atkinson Walker factory in Preston.** Michael Pollard collection.

Centre right: **By 1929 she was out of use in the shed at Aughnacloy. It is believed, that when she was rebuilt as a diesel on the CDR, that Henry Forbes sold her boiler to a laundry for more than he paid for the whole locomotive.** H.C.Casserley.

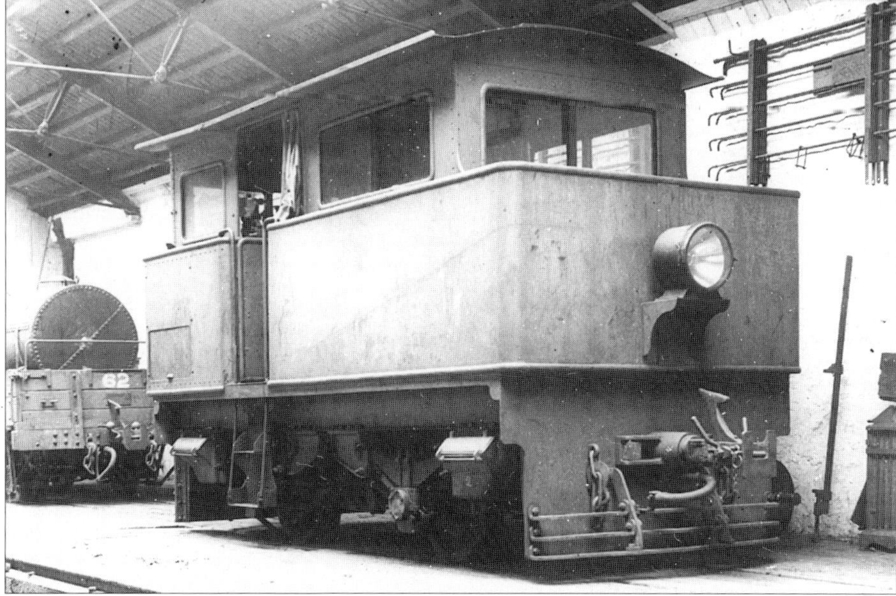

Bottom: **The CVR wagon stock, supplied by the Metropolitan Company, included two 15 ton bogie wagons supplied in 1904. These could be used for goods, cattle or on occasions such as Orangemen's specials on 12th July, they were fitted with seats and used to convey passengers.** H.C.Casserley.

Photographs on the opposite page:

Centre: **The Walker diesel rail lorry was delivered in 1933. It is seen here on the turntable at Ballygawley on 7th August 1937. In mechanical terms it was very similar to the railcar. On the closure of the CVR it eventually went to the CDR. Whilst it did not run on the County Donegal, we can be certain, that in true CDR fashion, every bit of it was used to keep the other railcars running.** Courtesy *Railway Magazine*.

Bottom: **The diesel railcar came in 1932. It was a 28-seat vehicle built by the Wigan based firm of Walkers. This was the first in a series of articulated diesel railcars powered by Gardner engines which Walkers were to build for the CDR and latterly the West Clare section of CIE, up to the 1950s. A solitary 5ft 3in version of the basic design was built for the Sligo, Leitrim & Northern Counties Railway (see *Irish Railways in Colour*, page 69), which at the time of writing languishes in deplorable condition in a siding at Mallow. Clogher Valley railcar No.1 seems to have been used mainly on the Fivemiletown to Tynan section. It was at Aughnacloy on 25th June 1937. We will encounter this railcar again later in the book as on the closure of the CVR it was acquired by the CDR and ran there until closure.** H.C.Casserley.

Chapter Two

THE NARROW GAUGE IN COUNTY ANTRIM

The once extensive narrow gauge railways of County Antrim were built by three independent companies. A fourth company was responsible for a short lived, but historically significant line, which we will also discuss in this chapter. Two of the lines made a junction at Ballymena, the other, the Ballycastle Railway had no physical connection with the other two. I am grouping these lines together on account of both their geographical proximity and because they all became part of the mighty empire of the London, Midland & Scottish Railway after 1923-24. The other 3ft gauge line in the county, the Giant's Causeway, Portrush and Bush Valley, is dealt with separately elsewhere.

Several things distinguished the Antrim lines from most of the other 3ft gauge railways in Ireland. They were among the first narrow gauge lines in the country, predating the Tramways Act of 1883, which was such a stimulus to the rise of the narrow gauge in the rest of the country. They were promoted as commercial enterprises in the normal 19th century fashion and were not dependent on baronial guarantees. Whilst the Ballycastle Railway was very much a branch, feeding into the broad gauge at Ballymoney, the two lines centred on Ballymena were promoted to tap mineral deposits. Ireland's general lack of such resources mark out these lines.

The broad gauge Belfast & Ballymena reached the latter town in 1848. It was extended to Coleraine in 1855 by the Ballymena, Ballymoney, Coleraine and Portrush Junction Railway. The B&B changed its name in 1860 to the Belfast & Northern Counties Railway and took over the BBC&PJ in 1861, thus happily dispensing with one of the most ponderous names in 19th century railway history. At about the same time the mining of iron ore began in the hills and glens north east of Ballymena. This ore could not be smelted locally owing to the lack of significant coal deposits in the area. For the first few years it was taken in horse drawn carts to small ports on the Antrim coast from where it was shipped to the industrial centres of the west of Scotland and Cumbria where a market for the ore was to be found.

In 1871 the Ballymena, Cushendall & Red Bay Railway was promoted to exploit this mineral traffic. Royal assent to its Act was given in July 1872. Significantly this Act allowed the railway to be built to a gauge between 2 and 3ft. The Ennis & West Clare Railway had been authorised the previous year to build to a narrow gauge, but was not proceeded with. There is no real evidence as to why or when the 3ft gauge was decided upon, though it is reasonable to surmise that the introduction of this gauge on the Isle of Man, at about the same time as the BC&RB was being promoted, may have influenced the decision.

Whilst the BC&RB was going through the elaborate formalities of the legislative process, the first 3ft gauge line in Ireland was being quietly made ready for operation up in the glens of Antrim, a short distance from where the BC&RB's line was to run. In 1872 the Glenariff Iron Ore & Harbour Company began their mining operations and to bring the ore down to a pier at Carrivemurphy, a private railway some four

B

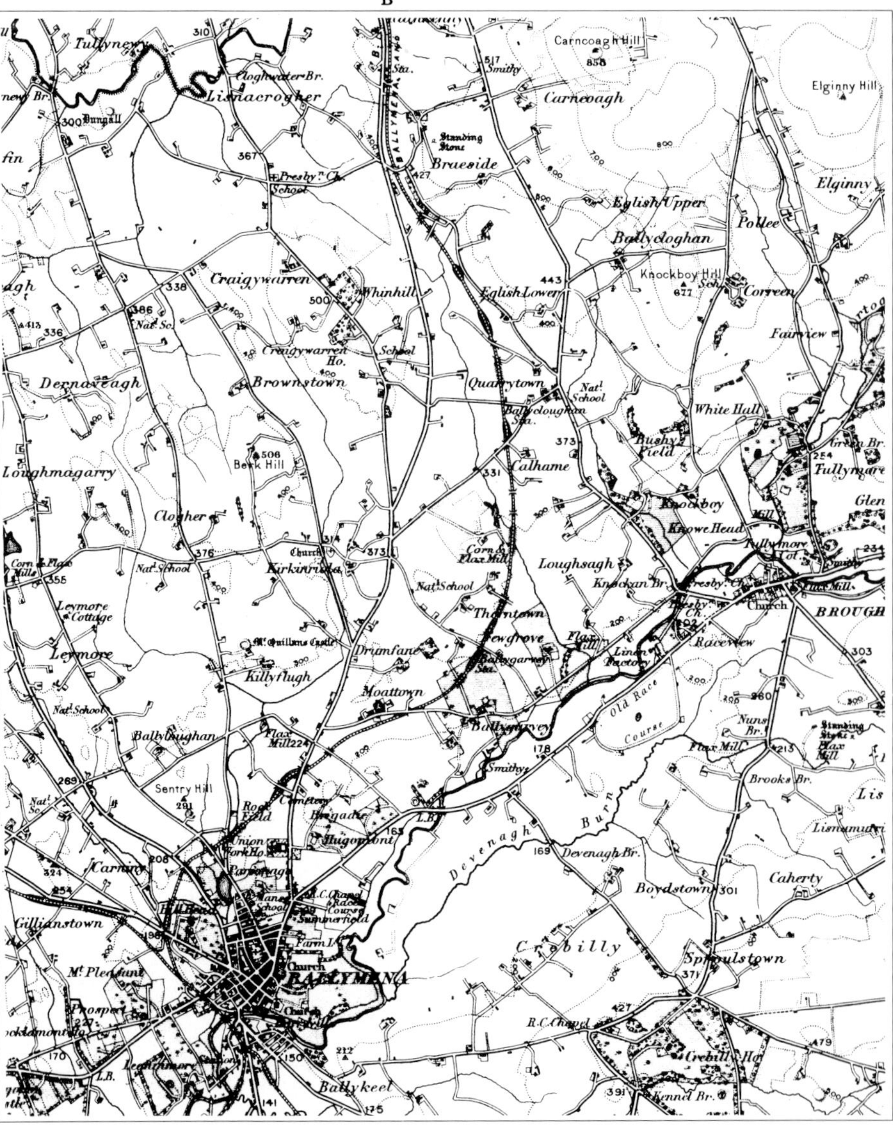

miles long was constructed. Two four-coupled 3ft gauge engines were obtained from Robert Stephenson and Company and these were the first Irish 3ft gauge locomotives to be put into service. Presumably because the line infringed no property rights being constructed on land owned by the Earl of Antrim who had leased mineral rights to the company, no Act of Parliament was needed. The GIO&H is remembered for its railway rather than its geological expertise. The high grade ore at the surface of its mine quickly ran out and within three years the mines and the railway had been abandoned. The engines lingered at the site until 1885 when the Earl of Antrim got a judgement against the company for monies owed to him. At the sale to liquidate the assets of the company, the engines were snapped up at bargain prices by the Lough Swilly Railway then in the process of converting its line to the narrow gauge.

The big problem facing the BC&RB, which was never resolved, was how to get its line, from a summit of over 1000ft, down to the coast in a distance of only about 4 miles. The line partially opened to Cargan in 1875. The company's capital was £90,000 in shares, with powers to borrow up to another £30,000 in loans. Funds were slow in coming in and the line was not completed to its terminus at Retreat, until 1876. Various schemes were mooted to get the line down to the coast including a plan by William Traill (of Giant's Causeway Tramway fame) to link it to the erstwhile Glenariff line, but all of these came to nought and the railway never did serve Cushendall and Red Bay, as promised in its title.

The BC&RB was purely a mineral line. No passenger trains were run. In the absence of a line to the coast its iron ore was brought down to Ballymena and shipped out over the B&NCR. Indeed the narrow gauge company owned some broad gauge wagons for this very purpose. At first the tonnages of minerals carried were remarkable. In 1880 and 1881 an average of 100,000 tons were conveyed. However the BC&RB was dangerously exposed by having one type of traffic which so dominated its revenues.

A depression in the iron trade in the mid-1880s plunged the company's finances into disarray and its Board had no alternative but to agree to a takeover by the B&NCR in 1884.

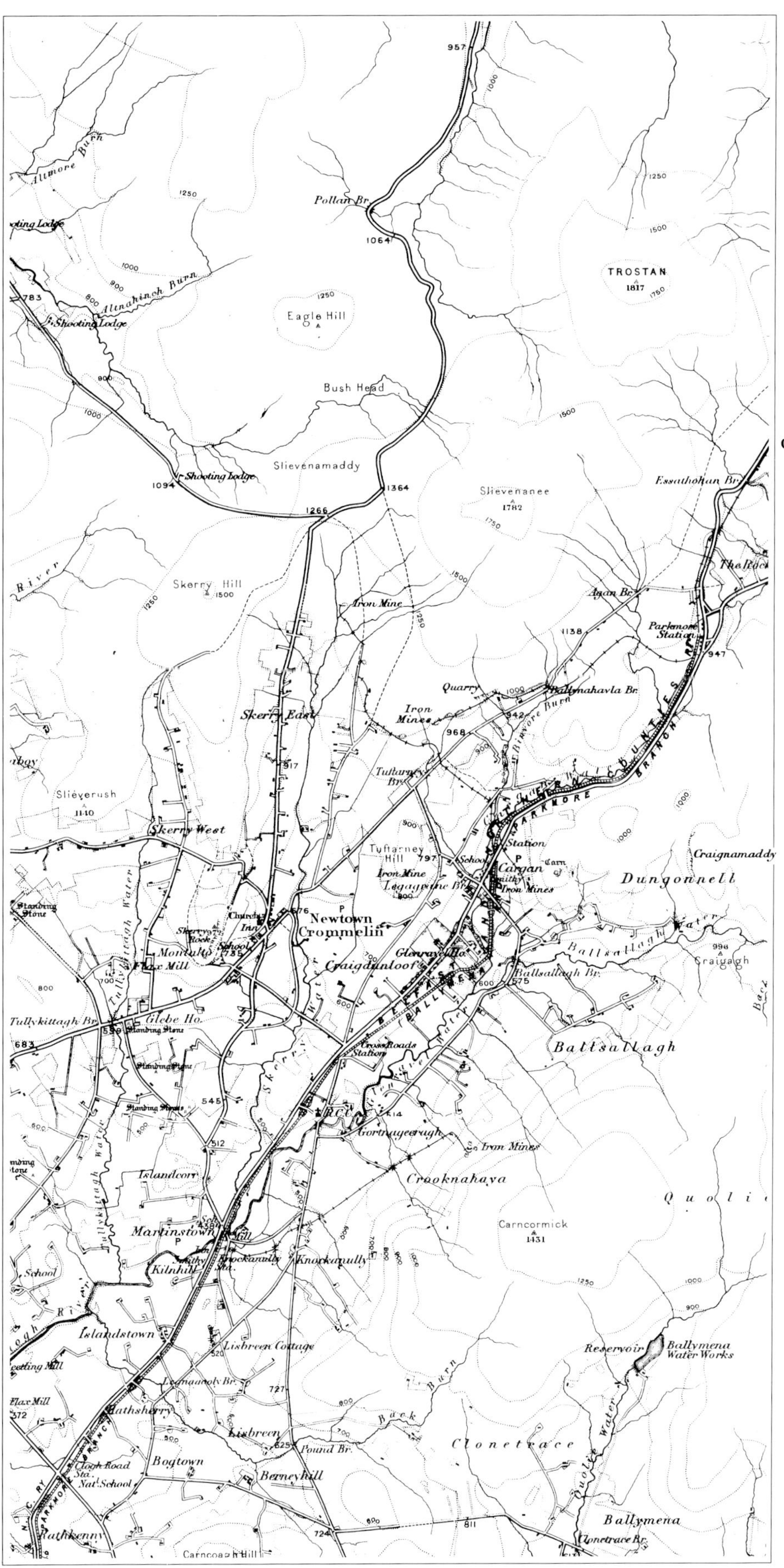

Copyright reserved, Ordnance Survey, Dublin. Reproduced from 1 inch series, sheet nos. 20, 14; revised 1900, 1900; published 1902, 1902 respectively. Scale 1 inch to 1 mile.

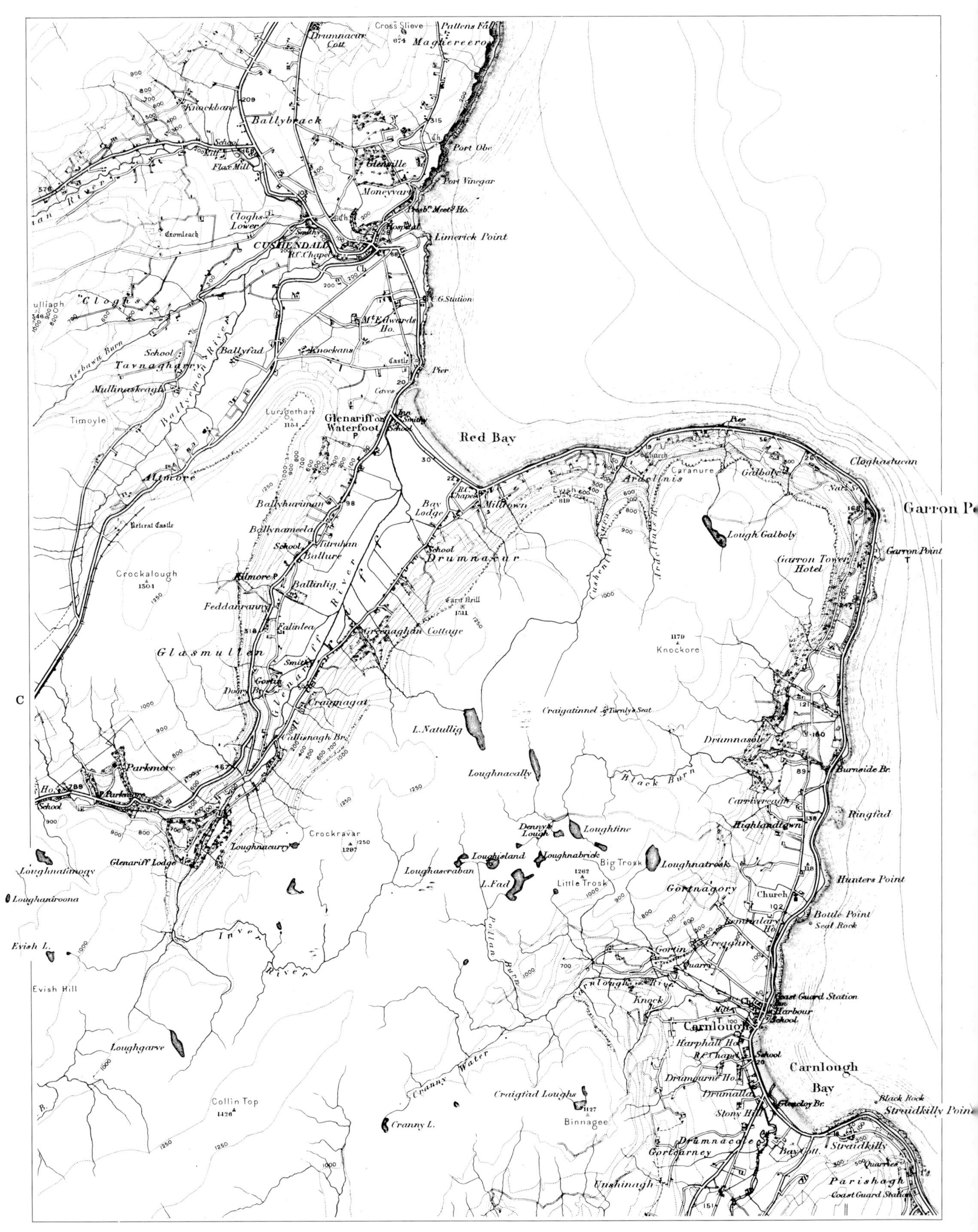
Cross Slieve
Pattens Fall
Drumnacur Cott.
Maghereeroe
Knockbane
Ballybrack
Port Obe
Glenville
Flax Mill
Port Vinegar
Moneyvart
Cloghs Lower
Cromleach
CUSHENDALL
R.C. Chapel
Limerick Point
C.G. Station
McEdwards Ho.
Knockans
Ballyfad
Tavnaghan
Mullinaskeagh
Timoyle
Lurigethan
Glenariff or Waterfoot
Red Bay
Altmore
Ballyhurinan
Bay Lodge
Milltown
Ardclinis
Caranure
Galboly
Cloghastucan
Garron P
Lough Galboly
Garron Point
Garron Tower Hotel
Retreat Castle
Ballynameela
Ballure
Drumnasar
Crockalough
Ballinlig
Feddanrany
Falinlea
Greenaghan Cottage
Knockore
Glasmullen
Craignagat
Craigatinnel
L. Natullig
Drumnasole
Parkmore
Callisnagh Br.
Loughnacally
Black Burn
Burnside Br.
Carriveagh
Ringfad
Highlandtown
Crockravar
Loughfine
Loughnacurry
Glenariff Lodge
Loughnatrosk
Big Trosk
Little Trosk
Loughascraban
L. Fad
Hunters Point
Loughnatinnogy
Loughaniroona
Gortnagory
Church
Bottle Point
Seal Rock
Evish L.
Evish Hill
Gortin
Creggan
Quarry
Knock
Coast Guard Station
Harbour
School
Carnlough
Harphall Ho.
R.C. Chapel
Carnlough Bay
Loughgarve
Drumnacole
Drumalla
Stony Hill
Glencloy Br.
Black Rock
Straidkilly Point
Collin Top
Cranny L.
Craigfad Loughs
Binnagee
Gortcarney
Straidkilly
Quarries
Unshinagh
Parishagh
Coast Guard Station

The second Antrim narrow gauge line to get its Act was the Ballymena & Larne which was authorised in 1874. By the end of the 1860s the port of Larne was growing in importance. Regular steamer services were being operated on the short sea crossing to Stranraer in south west Scotland. The broad gauge Carrickfergus & Larne Railway had opened in 1862 and attention was subsequently turned to making a railway link to the west to shorten the journey of those travelling to the port other than from Belfast. The first proposal was for a 5ft 3in line to Antrim. This was later dropped in favour of a narrow gauge line from Larne to Ballyclare. This scheme was expanded to extend the line to Ballymena and it was this which was submitted to Parliament in 1874. The B&L had a share capital of £136,000 and powers to raise up to £45,000 in loans. The first section from Larne to Ballyclare was opened in September 1877. Several visits from Colonel Rich of the Board of Trade were required before he was prepared to allow the line from Ballyboley, the junction of the branch to Ballyclare, to Ballymena to be opened in August 1878. The B&L terminus in Ballymena was initially at Harryville at the edge of the town. The line was extended into the B&NCR station in 1880 where it also made a connection with the BC&RB.

The B&L was a steeply graded line, rising in 12 miles, from sea level at Larne Harbour, to a summit at Ballynashee of 660ft, on gradients as steep as 1 in 36. Whilst the line depended heavily on mineral traffic, it carried passengers from the outset, unlike the Cushendall line. In its early years the B&L entertained plans for extensions to its system. One of these was for a line to Londonderry via Dungiven which was to cross the Foyle on a great viaduct and follow the GNR route into the city. Lack of funds put paid to this grand folly across some of the bleakest and most thinly populated parts of Ulster. The only extension to the original line to be built was a short addition of 1½ miles to the Ballyclare branch as far as Doagh which opened in 1884. By this date the B&L was suffering from the decline in the iron trade and after several years of financial uncertainty it followed the BC&RB into the embrace of the B&NCR in 1889.

The third line under consideration in this chapter is the Ballycastle Railway, authorised in 1875 and opened in 1880. The BR linked the seaside town of Ballycastle on the North Antrim coast to the B&NCR at Ballymoney, some 16¼ miles distant. Not all

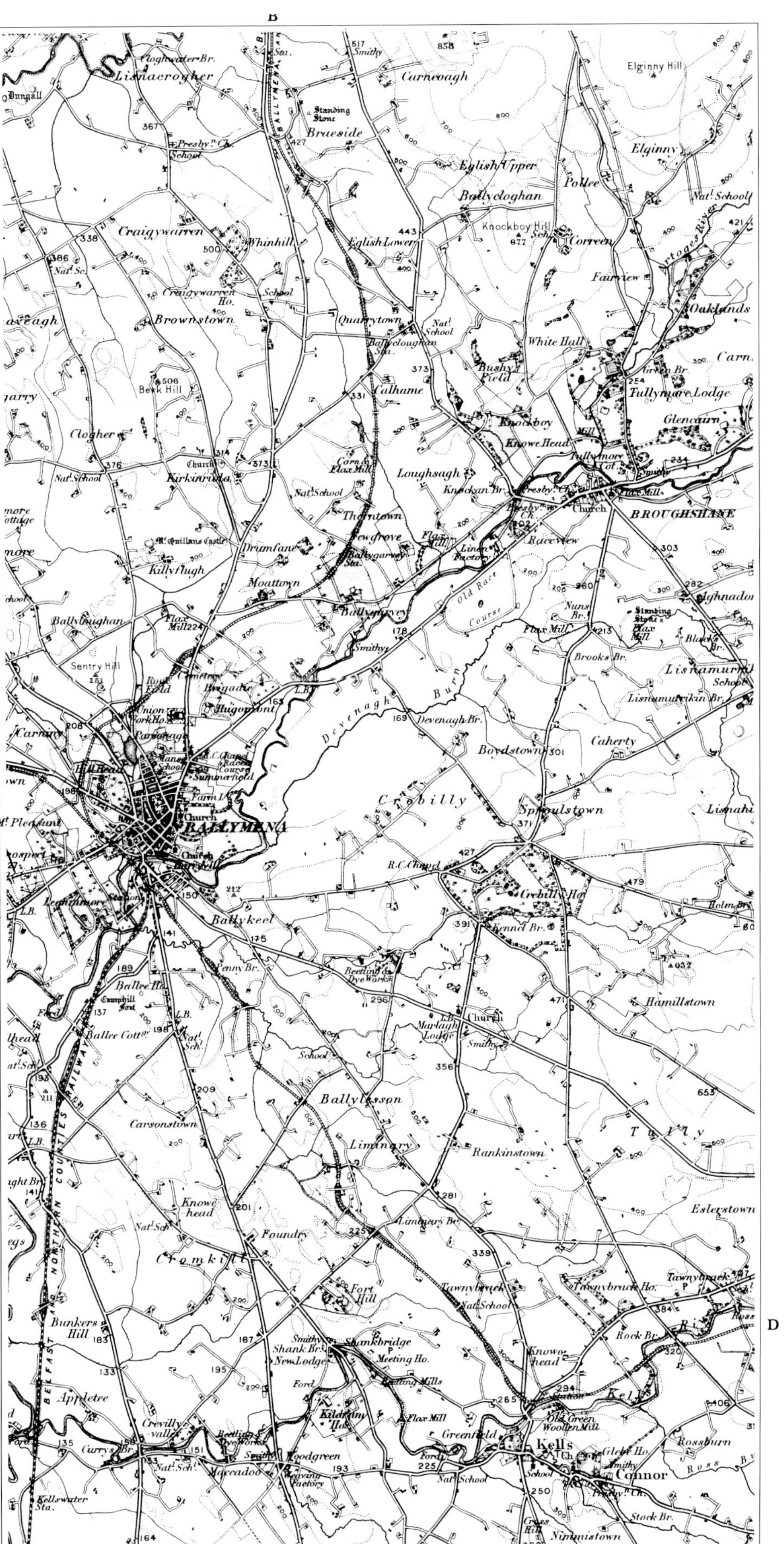

Copyright reserved, Ordnance Survey, Dublin. Reproduced from 1 inch series, sheet nos. 14, 20; revised 1900, 1900; published 1902, 1902 respectively. Scale 1 inch to 1 mile.

D
Deerfin
Ballynulto
Douglas Top
Douglas
Glen Head
Bractown
Crosshill
Mistyburn
Cross
Granagh
Greenhill Br.
Brae Hill
Lawtown
Glenhead
Whiteridge
Craighall
Nat. School
Moorfields
Shank Br.
The Battery
Shoptown
Glenwhirry
Reidstown
Glenville
Killylane Br.
Beetling & Dye Works
Bankhead
Battery Br.
Glenwhirry River
Pigtail Br.
Killy
Saughyards
Ross Lodge
Craigstown
Castlegore
Whappstown
Collin Ho.
Wee Collin
Ballynashee
Whanstown
Tildarg Hill
Elliotts Hill
Big Collin
Collin Vale
Maxwells Walls
Speerstown
Ballynashee Sta.
Braepark Br.
Shaws Hill
Breckenhill
Tildarg
Forthill
Barnish
Waterheadstown
Carnlea
Ballynashee Ho.
Lismacaffry
Tardree Mountain
Ballygowan
McVickersland
Peat Hill
Drumadarragh Hill
Galtstown
Castlehill
Islandkelly
Ballybracken
Walkmill
Five Corners
Frenchhill
Backside
Rashee
Springvale
Standing Stone
Flemingstown
Crawfordsland
Brownhill
Halftown
Duncansland
Ballyvoy Lodge
Brookfield
Rashee Lr.
Coggrey
Coggrey Ho.
Fairview
Ballyclare
Lady Hill
Scolboa
Mossside
Ballywoodock
Ballyclaver
Ballyclaver Ho.
Kilbride
Tumbling Br.
Thorndith
Grahamstown
Clareview
Flax Mill
Holestone
Dunamuggy
Kilbride Hall
Gribbinstown
Ballywee
Newmill
Fisherwick
Paper Mills
Tobergill
Doagh Station
Ballyhamage Ho.
Doagh
Donegore Hill
Size Hill
Sandymount
Hollybank Spinning Mill
Drumagorgan
Craigy Hall
Priests Town
Shaws Corner
Ballyvalley Br.
Smithy

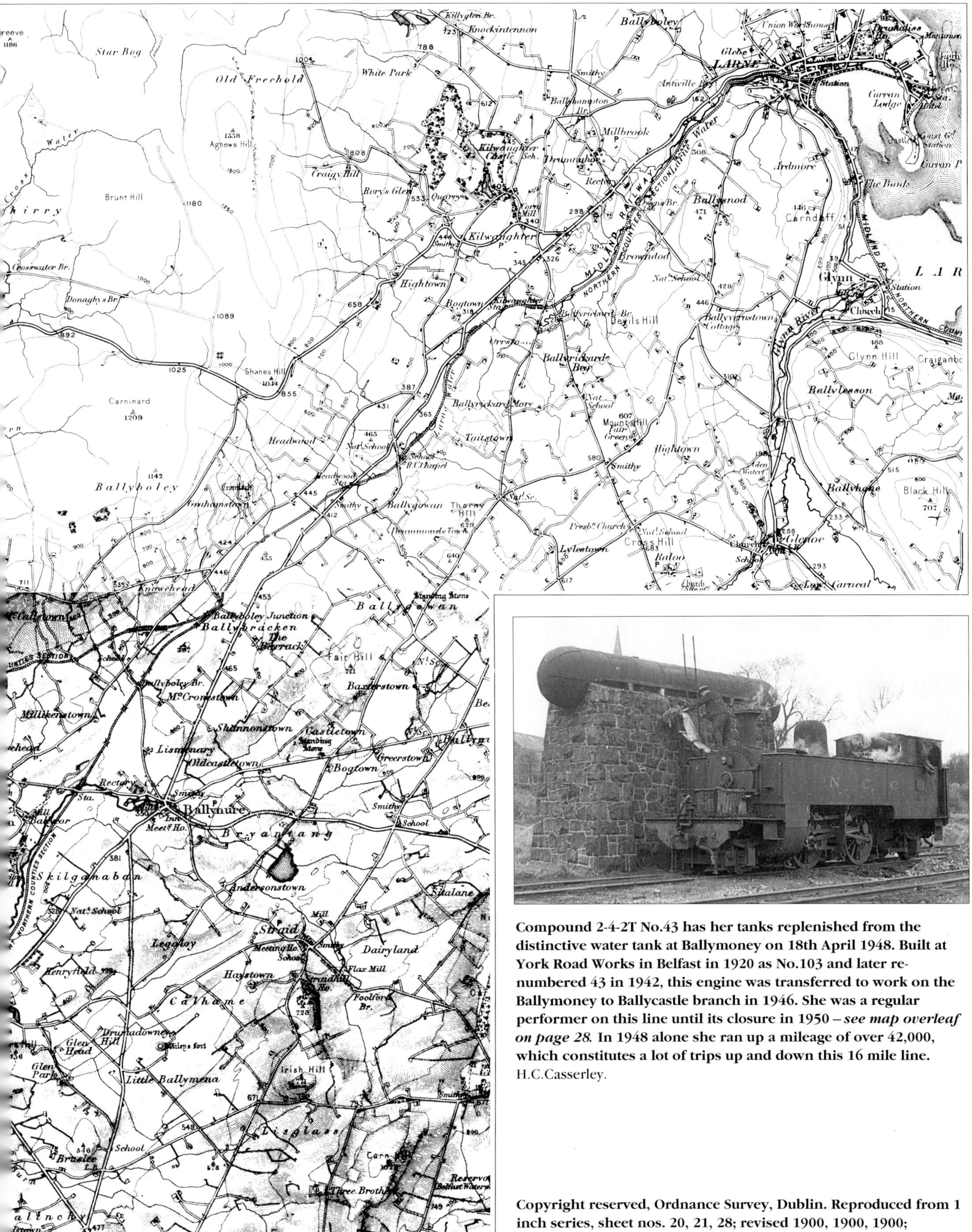

Compound 2-4-2T No.43 has her tanks replenished from the distinctive water tank at Ballymoney on 18th April 1948. Built at York Road Works in Belfast in 1920 as No.103 and later re-numbered 43 in 1942, this engine was transferred to work on the Ballymoney to Ballycastle branch in 1946. She was a regular performer on this line until its closure in 1950 – *see map overleaf on page 28.* In 1948 alone she ran up a mileage of over 42,000, which constitutes a lot of trips up and down this 16 mile line. H.C.Casserley.

 Reproduced from 1 inch series, sheet nos. 20, 21, 28; revised 1900, 1900, 1900; published 1902, 1902, 1902 respectively. Scale 1 inch to 1 mile.

the line's, £90,000 share capital was taken up when the line was promoted and this led to two problems. The BR cut corners with its permanent way. Very light track was laid to save money and the cost of improving this in later years was a severe drain on the company's modest resources. The concern's initial under-capitalisation meant that loans had to be raised to make up the difference and interest on these siphoned off a substantial proportion of the railway's income. This meant that dividends were scarce for ordinary shareholders even in the halcyon days before the Great War. The BR's finances had reached such a state by 1924 that its Directors resolved to close down the line and indeed services were suspended for some months. It thus very nearly became the first 3ft gauge line in Ireland to close down until an offer from the NCC to buy the line for £12,500 was received. Services resumed under the new owners in August 1924 and in the end the BR became the last of the Antrim lines to retain a passenger service. The end finally came in July 1950, by which time of course it had been taken over by the Ulster Transport Authority.

The locomotives of the Antrim lines were of considerable interest. The BC&RB's fleet consisted of three Black Hawthorn built 0-4-2 saddle tanks. Two of these lasted until 1923, having spent some time on the Cavan & Leitrim at the end of the 1914-1918 war. They had been sent there by the Railway Executive to assist in the construction of the extension of the Arigna branch. The B&L went to Beyer Peacock for their locomotives as did so many Irish railways. Of their first three engines, one was a 0-6-0 tank, the other two were 0-4-2Ts, very similar to those supplied by Beyer Peacock to the Isle of Man Railways at around the same time. The next B&L purchase was a unique 2-6-0 saddle tank built in 1880. Another 0-6-0T which arrived in 1883 completed its fleet. The BR began its services with three Black Hawthorn 0-6-0 saddle tanks which maintained the service until 1908 when two impressive looking 4-4-2Ts were ordered from Kitson's. This pair flattered to deceive. They lacked sufficient adhesion on their driving wheels and slipped and slithered on the steep grades and reverse curves of the Ballycastle line.

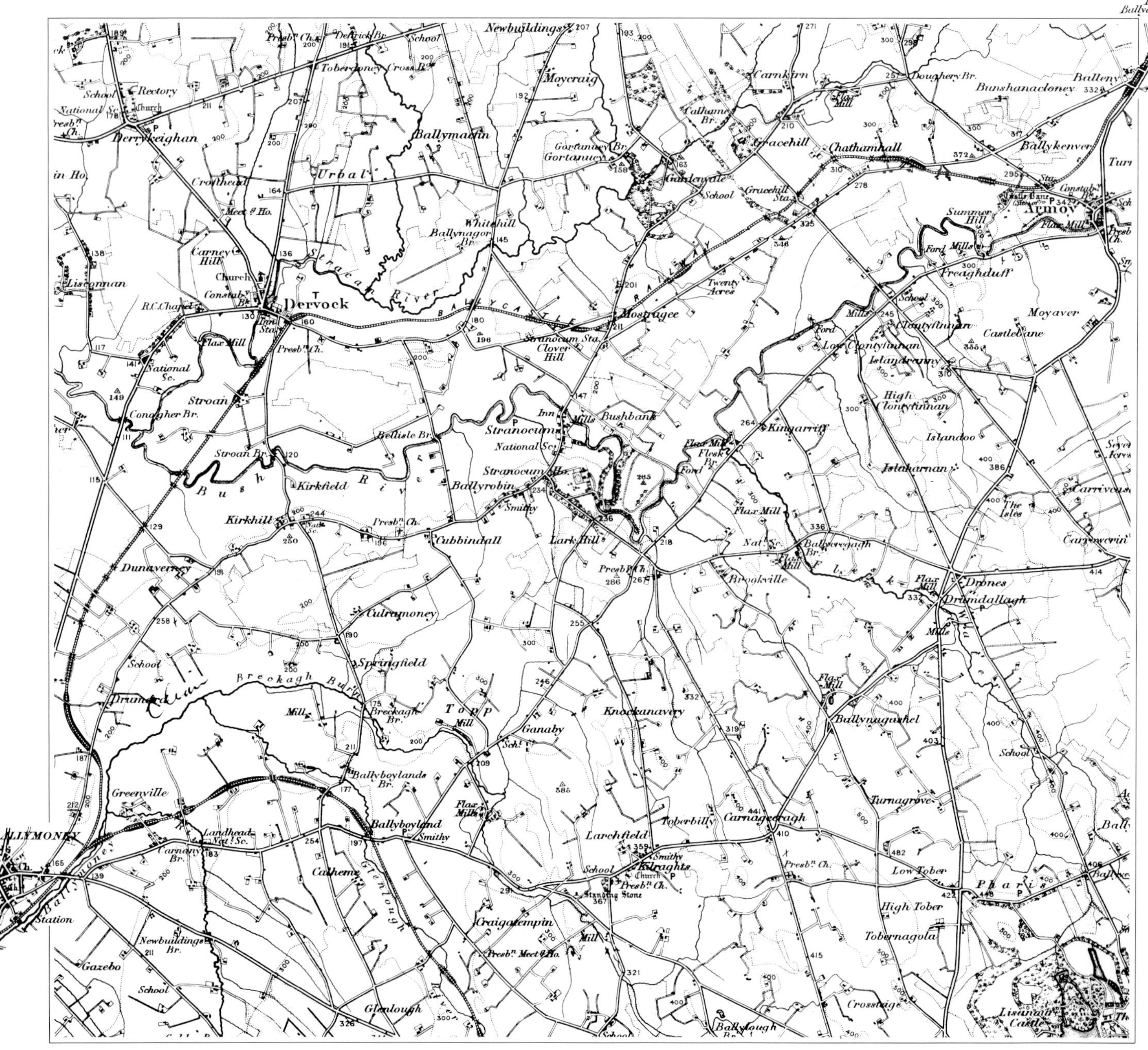

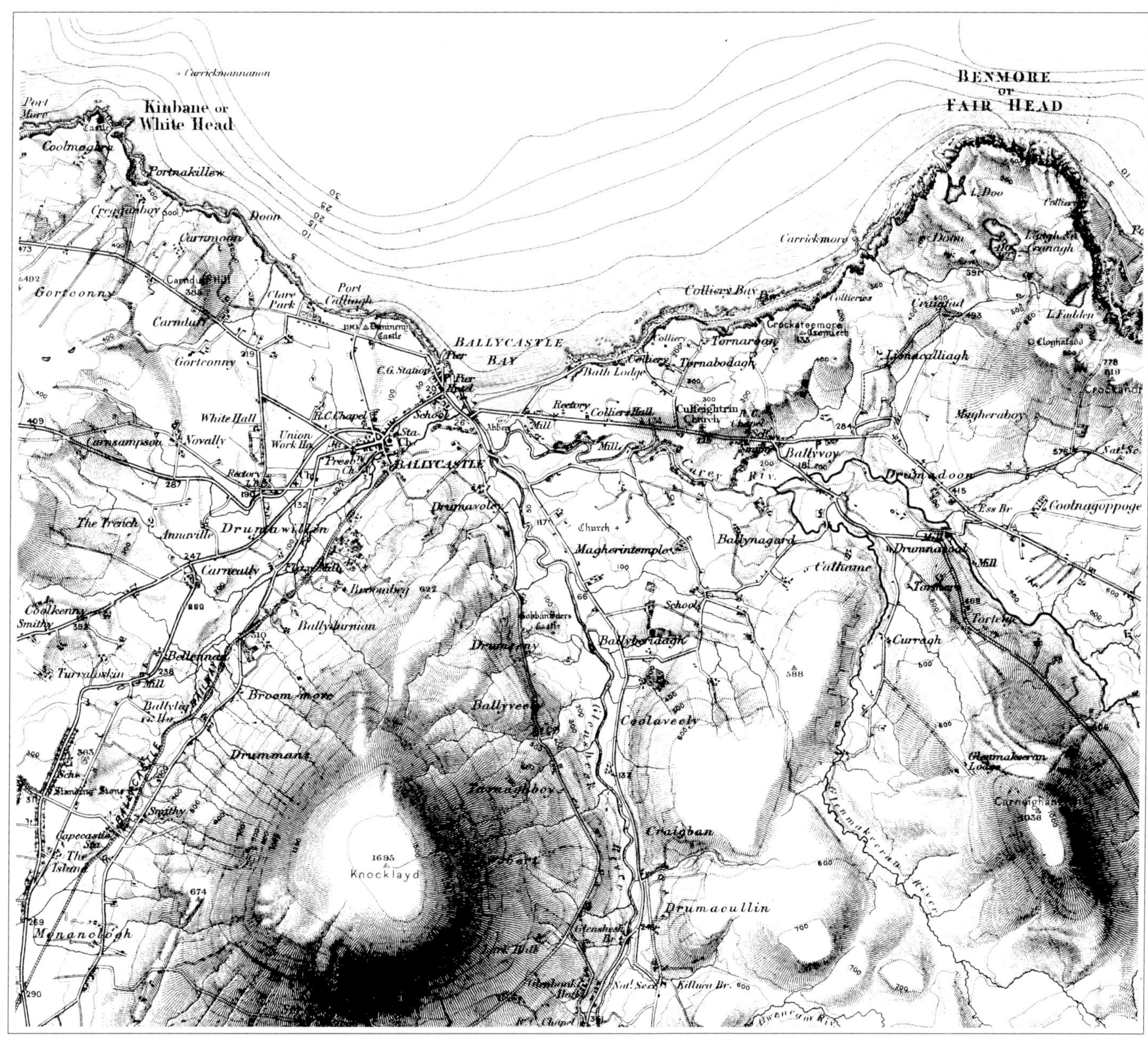

Copyright reserved, Ordnance Survey, Dublin. Reproduced from 1 inch series, sheet nos. 13, 8; revised 1900, 1900; published 1902, 1902 respectively. Scale 1 inch to 1 mile.

The BNCR and MR regimes brought additional motive power to their narrow gauge lines in the form of a delightful series of 2-4-2 compound tanks built between 1892 and 1920. The first pair were built by Beyer Peacock, the rest were constructed at York Road Works in Belfast. The B&NCR locomotive engineer at that period, Bowman Malcolm, was a firm believer in compounding for both his broad and narrow gauge engines. The first of the series was rebuilt in 1931 as a 2-4-4T, though in this form it had limited success even if it held the distinction of being the only locomotive of this wheel arrangement in service in the British Isles. The compound 2-4-2Ts were useful engines which lasted until the end of the Antrim lines. The locos on the narrow gauge in Antrim underwent several re-numberings and I will endeavour to unravel these in the captions to the photographs.

When the B&NCR took over the BC&RB, a passenger service was introduced on to what had previously been a freight only line. The permanent way was improved and signalling was introduced. Between 1885 and 1888 passenger trains were introduced in stages from Ballymena to Parkmore. The last section of the line from Parkmore to Retreat never carried passenger trains. The B&NCR realised the potential of the Antrim glens for tourism. The Company rented Glenariff and turned it into a sort of late Victorian theme park with paths for visitors, refreshment facilities and even a dark room that could be rented by photographers. Tourists were conveyed from Parkmore in horse cars to various destinations in the glens and ingenious round trips were devised, some of them from Larne along the famous Antrim coast road. Iron ore continued to be carried though the tonnages involved were much reduced from those conveyed in the line's early years. After the war, increasing road competition and a decline in the numbers lured by the blandishments of the glens led to a withdrawal of the passenger service in October 1930. On the same date passenger services from Ballyclare to Doagh on the B&L section were also suspended. Goods services carried on up to 1937 when the Rathkenny to Retreat section was completely closed.

Traffic from a creamery at Rathkenny kept the southern part of the BC&RB line open until June 1940 when this business was transferred to road vehicles and the line was abandoned.

The B&L had a longer innings than the BC&RB. Control from Belfast and ultimately, Euston, brought investment in locos and rolling stock. The most spectacular manifestation of this was in the form of the new carriages supplied in 1928 for the boat trains from Ballymena to Larne. These were by a long way the most luxurious coaches ever to grace an Irish narrow gauge line. They brought main line standards of comfort to the 3ft gauge, offering steam heating, electric lighting, lavatories and corridor connections to their patrons. Sadly they were only in service for five years. A bitter railway strike occurred in Northern Ireland in 1933 when the managements of the province's railway companies tried to impose pay cuts on their employees. During the course of the strike it was announced that passenger services from Ballymena to Larne and from Ballyboley Junction to Ballyclare, were not going to be resumed. At the same time the goods service from Ballyclare to Doagh was withdrawn and this section was to be closed completely. Goods trains continued to run between Ballymena and Larne until June 1940 when the line from Ballyboley Junction to Ballymena was closed. This left just the 12 mile section from Larne to Ballyclare open for freight only. In 1949 British Railways sold the former LMS lines in Northern Ireland to the UTA, an organisation famed for its antipathy to railways. The closure in 1950 of the paper mill at Ballyclare, which provided most of the traffic for the line that remained, allowed the UTA to bring the curtain down on its narrow gauge interests. The line from Larne to Ballyclare and the Ballycastle branch were both closed on the same melancholy day, 3rd July 1950.

Top: **The only locomotives owned by the BC&RB were three 0-4-2 saddle tanks built by Black Hawthorn which were delivered in 1874 and 1875. Numbered logically 1 to 3, and later renumbered 60 to 62 by the B&NCR, the first two lasted until 1923, the third was scrapped in 1908. They were renumbered a second time by the B&NCR in 1897 becoming this time 101A, 102A and 103A. This picture shows the first BC&RB engine on a passenger train at Ballymena before it was rebuilt and renumbered in 1897.** Ulster Folk and Transport Museum.

Centre: **The six locos bought by the B&L all came from Beyer Peacock. Three of these were 0-6-0Ts. Nos 2 and 3 arrived in 1877, No.6 dated from 1883. Under B&NCR ownership these became Nos 65, 66 and 67 in 1889 and 106, 107 and 108 in 1897. The reason for the B&NCR's double renumbering of its narrow gauge engines was that when they were first taken over the narrow gauge engines were allocated a block of numbers ahead of the broad gauge sequence which then stopped (in 1884) at 49. This underestimated the expansion of the broad gauge fleet therefore in the 1890s the narrow gauge engines had to vacate the numbers in the 60s which they occupied and jump to the 100s. No.108, on the turntable at Larne in this 1902 picture, is pretty much in its original condition.** Ken Nunn collection.

Above: **No.107, pictured in LMS days, has acquired Ross safety valves set in its dome. This was the first of the ex-B&L 0-6-0Ts to be scrapped, being withdrawn in 1931.** Len's of Sutton.

Top left, and centre left: **B&L No.5 was the only 2-6-0 saddle tank to run on the Irish narrow gauge. Built in 1880 it became No.68 and ultimately No.109 in subsequent re-numberings. Its nickname 'The Bruiser', was a reflection of its considerable power. These views of it were taken at Ballyboley Junction in 1930, four years before it was withdrawn.** H.C.Casserley.

Centre right: **No.105 was built by Beyer Peacock in 1878 as B&L No.4. Seen here in the shed at Larne, the similarities between her and the Manx engine pictured below, are very striking. No.105 was sold to the C&VBT in 1928: she is pictured on that line on page 32.** Charles P Friel collection.

Bottom left: **I have suggested that the adoption of the 3ft gauge in County Antrim, which led to it becoming Ireland's second gauge, was influenced by its introduction on the Isle of Man. Circumstantial evidence to back this contention may be found in the similarities between the two B&L 2-4-0Ts built in 1877 and 1878 and the Beyer Peacock engines of the same type supplied to the Isle of Man Railway in the 1870s. The B&L locos were supposed to be exact copies of Isle of Man Railway No.6 *Peveril*. I turned to that well known historian of the railways of the Isle of Man, Robert Hendry, for a picture of No.6 in its original condition, but as it had been rebuilt relatively early in its career, he suggested that a comparison could best be made with the former Manx Northern Railway 2-4-0T, seen here as Isle of Man Railway No.14, *Thornhill*. This engine was built in 1880 but was the last of the type to remain in original condition.**
H.J.Stretton-Ward, R.P.Hendry collection.

Top left: **No.105 finished its days on the Castlederg & Victoria Bridge Tramway where it was seen in June 1930. The dome, cab and many other features are identical to those on the IOMR engine.** H.C.Casserley.

Centre left: **The locomotive fleet of the Ballycastle Railway was very straightforward, consisting of five engines of two types. Three Black Hawthorn 0-6-0 saddle tanks were purchased for the commencement of services in 1879 and 1880. One of these, No.2 *Countess of Antrim,* is arriving at Ballymoney with a train from Ballycastle on 6th May 1920.** Ken Nunn collection.

Centre right, and bottom left: **The only other BR locos were the two Kitson built 4-4-2Ts of 1908. Their lack of adhesion diminished their usefulness and when the LMS/NCC took over they were transferred to the B&L section. Their cabs and boiler mountings were cut down to comply with that line's loading gauge. Originally numbered 3 and 4 on the BR, they became NCC Nos 113 and 114. Both were photographed in NCC days at Larne.** Both Len's of Sutton.

Opposite page, centre left: **The B&NCR locomotive engineer Bowman Malcolm was a strong advocate of compound working. This practice used the steam generated by a locomotive's boiler twice. Steam was first expanded in a high pressure cylinder and was then used again in a low pressure one before it was expelled through the chimney. He introduced compound working in engine designs for the broad gauge from 1890 on and the principle was applied to a pair of narrow gauge 2-4-2Ts built by Beyer Peacock in 1892. The two engines were first numbered 69 and 70, later becoming Nos 110 and 111. This broadside view of the latter was taken in LMS days.** Len's of Sutton.

Top and centre right: **In 1931 No.110 was radically rebuilt as a 2-4-4T, the only engine of this wheel arrangement ever to run in Ireland. The bogie at the rear enabled a substantial coal bunker to be added to the loco. The 'new look' 110, though more powerful, was not a success and it seems to have been used as little as possible. The unique 2-4-4T was scrapped in 1946.** Both Len's of Sutton.

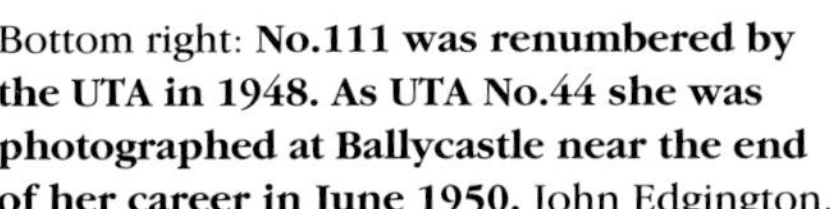

Bottom right: **No.111 was renumbered by the UTA in 1948. As UTA No.44 she was photographed at Ballycastle near the end of her career in June 1950.** John Edgington.

Top: **No further narrow gauge engines were introduced until 1908 when a further 2-4-2T compound was built, this time at York Road Works in Belfast. Numbered 112 up to 1920, then 102 until 1939 and subsequently No.42, this engine was rebuilt in 1930 with a new bunker at the rear. This dates our picture of her as having been taken in the 1930s.** Len's of Sutton.

Centre left: **1890 saw another 2-4-2T emerge from York Road. Numbered at first 113, it became 101 in 1920 and finally in 1939, No.41. As No.101 it was seen at Larne on 22nd May 1922.** Ken Nunn collection.

Bottom left: **No.103, built in Belfast in 1919 had the relatively short career of less than twenty years, being scrapped in 1938. Photographed at Larne in August 1930, astonishingly, for a loco on the Antrim narrow gauge, she retained the same number throughout her career.** H.C.Casserley.

Opposite page, top left: **The last of the compounds and the last engine built for the narrow gauge lines of County Antrim was No.104 which appeared in 1920. Another product of York Road works, she was renumbered 43 in 1942. Seen on duty on the Ballycastle line in April 1948, No.43 was not scrapped until 1954. If she had managed to hang around intact for another few years she might have made it to Belfast Transport Museum. Alas this was not to be and the last survivor of this successful and attractive class of engines went the way of so many others.**

Top right: **The climb out of Larne was known as Inver bank and provided a severe challenge for locomotives heading west and for the brakes of trains going down towards the coast. The bank offered gradients of 1 in 36 and 1 in 44 in just over a mile. 2-4-2T No.101 pounds up the bank with a long train of coal and livestock wagons in the 1920s.** R.C.Ludgate collection.

Centre: **This picture of Beyer Peacock 2-4-0T No.64 at Larne must have been taken between 1889 when the loco was given this number, and 1897 when it became No.105.** Charles P Friel collection.

Right: **The former BR loco, 4-4-2T No.113 heads a short coal train out of Larne. For a locomotive with a reputation for slipping, ten loaded coal wagons and a brake van was probably about her limit on the stiff climb out of Larne.** W.Robb MBE, courtesy W.T.Scott.

Top left: **Ballyboley, 7¾ miles from Larne, was the junction for the branch to Doagh which can be seen diverging to the right of No.109 and its coal train in this 1933 picture. The 2-6-0 saddle tank is about to pass a diesel engined railcar built by a Belfast firm for a railway in South America which was tried out on the Larne to Ballymena line before it went overseas. The Antrim narrow gauge lines themselves remained steam worked from beginning to end.** R.C.Ludgate collection.

Centre left: **4-4-2T No.113 pauses at Ballyboley with a coal train in June 1945.** D.G.Coakham.

Centre right: **2-4-2T No.42 is at Ballyboley on 28th July 1949 with a train of wagons containing wood pulp for the mill at Ballyclare. The railway was now in the hands of the UTA, the fifth owners of the line after the B&L, the B&NCR, the MR and the LMS. The closure of the paper mill in 1950 gave the UTA the opportunity to close this, the last remaining part of the B&L.** D.G.Coakham.

Bottom: **No.113 and a brake van pause at Ballyboley on the way back from taking a coal train to the paper mill at Ballyclare. By this time, 1945, the main line beyond Ballyboley to Ballymena had been closed and lifted and the traffic generated by the paper mill had become the line's staple traffic.** R.C.Ludgate.

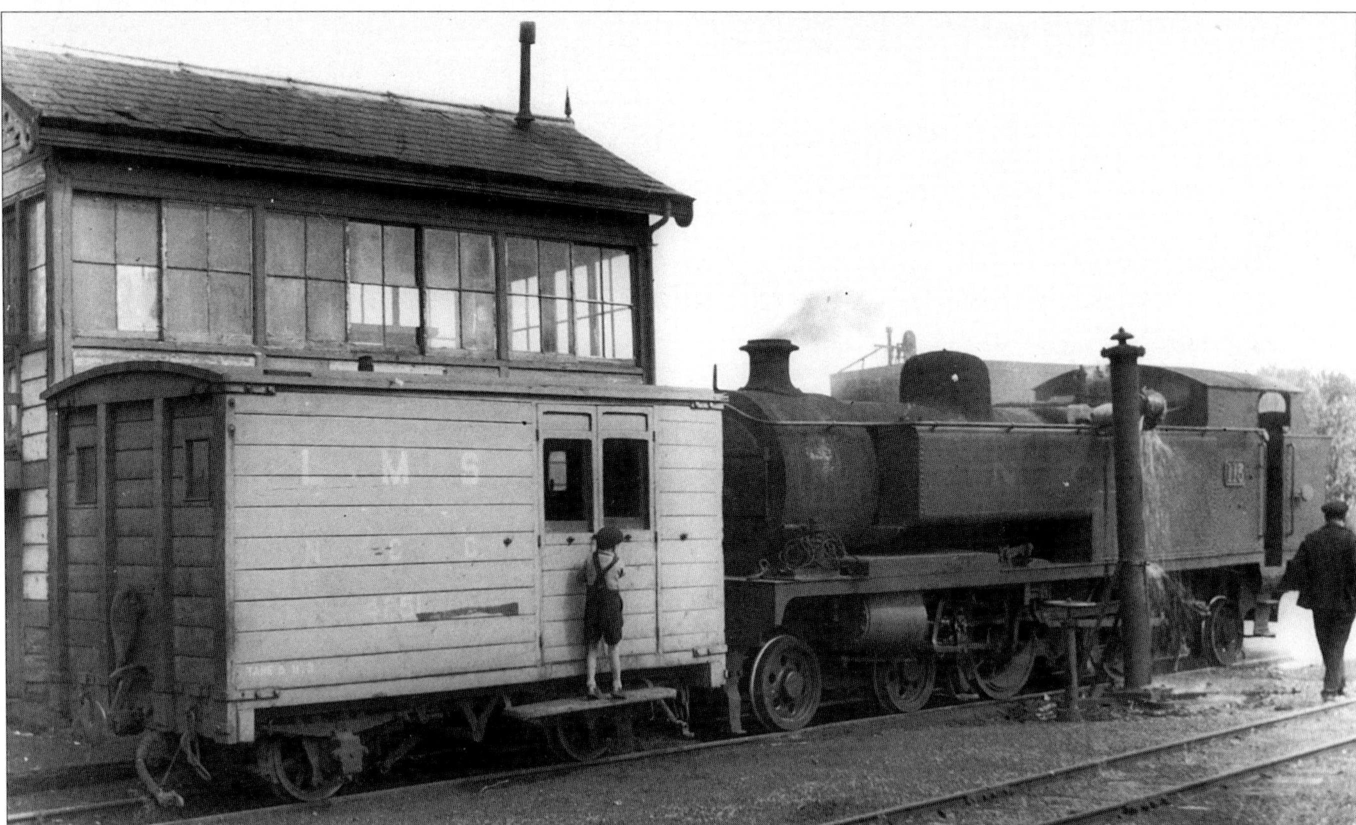

Top: **When Henry Casserley travelled on the Doagh branch on 9th August 1930 'The Bruiser' was in charge of the modest branch train.**

Above: **The short extension from Ballyclare to Doagh was opened in 1884. Passenger services were withdrawn from this section on 1st October 1930.** H.C.Casserley.

Right: **No.113 approaches the siding leading into the mill at Ballyclare in June 1945.** D.G.Coakham.

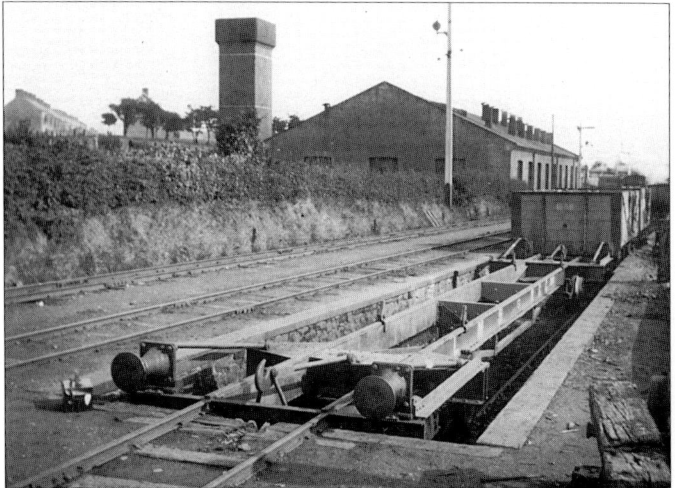

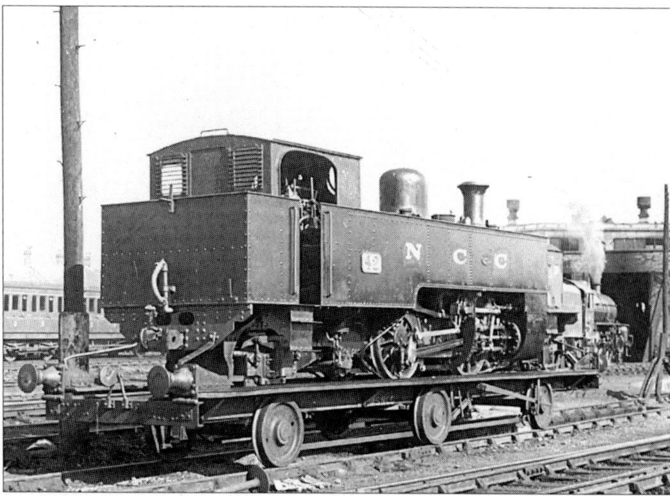

Top left: **Among the more unusual vehicles in the vast inventory of the LMS were the three wagons which were used to bring narrow gauge vehicle to Belfast for repairs and overhauls. The transporter wagon was run into a special bay and the narrow gauge stock was shunted on to the 3ft gauge rails on the wagon's body. One of the wagons and the loading bay at Ballymena were photographed in 1930.** H.C.Casserley.

Top right: **Narrow gauge compound 2-4-2T No.42 is seen on 6-wheel transporter wagon No.3094, at York Road in April 1948. One of the NCC's famous Moguls can be seen in the shed ahead of it.** H.C.Casserley.

Above: **At Ballymena, where the narrow gauge tracks shared the main line station, through running from the Parkmore line to Larne was possible. This general view of the station, taken in 1938 after narrow gauge passenger services had ended, shows in the foreground the narrow gauge platform line crossed by a broad gauge siding, with the Up and Down broad gauge platforms, to the right.** H.C.Casserley.

Right: **Ballymena was one of the few places in Ireland where mixed gauge tracks could be seen. In LMS days both gauges shared the one engine shed as this 1938 view shows.** H.C.Casserley.

Left: **The first B&L locomotive, No.1, later No.63 and as seen here, No.104, was built by Beyer Peacock in 1877. She is seen leaving Ballymena with a train to Larne at the turn of the century. The B&NCR broad gauge tracks to Belfast are in the foreground. The lower quadrant semaphore signals were later replaced by somersault signals.**
Charles P Friel collection.

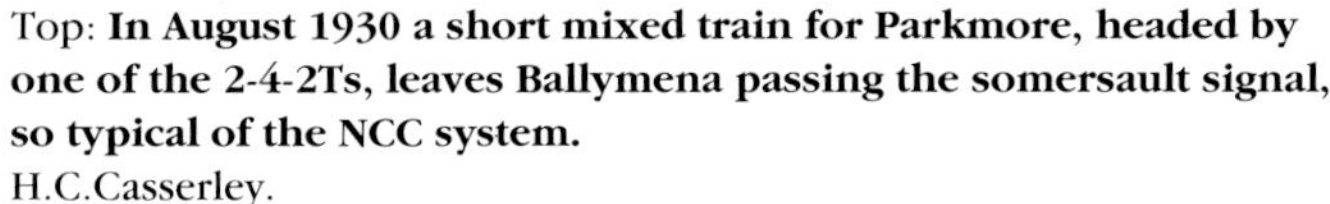

Top: **In August 1930 a short mixed train for Parkmore, headed by one of the 2-4-2Ts, leaves Ballymena passing the somersault signal, so typical of the NCC system.**
H.C.Casserley.

Centre left: **In the last years of the passenger service on the Ballymena to Larne line the NCC introduced a new train which, in terms of passenger comfort, was far in advance of anything which had been seen before on the narrow gauge in the British Isles. Coaches 350 to 353, built in Belfast, had electric lighting, steam heating, lavatories and corridor connections. They were put in service on the boat trains from Ballymena which connected with the steamers to Scotland at Larne Harbour. The boat express covered the 25 miles in about an hour with one stop. 4-4-2T No.113 and three of the 50ft long coaches are seen here at Larne Harbour. When passenger services between Ballymena and Larne were withdrawn the coaches saw further service on the Ballycastle line and three of these 1928 built coaches finished their days on the CDR.** R.C.Ludgate collection.

Centre right: **Coach No.353, a brake composite with two each 1st and 3rd class compartments, was photographed after the end of passenger services, somewhat the worse for wear.**
R.C.Ludgate.

Above: **For the introduction of passenger services on the BC&RB line in the mid 1880s, the B&NCR, between 1886 and 1898, built in Belfast, ten 8-wheeled vehicles, which were referred to as tramcars. The first of these, No.306, is seen here. This was an all-3rd, seating 40 passengers in two saloons fitted with longitudinal seats. These vehicles had pivoted fall plates which allowed passage through the train, and verandahs from which tourists could view the splendours of the Antrim Glens. As built, they had panelled sides and more steeply curved roofs –** ***see page 30.*** **The flatter roof and the matchboard sides were the result of a later rebuild.** R.C.Ludgate.

Above centre: **Like the Ballymena lines, the Ballycastle Railway had a convenient cross platform interchange with the Belfast to Londonderry broad gauge line of the B&NCR and its successors. At Ballymoney station on 10th August 1930, the 2.55pm train for Ballycastle waits for the off, headed by 0-6-0T No.106 which had been built for the B&L in 1877.** H.C.Casserley.

Top left: **Ten years earlier one of the original BR locos, No.2 *Countess of Antrim*, heads the 5.30pm departure to Ballycastle on 4th May 1920.** Ken Nunn collection.

Bottom left: **On 18th April 1948, 2-4-2T No.43 brings a train from Ballycastle into Ballymoney station. Extra supplies of coal were carried in the wicker baskets in front of the smokebox.** H.C.Casserley.

Top right: **Pigeon baskets were a common sight on Irish railway stations. On 2nd July 1948 staff at Ballycastle release birds which were about to undertake the long journey to Mallow in County Cork.** W.Robb MBE, courtesy W.T.Scott collection.

Above: **This view of Ballycastle in the late 1940s shows that it offered everything that you might expect from the terminus of a narrow gauge branch line. It has a single platform, an engine shed, sidings and a loading bay for livestock. It just cries out to be modelled! Perhaps the only surprising element of the picture is the corridor connection at the end of the coach in the platform.** R.C.Ludgate.

Below: **A delightful portrait of 2-4-2T No.43 as it takes water outside Ballycastle shed in 1949.** W.Robb MBE, courtesy W.T.Scott collection.

Above: **In their last year of service and bearing the railway equivalent of the pirates' 'black spot', the UTA logo, on their tanks, 2-4-2Ts Nos 41 and 44, the latter an 1892 engine still going strong, await their next call of duty on 26th June 1950, at Ballycastle shed.** John Edgington.

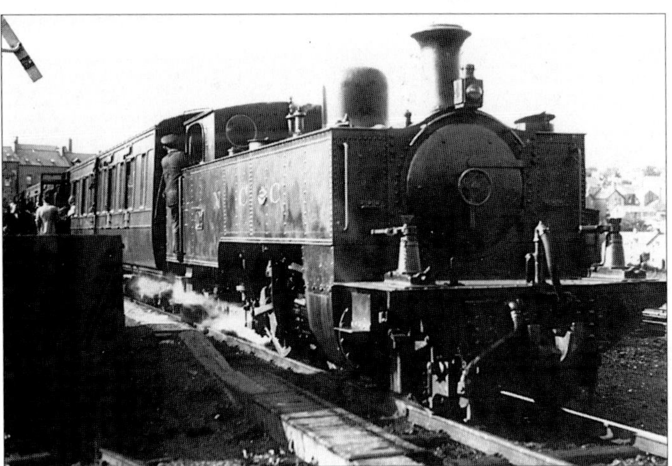

Above: **The 2-4-2Ts dominated services on the Ballycastle line following the NCC take over. On 13th June 1936, No.102 has the road for the 6.40pm departure from Ballycastle though passengers are still boarding the train.** W.Robb MBE, courtesy W.T.Scott collection.

Above: **The same train with the three corridor coaches at its head, gets under way over the viaduct outside the station and off towards Ballymoney.** W.Robb MBE, courtesy W.T.Scott collection.

Above: **On 26th June 1950, a much more modest formation is headed by No.41 at the same location. The train is the 6.20pm to Ballymoney.** John Edgington.

Chapter Three

THE GIANT'S CAUSEWAY TRAMWAY

THERE was one more narrow gauge line in County Antrim in addition to those dealt with in the last chapter. It was so singular in its nature and, in its own right, so significant in the history of railways in the British Isles, that it would have been invidious to have included it with the others. Its full title was the Giant's Causeway, Portrush and Bush Valley Railway and Tramway Company Limited, more commonly known as the Giant's Causeway Tramway. While it missed out by a matter of weeks from being the first electric railway in the British Isles, that honour going to the Volk's Electric Railway along the seafront at Brighton, the Irish line demonstrated, over a much longer distance than the Brighton one, the potential of electricity as a motive force for railways, in a way that had never been seen before in these islands.

The origins of the railway were not all that different from some of the other lines we have examined. In the 19th century if your town or district was not linked to the railway network it was felt to be missing out in all kinds of ways. This was the motivation to connect the small town of Bushmills in north Antrim, either along the coast to the rapidly developing resort of Portrush or inland by means of a line to make a junction with the Ballycastle Railway, at Dervock.

A public meeting was held in Bushmills in October 1879 chaired by Dr Anthony Traill, whose brother William made a significant contribution to the discussion. Though the Traill brothers came from a local family, Anthony was a fellow and later Provost of Trinity College in Dublin and William had taken an engineering degree at that university. The meeting decided to support two railways. The first of these, which was never built, was to run from the Giant's Causeway to Dervock on the BR. It was hoped that this could be extended in time to Rathkenny on the BC&RB and ultimately provide through running from Bushmills to Larne over the B&L. The other line mooted at this meeting is the one that concerns us; a tramway along the coast to Portrush. When parliamentary assent was given to this line in August 1880 it is significant to note that authority was provided to work the line using electricity.

The Traills' connections with the academic world through Trinity College was the key to their championing the use of electricity. They were in touch with such figures as Sir William Thompson, later to become Lord Kelvin, and Dr William Siemens. These men, involved in research into the practical applications of electricity, both took stock in the company, and indeed, Siemens became a director. At first the line was to be electrified on the two rail system which had been used on various experimental railways already in being. By this method, familiar to all railway modellers, the two rails were insulated from each other and were used as positive and negative conductors as well as the running rails. Leakage of current, especially in wet weather, put paid to this idea and it was decided to adopt a third rail system, with the conductor rail located on the seaward side of the tram, away from the public roads along which the track was to run for most of its length. Initially electricity was generated by a steam driven dynamo while a hydro-electric power station was constructed at Walkmills near Bushmills.

Construction began on the Bushmills to Portrush section in September 1881 and the line was inspected and approved by the Board of Trade in January 1883. It was not permitted to have the third rail running through the streets of Portrush and Bushmills at either end of the line so two steam tramway locomotives were acquired to work on these sections and also to handle the goods traffic which was expected to develop. The line cost £21,000 to construct and was formally opened by the Lord Lieutenant in September 1883. At the official opening Anthony Traill told the assembled guests that services had begun in February 1883, presumably using the steam locomotives. We know that trips in the electric cars were advertised as a novelty in the summer of 1883. Because of problems with the power station regular electric services did not begin until November. The VER in Brighton opened in August 1883, but as this was only a quarter of a mile long and did not present any of the complexities of the Giant's Causeway line, even though it pipped the Irish line at the post for the right to be called the first electric railway in the British Isles, the latter must be considered as the first serious application of this new form of traction in these islands.

The tramway was laid to the 3ft gauge and was single track throughout. At first there were five passing loops though three more were added later. The conductor rail was not erected alongside the loops, cars had to coast in and out of these. Where the line crossed farm tracks there was a gap in the conductor rail. Electrical connections were maintained through cables buried in the ground at these places and pick up shoes on both the motor cars and the unpowered trailers enabled power collection to be maintained over the gaps. In 1885 plans to extend the line to the Giant's Causeway from Bushmills were revived as was the scheme for a conventional steam narrow gauge line to join the BR at Dervock. Only the extension of the tramway could be funded and the line to the famous basalt rock formation which was and is one of Ireland's premier tourist attractions, was opened in July 1887. In the decades that followed, many hundreds of thousands of visitors were conveyed to the Causeway by the tramway. Whether some of these came away with the impression it left on Dr Johnson, as recorded by Boswell, that 'it was worth seeing but not worth going to see', we do not know. Perhaps if the great lexicographer had been conveyed to the Causeway in the comfort of an electric tram he might have been more favourably disposed to the place.

It is not surprising, that as a pioneer of electric traction, the Giant's Causeway had its fair share of teething problems. In the early days it was very difficult to measure the voltage being delivered from the power station with any accuracy. Leakage of current was also a constant problem. A third steam engine was delivered in 1886 and the mileages worked by the steam engines were constantly greater than those worked by electric traction. As an example, in 1888 steam mileage was 23,588 whilst that of the electric tramcars was 12,886, eloquent testimony to the difficulties of using the new technology. The tramway worked off a theoretical supply of 250 volts and during the Board of Trade inspection the famous incident occurred when William Traill removed his trousers and sat on the live rail to prove that it was perfectly safe. However an accident in 1895 brought the wisdom of the third rail into question. A cyclist came off his machine and was thrown onto the live rail. He died shortly afterwards. When the fatality was investigated by Major Cardew of the Board of Trade he discovered that the voltage fluctuated up to a high of 310 volts and averaged 290 and that only three warning notices could be seen along the whole length of the line. He insisted that the use of electrical power should be suspended until the live rail was either boxed in or was raised 8ft above the ground. The only satisfactory solution was to introduce an overhead wire to replace the third rail. The lowest tender the company received for this work was for £15,000, a sum which it was unable to afford, so William Traill resigned his directorship and undertook the work himself for a payment of £8,000 in shares and debentures. Overhead operation began in July 1899.

By this time electric traction was much more commonplace. The Giant's Causeway Tramway joined the growing ranks of conventional electric tramways. It settled down to play its part in the tourist trade of the Causeway coast. The line was never terribly prosperous; a wet summer could make a large dent in its finances. It was purely a passenger line, the goods traffic confidently predicted by its promoters never materialised. Steam traction was not finally dispensed with until the 1920s, the last two steam locomotives being sold off eventually in 1931. Its tourist traffic faced stiff competition from buses and charabancs both before and after the 1914-1918 war. Like the other Irish railways the tramway was taken over by the Railway Executive during the war for which it received £8,437 in compensation in 1921. The directors offered the line for sale first to the MR in 1903 and later in the 1920s several times to the LMS, though neither larger company was tempted.

George Behrend, the English travel writer and railway enthusiast, has provided me with an interesting account of his impressions of the line which he visited just before the outbreak of the Second World War.

'The war was coming, my parents said, so they let me leave school as soon as I had passed the necessary exams for University, and given the required term's notice. My school friend was Scottish, and we drove together to Stranraer from Marlborough, via Aberdeen. My parents would not let us travel abroad, while promptly going off themselves. So we went to Northern Ireland. The Irish were completely baffled that a Scot and southern English should be happily travelling together. The English were considered deplorable, but Scots were oppressed fellow Celts.

'We arrived at Larne, the car was craned off the ship and we drove to Portrush to see the Giant's Causeway Tram. It was only 8 miles or so long; so the trams ran frequently, as trams should; roughly every 15 minutes or more, I think; or maybe every 10 minutes. At any rate there were a great number of cars. And it was a proper tram, like in Europe, not an ungainly English double decker drawn up in the middle of the road. The tram was safely at the kerbside. Moreover it was not a single car, but a single deck tram hauling a trailer. Soon it was time for the tram to leave. Its driver signalled to us to get aboard, so we dodged across the road among the few motor cars and many donkey carts and pony traps. This side of the trailer was quite open, with a running board all along the side, and grab handles to heave yourself in by. We settled for the trailer car, in preference to the stuffy tramcar, on whose open end platforms, only the driver and conductor might stand. The trailers looked older than the trams. It started off, like trams anywhere, along the side of the road; on the left, so no battling with traffic until coming back. Outside Portrush, it settled on the verge, brushed by a hedge most of the way which was why the doors were on one side only, and not usable from the kerbside. No one wanted brambles in their faces: it was not an unusual arrangement at all. Beyond the hedge lay some fields, then the sea.

'Tram and trailers swayed, as 4-wheelers do, on indifferent track. The trolley jumped off the wire as we went over the run-round loop points at Portrush, but the conductor was ready for this, and had the pole back up on the wire again so quickly that the driver barely noticed. Another tram was approaching the other way, and the conductor took advantage of the pause to transfer himself to the trailer, before it arrived. Then we set off again, the conductor clambering along the running board, and hooking his arm round the roof stanchions to leave both hands free for issuing the tickets. The trailer was, you see, a toast-rack car, but the term was not known to us then. The lurching was chronic, the conductor slow, anyone less experienced would have undoubtedly been thrown off, or broken his elbow which held his weight. A particularly nasty bit of track scared even the conductor whose nonchalance was so notable at the beginning. But just as I thought he would go flying, I suddenly was aware that the tram no longer sailed along at 20-25 miles an hour but was stopping though no one was waiting to get on, nor had got up to get off.

'A violent banging on the gong sent the conductor scurrying along the footboard as the tram slowed down, then he jumped rather acrobatically onto the tram's step, and I noticed that the pole was waving in the air, again. This time he was not nearly so adroit, as he missed the wire – more clanging on the gong, as the driver furiously wound the hand brake to stop the tram running backwards. It was clear the tram objected as much as its driver at being stopped on a hill, requiring careful twiddling of the handles to get going again without damaging the motors. Shortly afterwards, we stopped docilely in another loop for no apparent reason, and the conductor finished collecting his fares. I could not understand the agitation for speed, followed by this placid pause, not realising at the time that the antiquity of the cars and their motors was the reason for indecent haste not to stop on the rise. Presently another tram came from round the corner out of sight. The corners were hidden by hills their summits about a mile or so away to the right. The tram drivers had no signals, yet at the next loop here was another tram, waiting for us. The loop was round another corner, and we whizzed by at top speed. It appeared to be Irish magic – but then I was not looking for small boys up the mountain on the right, waving white and red flags at the tram drivers. By now the conductor had taken the fares and spent the rest of the way to Bushmills, nursing the pole, which frequently de-wired. We clattered through another loop, then round another corner and here was Bushmills distillery and tram depot.

'The tram now did a U-turn to the left, the depot fan being on the right, a straight run in from Portrush. Now the tram bounded across country making for the coast. The track ran much straighter than beside the sinewy road, and then ended in what appeared to be the middle of nowhere. A track led round a bluff, and beyond was the famous Causeway with its hexagonal rock formation. My greatest recollection was of finding the Causeway rather dull. The rock formation is extraordinary and a few people came to look at it. After Bushmills the tram had been nearly empty. The tram was infinitely more enticing than the Causeway, to me at least, giving Giant-size pleasure. Even in 1939 we could say "They don't have electric trams like this any more!" '

During the Second World War the line was busy. A great number of American servicemen were based in Northern Ireland and many of these visited the Giant's Causeway. A winter service was introduced in 1940 for the first time since the 1920s and this lasted until 1947. George Behrend has noted above the poor condition of the track and overhead in 1939 and this was exacerbated in the subsequent years. Faced with falling receipts and a lack of funds to refurbish the line, the directors again tried to sell the tramway, this time to the UTA, which declined to take it on. A predictable lack of interest from the government of Northern

Ireland who shortsightedly refused to provide a subsidy for what was a considerable tourist attraction in its own right, as the age of the electric tramway everywhere was on the wane, led the directors to the reluctant conclusion that they must abandon the tramway which ran for the last time on 30th September 1949.

Copyright reserved, Ordnance Survey, Dublin. Reproduced from 1 inch series, sheet no.7, revised 1910, published 1912. Scale 1 inch to 1 mile.

Bottom left: **This photograph was taken on 28th September 1883, the day of the official opening. It shows at the controls of the tram, the Lord Lieutenant of Ireland Earl Spencer, the great great grandfather of the present Princess of Wales.**
Michael Pollard collection.

Bottom right: **Steam locomotive No.3 *Dunluce Castle* was delivered in 1886 by Wilkinsons who supplied all the four locomotives on the line. These machines were crewed by a single man who had access to the fuel bunker and the fire doors from one end of the locomotive only. As there were no turntables on the tramway this meant that it was possible to fire the locomotive when it was in motion on one leg of the journey only. When the driver was at the end away from the coke bunker he could only fire when the engine was stopped.** Michael Pollard collection.

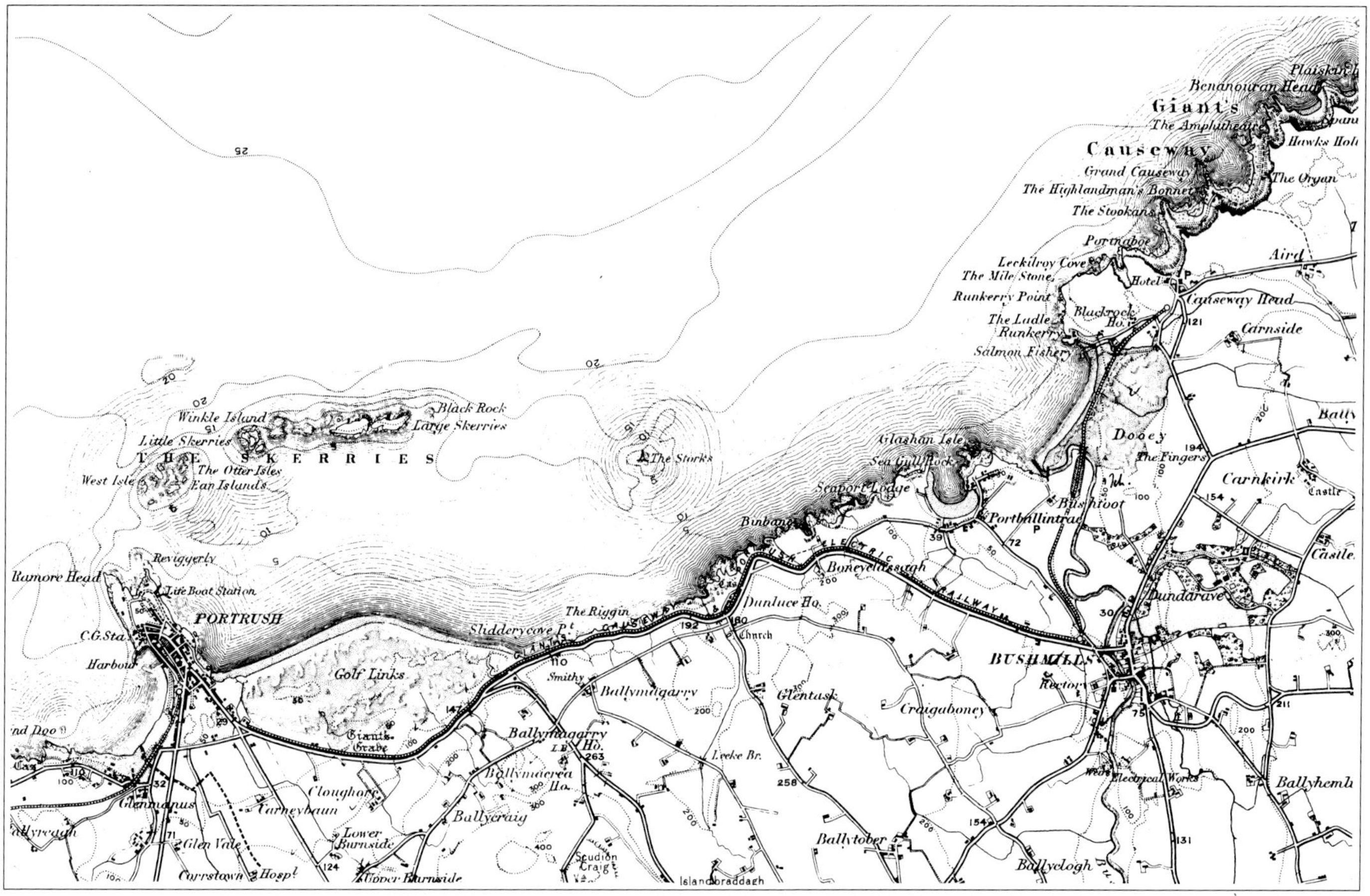

Above: **The steam locomotives had their motions enclosed in classic tramway fashion. Here the roof and the upper cladding have been removed from No.4 *Brian Boroimbe* to reveal the locomotive's vertical boiler. Nos 3 and 4 remained on the line until 1931 when they were sold to a contractor who was building a breakwater at the mouth of the River Bann, a short distance along the coast to the west of Portrush.** Michael Pollard collection.

Above: **The hydro electric power station at Walkmills on the River Bush was one of the very first such installations in the British Isles. A weir was built across the river above the power station, which had the effect of creating a supply of water in a sort of a natural dam which could be drawn upon to supply the turbines. This made the power supply less dependent on the vagaries of a free flowing river.** Michael Pollard collection.

Centre left: **A view inside the power station. The spoked wheels projecting from the walls were used to control the gates which governed the flow of water and thus the output from the turbines. The dials affixed to the walls are the voltmeters for the two turbines.** Michael Pollard collection.

Bottom left: **A tramcar and two trailers head for Bushmills through the streets of Portrush in this lovely Edwardian view taken at Methody Corner, at the junction of Main and Causeway Streets. The last vehicle is No.18, a seven bench toast-rack trailer seating 28 passengers, which was acquired in 1897.** Michael Pollard collection.

Opposite page, top left: **This is car No.24, the last item of rolling stock acquired for the tramway. It was bought from the then recently closed 3ft 6in gauge tramway system in Dunfermline in Scotland, in 1937. It had been an open topped double decker but was re-gauged and converted to the form seen here at Portrush.** Michael Pollard collection.

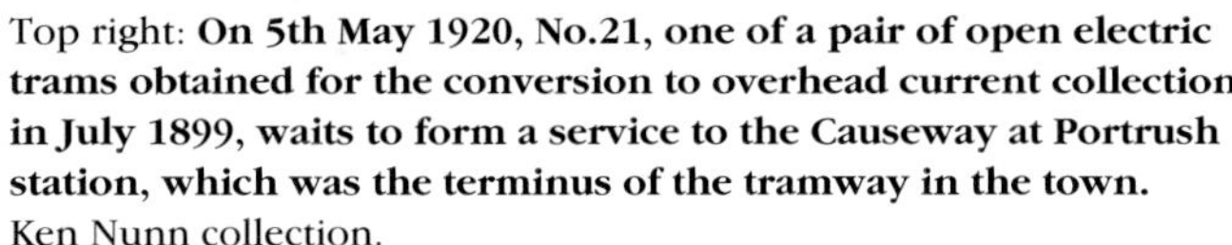

Top right: **On 5th May 1920, No.21, one of a pair of open electric trams obtained for the conversion to overhead current collection in July 1899, waits to form a service to the Causeway at Portrush station, which was the terminus of the tramway in the town.** Ken Nunn collection.

Centre right: **No.21 and its trailer form the 10.15am service to Bushmills on 5th May 1920. The tram is seen on the outskirts of Portrush. The canvas screens which were there to provide some protection for passengers in inclement weather have been partially rolled back.** Ken Nunn collection.

Bottom: **No.9 was delivered as an enclosed trailer around 1890 and was converted to a powered tramcar in 1909. It was normal to run open and closed vehicles together to offer passengers a choice of accommodation depending on the weather. In the last year of the service, 1949, No.9 heads one of the toast-rack trailers, on the passing loop at the White Rocks near Portrush.** Michael Pollard collection.

Chapter Four

THE PORTSTEWART TRAMWAY

THE PORTSTEWART Tramway recorded two firsts in its 44 year history. It was the first roadside steam tramway to be constructed in Ireland but it also had the melancholy distinction of being the first conventional Irish narrow gauge line to close down. In some ways its story is so typical of many of the minor lines in the British Isles. In the late nineteenth century the steam locomotive and the iron road were the only realistic alternative to the horse as a means of transporting people and goods and yet in a short space of time this type of technology was being challenged and usurped by the internal combustion engine, something which the Victorian promoters of these lines could never have envisaged.

Portstewart today is an attractive seaside town in County Londonderry but in the middle of the nineteenth century it was a tiny fishing village. When the railway from Ballymena to Portrush was being promoted in the 1850s, the local landowner refused to allow the line to go near Portstewart. A station was built 1½ miles away at Cromore which was called Portstewart in the timetables. The inevitable occurred, and as happened so often in the last century, the coming of the railway acted as a catalyst to the development of Portrush. Dotted around the coasts of the British Isles today are flourishing towns and resorts which were created in large measure by the coming of the railway in the nineteenth century.

As Portrush flourished, Portstewart stagnated and attempts began to get a branch line or a tramway to connect the latter to the main line. Unsuccessful schemes were mooted in 1861 and 1871. Four years later the 1871 scheme was revived under the provisions of the Tramways Act of that year. This Act had introduced two significant changes to existing railway legislation. It allowed steam traction to be used on tramways and introduced procedures whereby the promoters of local lines in Ireland could dispense with the expensive business of obtaining an Act of Parliament, and could apply instead to the Lord Lieutenant for an Order in Council to build their line. This course of action was followed by the promoters of the Portstewart Tramway Company who were granted their Order in Council in April 1880.

The Company needed to raise capital of £5,000 to construct their line and £2,000 of this was subscribed by the Belfast & Northern Counties Railway which had taken over the Ballymena to Portrush line in 1861 and was likely to be the main beneficiary of a tramway from Portstewart to its distant main line station. The tramway was built to the 3ft gauge and was 1 mile 62 chains long. It was single track with two passing loops. Most of the permanent way consisted of conventional sleepered railway track but tram rails were used for the line's passage through the streets of Portstewart. Track laying had been completed by April 1882 and the line was inspected and passed for service in June of that year.

The service was largely dictated by the arrival and departure of trains at the station. The first loco was a Kitson standard tramway 0-4-0T with its wheels and motion enclosed by distinctive tramway skirts. This loco, which cost £650, was coke fired and could be driven from either end. It was fitted with a form of condensing gear to enable it to comply with the then existing Board of Trade regulations which insisted, in the words of that wonderful piece of Victorian railway jargon, that such engines must, 'consume their own steam'. A second engine, identical to the first, arrived in 1883, and these two machines handled all the traffic up to 1900 when they were joined by another Kitson engine. The third locomotive had slightly smaller wheels and a consequently greater tractive effort and its delivery completed the line's locomotive fleet. On the commencement of services one open top double deck tramcar, one single deck toast-rack car and a 4-wheel van formed the line's entire rolling stock. These were supplemented by two bogie cars delivered in 1897 and 1899 respectively.

At first the tramway was moderately successful but by October 1892 the Company was bankrupt and a Receiver appointed. It struggled on until 1897 when its creditors petitioned that it should be put up for sale. The only offer was one of £2,100 from the B&NCR who thus acquired the line in that year. The B&NCR was taken over in turn by the English Midland Railway in 1903 and at the grouping of Britain's railways in 1923 the humble Portstewart Tramway became a tiny part of the great empire of the London, Midland and Scottish Railway.

By 1925 the track of the tramway was in very poor condition and the Northern Counties Committee, which ran the Ulster lines of the LMS, was reluctant to invest in what must have seemed even then, an anachronism. Closure was announced and the last tram ran on 30th January 1926. The trams were replaced by a service of motor buses. As well as being the first Irish narrow gauge railway to succumb, this may well have been the first instance in the British Isles, of what was to become known in the 1980s, by that ghastly word, bustitution. Sadly it was not to be the last.

As a footnote to the tramway's history it must be said that it has one final claim to fame in that 2/3rds of its locomotive fleet has been preserved. On the closure of the tramway it was realised that even in 1926 the steam tramway locomotive was becoming an increasing rarity and thus No.1 was dispatched to a museum in Hull. No.2, having reposed at York Road Works in Belfast for many years, escaping both the drive to collect scrap metal during the Second World War and the attentions of the Luftwaffe, whose raids caused a great deal of destruction to the York Road installations in 1941, is now safely in the care of the Ulster Folk and Transport Museum. Who knows, given the miracles that railway preservationists have achieved, it might even steam again some day.

Opposite page. **Ken Nunn visited and photographed the tramway on 5th May 1920 On that day the original locomotive No.1, was on duty. This had changed very little since it had been delivered in 1882 from the premises of Kitson and Company in Leeds. This 0-4-0 tramway locomotive had a wheel base of 5ft and wheels which were 2ft 4in in diameter. The loco was fitted with controls at each end and was driven and fired by one man in what could be described as an early example of one person operation. Before setting out, the driver would build up the fire in order to generate enough steam pressure for the journey.**

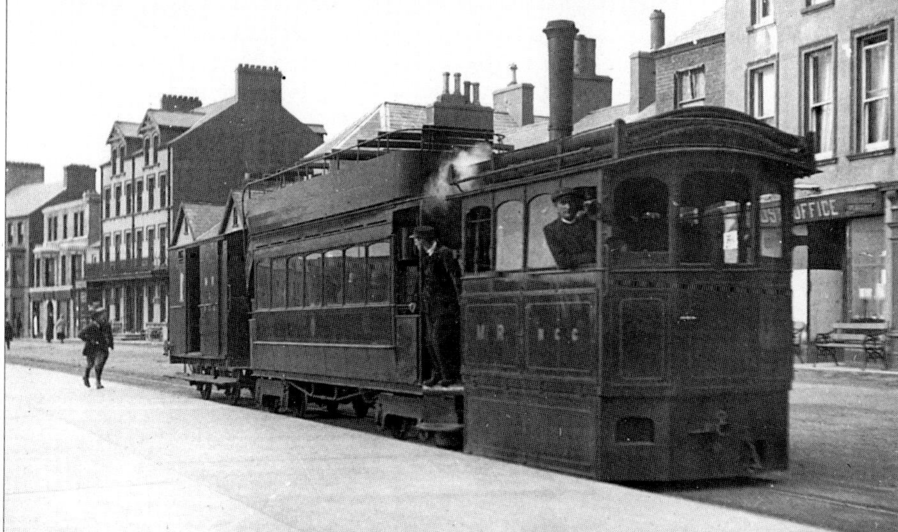

Top left: **Having backed onto its train which is made up of 1897 built bogie tramcar No.1 and the 4-wheel luggage van, supplied at the same time as the engine for the opening of the line in 1882, the cavalcade which is forming the 4.30pm to Portstewart from the station, gets under way. The remains of the condensers can be seen on the roof of the locomotive.**

Top right: **No.1 is running around its train at Portstewart station.**

Centre left: **A later service the same day; the 6.10pm departure from the station, is seen in the streets of Portstewart as it heads towards its terminus at The Parade. This location is now known as The Promenade.**

Bottom: **After a series of ups and downs of fortune; Loco No.2, a Kitson 0-4-0T, built in 1883 (maker's number T84) went to the Belfast Transport Museum for preservation. In 1993, along with the other exhibits, it was moved to splendid new premises at Cultra in County Down.** John Edgington.

Copyright reserved, Ordnance Survey, Dublin. Reproduced from 1 inch series, sheet no.7; revised 1910; published 1912, respectively. Scale 1 inch to 1 mile.

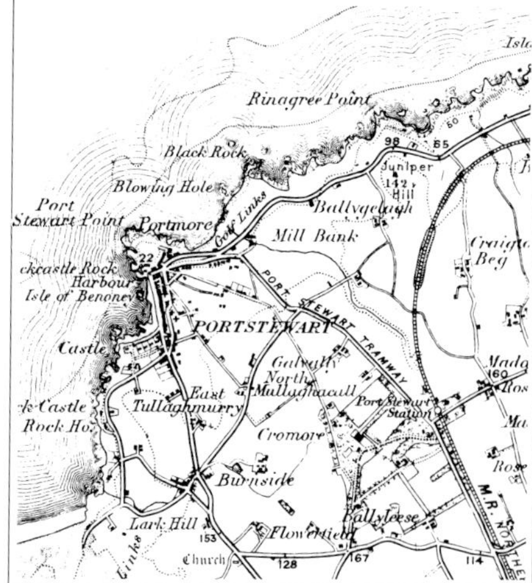

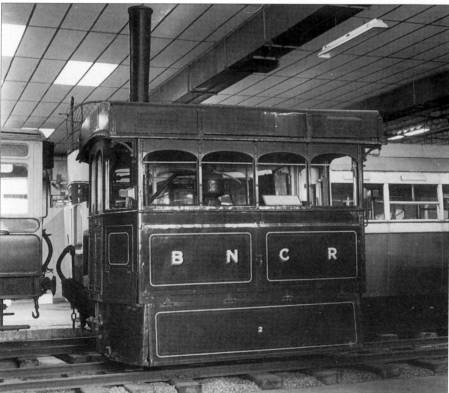

Chapter Five

THE LONDONDERRY & LOUGH SWILLY RAILWAY

THE Londonderry & Lough Swilly Railway Company was the second largest narrow gauge operator in Ireland with, at its peak, a route mileage of 99. Like the first section of what was to become the CDR and the first stretch of the CB&P it began life as a broad gauge line.

The origins of the L&LSR go back to 1852 when a line was authorised from Derry to Carrowen on the shore of Lough Swilly, a distance of some 8¾ miles. At first the company was known as the Lough Foyle & Lough Swilly, changing its name to the more familiar L&LSR in 1853. Construction did not begin until 1860 and the first train ran to a pier at Farland Point on Lough Swilly in December 1863, from where small craft served communities along the shore of the lough. An Act of 1861 provided powers to extend the line up the eastern shore of Lough Swilly to Buncrana, some 12 miles from Londonderry. Trains to Farland Point were suspended shortly after the opening of the line to Buncrana in 1864 and the track to the pier was lifted in 1877

In the early 1860s another line which was to become part of the L&LSR system was promoted. This was the Letterkenny Railway which originally planned to build a line from Letterkenny to near Saint Johnstown on the Londonderry & Enniskillen (later GNR) line between Derry and Strabane. The direction of the LR line was changed and its Act of 1863 authorised a line from Letterkenny to make a junction with the L&LSR and hence over their tracks to Londonderry. A mere 20 years elapsed before this line was eventually built. The usual problem of lack of finance caused the delay until finally in 1880 baronial guarantees were offered by the County Donegal Grand Jury, but only on condition that the line was built to the 3ft gauge. The L&LSR offered to convert its existing line to the narrow gauge at this point and after more financial difficulties, resolved only by a loan of £85,000 from the Board of Works, the LR opened for business on 30th June 1883. The new line met the L&LSR at what became known as Tooban Junction 6 miles from Derry. The L&LSR did not convert its line to the narrow gauge until March 1885 though it had narrow gauge rolling stock from 1883 with which to work the Letterkenny line. The independence of the LR lasted only until 1887 when, unable to pay the interest on its Board of Works loan, the Board took it over though the Swilly Company continued to work it.

The next extensions to the Swilly system were due to that most enlightened piece of legislation, the Railways (Ireland) Act of 1896. This Act allowed government grants to be made available for the construction of railways in the so called congested districts, the official misnomer for areas of acute poverty and underdevelopment. The legislation shifted the balance of the financial burden involved in railway construction from local to central government.

The first line built was an extension from Buncrana, north to Carndonagh, a distance of 18½ miles. Carndonagh was a small town near the top of the Inishowen Peninsula some 11 miles from Malin Head, Ireland's most northerly point. Most of the money for this line, which opened on 1st July 1901, came from the Public Works Loan Commissioners. In 1898 plans were put forward for a much longer new line which became known as the Letterkenny & Burtonport Extension Railway.

It can be argued that the L&BER was either a noble attempt to open up a desolate and desperately poor area or a colossal waste of money. It certainly would not have been built without the £300,000 of public money sunk into it. It was the epic of the Irish narrow gauge. Burtonport was a tiny fishing village in west Donegal. To get there the line meandered along for 49¾ miles through some of the bleakest and poorest countryside in Ireland. Some of its stations were miles from the villages they purportedly served. A difficult line to construct, its main engineering feature, the 380 yards long Owencarrow Viaduct, was so exposed to gales coming in from the north that in both 1906 and in 1925, trains were blown off it. In the case of the 1925 accident four passengers were killed. The contractor who built the line recorded how whole sections of the formation, ballasted and ready for the track, sank into the boggy ground. When the line opened in 1903 the 74¼ mile journey from Derry to Burtonport was the longest through run on the Irish narrow gauge, a journey requiring at least five hours in the train.

The L&BER was a separate company though worked by the Swilly. Its rolling stock had its own number sequence and carried the letters L&BER to distinguish them from the rest of the L&LSR fleet. Though the locos acquired for the extension carried L&LSR running numbers they should not, in theory at least, have been used elsewhere. In practice this was far from the case.

The same strictures applied to locos bought for the Carndonagh line and at one point the Board of Works summonsed the L&LSR for using Carndonagh engines on the line to Letterkenny.

In 1905 the Board of Works was also becoming increasingly concerned about the state of the L&BER and the manner in which it was being worked. Joseph Tatlow, the manager of the Midland Great Western Railway was commissioned to report on the line in 1905 and again in 1917. His findings confirmed the Board's worst fears and in 1917 the management of the extension was made the direct responsibility of Henry Hunt, the Swilly's General Manager, who had not long before joined the Company from the English Great Central Railway.

At this point it is worth reflecting on the Swilly's locomotive fleet, for the Burtonport Extension was responsible for the delivery of some of the most remarkable engines ever to run on the narrow gauge in the British Isles. The stock of the original 5ft 3in line was unexceptional, consisting of six 0-6-0 tank engines. The first narrow gauge locomotives were three 0-6-2Ts built by Black Hawthorn. These were followed by another engine from the same manufacturer in 1885, this time a 0-6-0T. The same year saw the arrival of two 2-4-0Ts obtained second hand from a defunct iron ore line in County Antrim.

In 1899 the first of the Swilly's big engines appeared, two 4-6-2Ts Nos.5 and 6 (later Nos.15 and 16), built by Hudswell Clarke. The Swilly was the only operator in Ireland, on either gauge, to use engines of this notation.

Two similar machines were supplied by the same builder in 1901 for the opening of the Carndonagh line and further pairs of 4-6-2Ts were built in 1904 by Kerr Stuart and in 1910 by Hawthorn Leslie.

For the opening of the Burtonport line four 4-6-0Ts were ordered from Andrew Barclay. These engines carried the initials L&BER on their tanks. Though seemingly limited in terms of their coal and water capacity for a line the length of the Burtonport extension they were popular engines and lasted until the system closed in the 1950s.

The last four engines acquired by the L&LSR were the most magnificent machines ever to grace narrow gauge tracks in the British Isles. In 1905 Hudswell Clarke supplied two 4-8-0 tender engines for use on the Burtonport line. These locomotives weighed 58¾ tons, had Belpaire fireboxes and flangeless leading drivers to help them get round sharp curves. Designed by James Conner the tenders could carry 1,500 gallons of water and hold four tons of coal. These were the only narrow gauge tender engines to run in Ireland; indeed they were the only 4-8-0 tender engines of any kind to run in the British Isles. They were enormous machines for the 3ft gauge and they looked more like the sort of locomotives one would expect to see in India or in southern Africa than in Ireland. With their great coal and water capacity they were ideal locos for the Burtonport extension; epic engines for an epic line. No.11 was worked so hard that she was worn out and withdrawn by 1933. Her sister No.12 lasted to the end of the Swilly, if only the line had survived a few more years she would undoubtedly have been preserved.

The final pair of engines supplied to the L&LSR were equally as spectacular as the 4-8-0s. These were a pair of 4-8-4Ts supplied by Hudswell Clarke in 1912. Again they were unique, the only engines of this wheel arrangement to run on any gauge in the British Isles. Designed by Ingram Sutcliffe, the L&LSR Locomotive Superintendent from 1911 to 1914, they weighed over 50 tons and had a tractive effort of 17,350lbs which was greater than many broad gauge engines of this period. Numbered 5 and 6, they survived up to 1953 but sadly like the rest of the Swilly locos they were cut up for scrap when the line closed.

It might be thought that the L&LSR and the CDR, both operating large narrow gauge systems in the same county, would have had cordial relations. In fact the opposite was the case – there was a coldness, almost an indifference between the two lines which potentially had so much in common. Until the CDR's line from Strabane to Letterkenny was completed in 1909 the only connection between the two systems was a circuitous one along the mixed gauge tracks of the Londonderry Port and Harbour Commissioners. Even when the CDR reached Letterkenny it operated out of its own station adjacent to the L&LSR one. It might have seemed more logical for the two concerns to share the existing Swilly station rather than have the CDR go to the expense of building a new one. Letterkenny's two narrow gauge stations were however linked by a spur. During the First World War the Irish Railways Executive Committee forced a measure of co-operation on them in the

matter of loco repairs and the pooling of rolling stock but that was as far as it went. Through ticketing arrangements were unknown though in the 1930s Henry Forbes, the CDR's famous manager, organised excursions from the Donegal system through Letterkenny to the religious centre of Doon Well on the Burtonport line. In 1922 Henry Hunt asked Forbes to allow the L&LSR to try out one of the CDR's 2-6-4Ts on the Burtonport line, prior to ordering new engines. Forbes prevaricated to such an extent that this intriguing narrow gauge locomotive exchange never materialised and in any event the Swilly ordered no new engines.

The division of Ireland in 1922 caused the L&LSR the gravest disruption. Because part of its line was in Northern Ireland it was not considered for inclusion with the GSR. More seriously, because the city of Derry and its natural economic hinterland were now in two different countries, the delays for customs examination and the realignment of north Donegal's economic activity to match the new political boundaries, undermined the railway's traffic patterns. The Swilly was losing money as early as 1925 and was kept afloat by grants from both Governments.

In 1927 a request was made by the Directors of the L&LSR to the CDRJC that they consider taking over the working of the Swilly system. The Joint Committee declined to enter into negotiations on this request and also declined a similar approach, this time, from the Government of Northern Ireland, in 1930. The prospect was thus lost of a unified 223 mile narrow gauge system. This would certainly have led to savings but whether it could have withstood the pressure of road competition any better is debatable.

The L&LSR began to contract in the 1930s. The line to Carndonagh was closed in November 1935 and at the same time regular passenger services were withdrawn to Buncrana. Buncrana trains were reinstated during the Second World War, not finally ending until 1948, and excursions to Buncrana lasted up to the end in 1953. The Burtonport extension closed in June 1940 and part of the track was lifted. However the section from Letterkenny to Gweedore reopened for freight in February 1941 because of wartime shortages of oil for the replacement motor vehicles. Passenger services to Gweedore began again in March 1942 and continued until January 1947. Freight traffic to both Buncrana and Letterkenny continued up to July 1953 when Swilly rail services finally ceased. The Company had begun operating bus and lorry services in the 1920s and long after the Company's trains had ceased to run visitors to Londonderry and Donegal could see these vehicles still proudly proclaiming that they were the property of the Londonderry & Lough Swilly *Railway* Company.

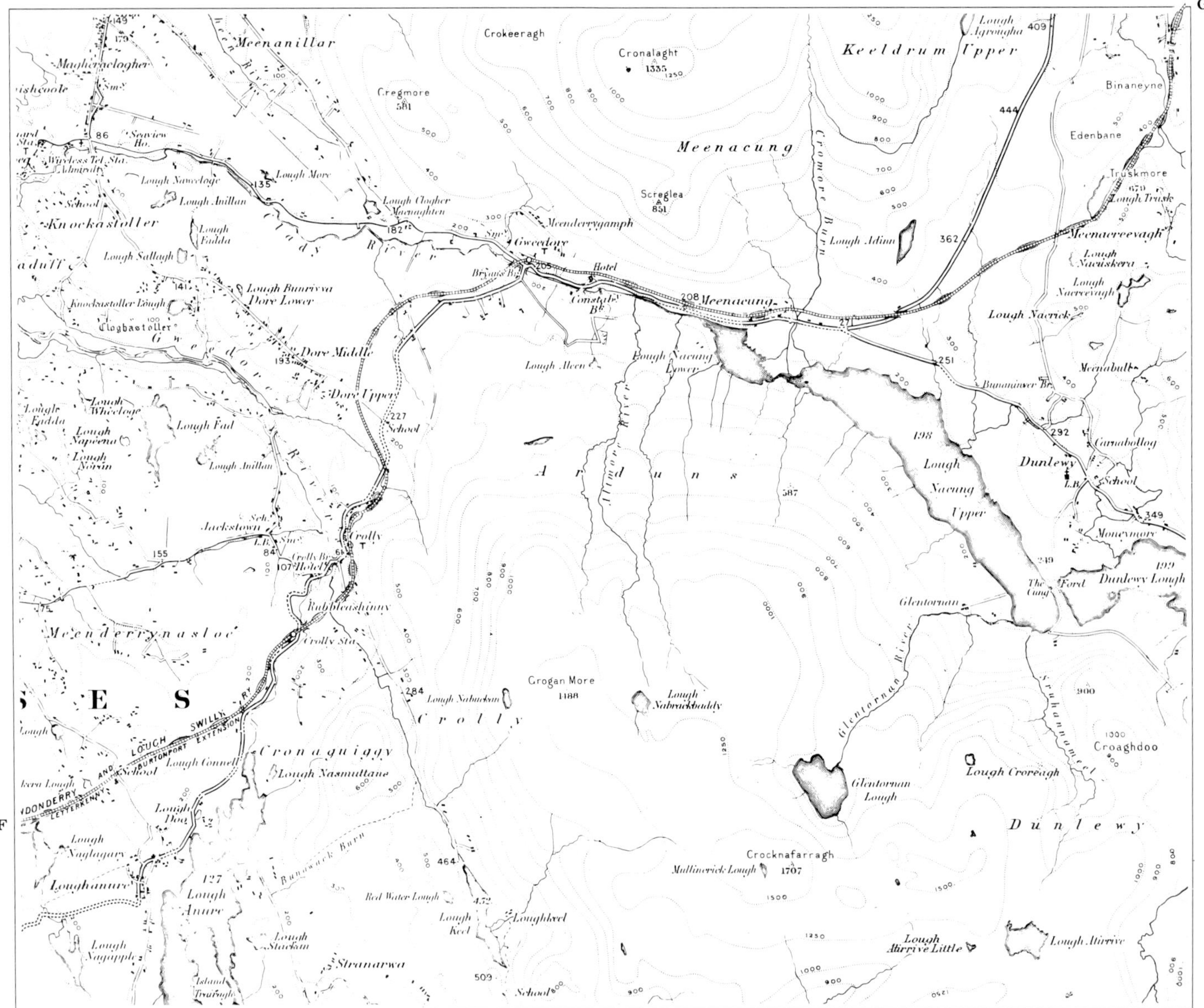

Right: **The most logical way of dealing with the locos of the L&LSR is in the order in which they were supplied. Before looking at the 3ft gauge locos, I have been most fortunate in finding a rare picture of one of the Swilly's 5ft 3in engines, albeit in the ownership of another company. The Cork & Bandon Railway's 4-4-0T No.14 was built by Sharp Stewart in 1876 as an 0-6-0T for the Lough Swilly company. It was originally named *St Patrick.* At the auction of the L&LSR's broad gauge effects in 1885 the engine was snapped up by the C&B. It moved to the other end of Ireland where it was rebuilt eventually as a 4-4-0T, in which condition it was photographed at Cork in the 1890s.** W.H.Butler Collection.

Above: **The Swilly's first narrow gauge engines were three 0-6-2Ts supplied by Black Hawthorn. The first was built in 1882, the other two the following year. No.1, seen here at Pennyburn around the turn of the century, was used on the construction of the DR's Glenties line in the 1890s.** Charles P Friel collection.

Above right: **In this picture of No.2 *Londonderry,* the long gap between the rear coupled wheel and trailing wheels, which was a feature of these engines, may be noted.** Charles P Friel collection.

Right: **No.1 *J.T.Mackey* has just arrived at Buncrana in this turn of the century view.** Charles P Friel collection.

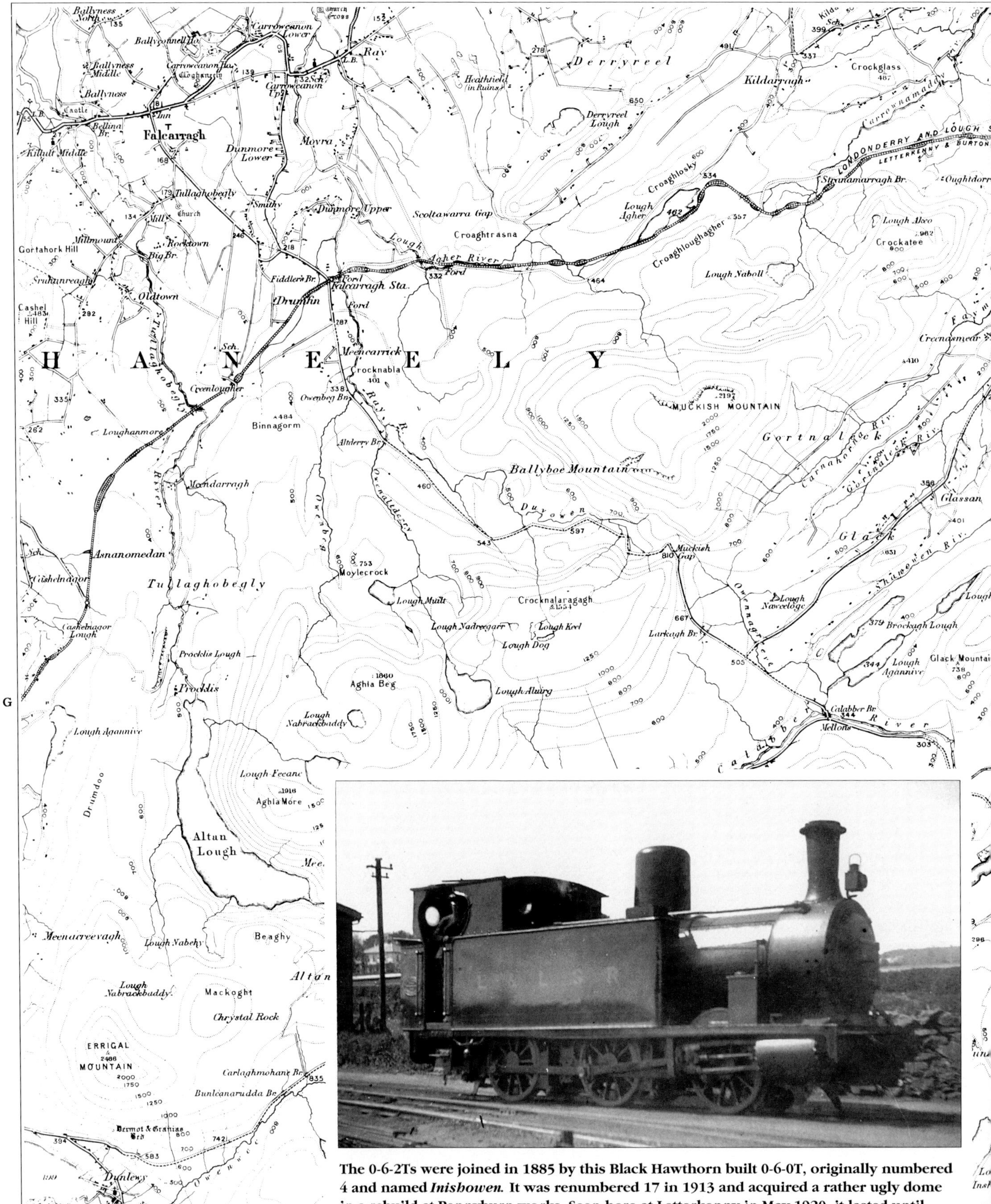

The 0-6-2Ts were joined in 1885 by this Black Hawthorn built 0-6-0T, originally numbered 4 and named *Inisbowen.* It was renumbered 17 in 1913 and acquired a rather ugly dome in a rebuild at Pennyburn works. Seen here at Letterkenny in May 1920, it lasted until 1940. Ken Nunn collection.

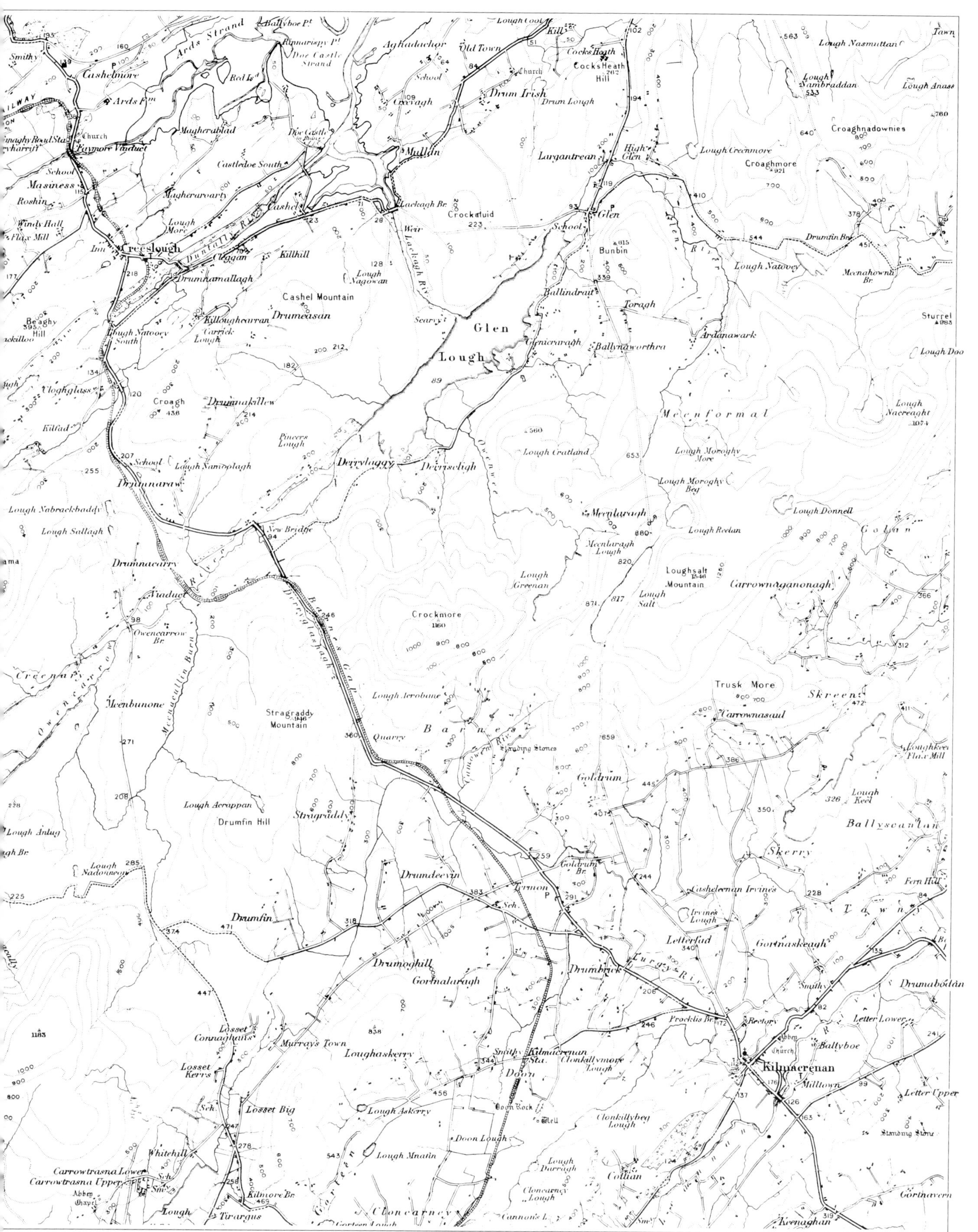
Ards Strand
Ballyboe Pt.
Doe Castle Strand
Aghadachor
Old Town
Kill
Cocks Heath
Cashelmore
Ards Fm.
Red Id.
Magherablad
Doe Castle
School
Church
Carragh
Drum Irish
Drum Lough
Mullin
Largantrean
High Glen
Lough Creenmore
Croaghmore
Croaghnadownies
Lough Nasmuttan
Lough Nambraddan
Lough Anass
Faymore Viaduct
Castledoe South
Masiness
Roshin
Windy Hall
Flax Mill
Magheraroarty
Cashel
Lough More
Lackagh Br.
Crockatuid
Glen
School
Bunbin
Creeslough
Duntally
Cloggan
Killhill
Drumnamallagh
Lough Nagowan
Lackagh Rr.
Glen River
Lough Natooey
Drumfin Br.
Meenahowna Br.
Cashel Mountain
Drumeasan
Killoughcarran
Carrick Lough
Ballindrait
Toragh
Beaghy Hill
Lough Natooey South
Glen Lough
Gortnicraragh
Ballynaworthra
Ardanawark
Sturrel
Lough Doo
Cloghglass
Croagh
Drumnakillew
Kilfad
Meenformal
Lough Nacreaght
Pincers Lough
School
Lough Namoolagh
Derrylaggy
Derryscligh
Lough Cratland
Lough Moroghy More
Lough Moroghy Beg
Drumnaraw
Lough Nabrackbaddy
Lough Sallagh
New Bridge
Meenlaragh
Lough Reelan
Lough Donnell
Meenlaragh Lough
Drumnacarry
Lough Greenan
Loughsalt Mountain
Lough Salt
Carrownaganonagh
Viaduct
Owencarrow Br.
Crockmore
Barnes Gap
Owencarrow
Creenary
Meenbunone
Stragraddy Mountain
Lough Aerobane
Quarry
Barnes
Trusk More
Skreen
Carrownasaul
Standing Stones
Goldrum
Loughkeel Flax Mill
Lough Keel
Lough Acrappan
Drumfin Hill
Stragraddy
Ballyscanlan
Lough Anlug
Lough Nadoaneon
Skerry
Drumdeevin
Goldrum Br.
Termon
Sch.
Cashelcenan Irvines
Irvines Lough
Fern Hill
Drumfin
Letterfad
Gortnaskeagh
Drumoghill
Gortnalaragh
Drumbrick
Lurgy River
Drumabodan
Procklis Br.
Rectory
Letter Lower
Losset Connaghans
Murrays Town
Loughaskerry
Kilmacrenan Sta.
Clonkallymore Lough
Church
Ballyboe
Kilmacrenan
Milltown
Losset Kerrs
Doon
Letter Upper
Sch.
Losset Big
Lough Askerry
Doon Rock
Well
Clonkillybeg Lough
Doon Lough
Standing Stone
Whitehill
Lough Mnatin
Lough Darragh
Collian
Carrowtrasna Lower
Carrowtrasna Upper
Abbey Chapel
Kilmore Br.
Cloncarney Lough
Gortnavern
Lough
Tirargus
Cloncarney
Gorteen Lough
Cannon's L.
Keenaghan

H

H

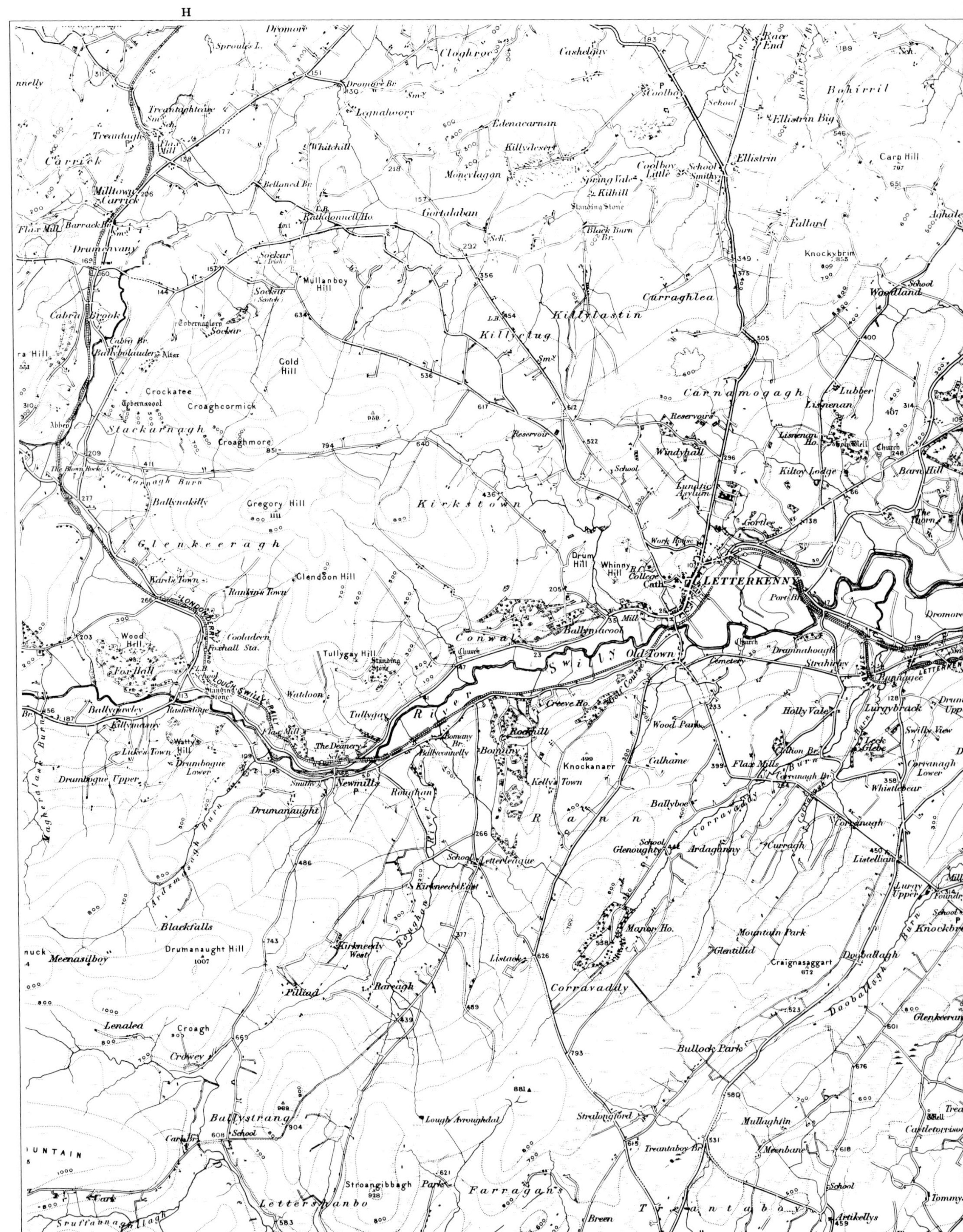
Dromore
Cloghroe
Cashelgay
Race End
Bohirril
Coolboy
School
Ellistrin Big
Logahoory
Edenacarnan
Treantaghteane
Treantagh
Carrick
Whitehill
Killydesert
Carn Hill
797
Moneylagan
Coolboy Little
Ellistrin
Spring Vale
Kilhill
Milltown
Bellaneed Br.
Rathdonnell Ho.
Gortalaban
Standing Stone
Black Burn Br.
Fallard
Flax Mill
Barrack Hill
Drumenvany
Sockar
Irish
Sockar
Scotch
Mullanboy Hill
Knockybrin
858
Woodland
Cabra Brook
Killylastin
Carraghlea
Killyclug
Cabra Br.
Ballybolauder
Altar
Cold Hill
Carnamogagh
Lubber
Lisnenan
Crockatee
Croaghcormick
Stackarnagh
Reservoirs
Reservoir
Croaghmore
Windyhall
Lisnenan Ho.
Church
Kiltoy Lodge
Barn Hill
Stackarnagh Burn
Ballynakilly
Gregory Hill
Kirkstown
School
Lunatic Asylum
Gortlee
The Thorn
Glenkeeragh
Work House
Drum Hill
Whinny Hill
R.C. College
Cath.
LETTERKENNY
Glendoon Hill
Karl's Town
Rankin's Town
LONDONDERRY
Port Br.
Dromore
Wood Hill
Cooladeen
Foxhall Sta.
Conwal
Ballymacool
Mill
Fox Hall
Tullygay Hill
Standing Stone
Swilly
Old Town
Cemetery
Dromnahoagh
Strahirley
Bunnagee
LOUGH SWILLY RAILY
Watdoon
River
Creeve Ho.
Tullygay
Rockhill
Ballygawley
Killymasny
Flax Mill
The Deanery
Bomany Br.
Ballyconnelly
Bomany
Wood Park
Holly Vale
Lurgybrack
Swilly View
Leck Glebe
Watty's Hill
Luke's Town
Drumbogue Lower
Drumbogue Upper
Newmills
Roughan
Knockanarr
Kelly's Town
Calhame
Flax Mills
Carranagh Br.
Corranagh Lower
Whistlebear
Drumanaught
Ballyboe
Ran
Corravaddy
Corranagh
School
Glenoughty
Ardagunny
Curragh
Listellian
Magheradaw Burn
Ardsmasagh Burn
River
Letterleague
Kirkneedy East
Lurgy Upper
Knockbrack
Blackfalls
Roughan
Manor Ho.
Mountain Park
Meenasilboy
Drumanaught Hill
1007
Kirkneedy West
Listack
Glentillid
Craignasaggart
872
Doobalagh
Doobalagh Burn
Pilliad
Rareagh
Corravaddy
Lenalea
Croagh
Glenkeeran
Crowey
Bullock Park
Ballystrang
School
Lough Avoughdal
Stralongford
Mullaghfin
Castletorrison
Carn Br.
Treantaboy Br.
Meenbane
MOUNTAIN
Stroangibbagh
Park
Farragans
School
Lettershanbo
Breen
Treantaboy
Artikellys
Tommy
Cark

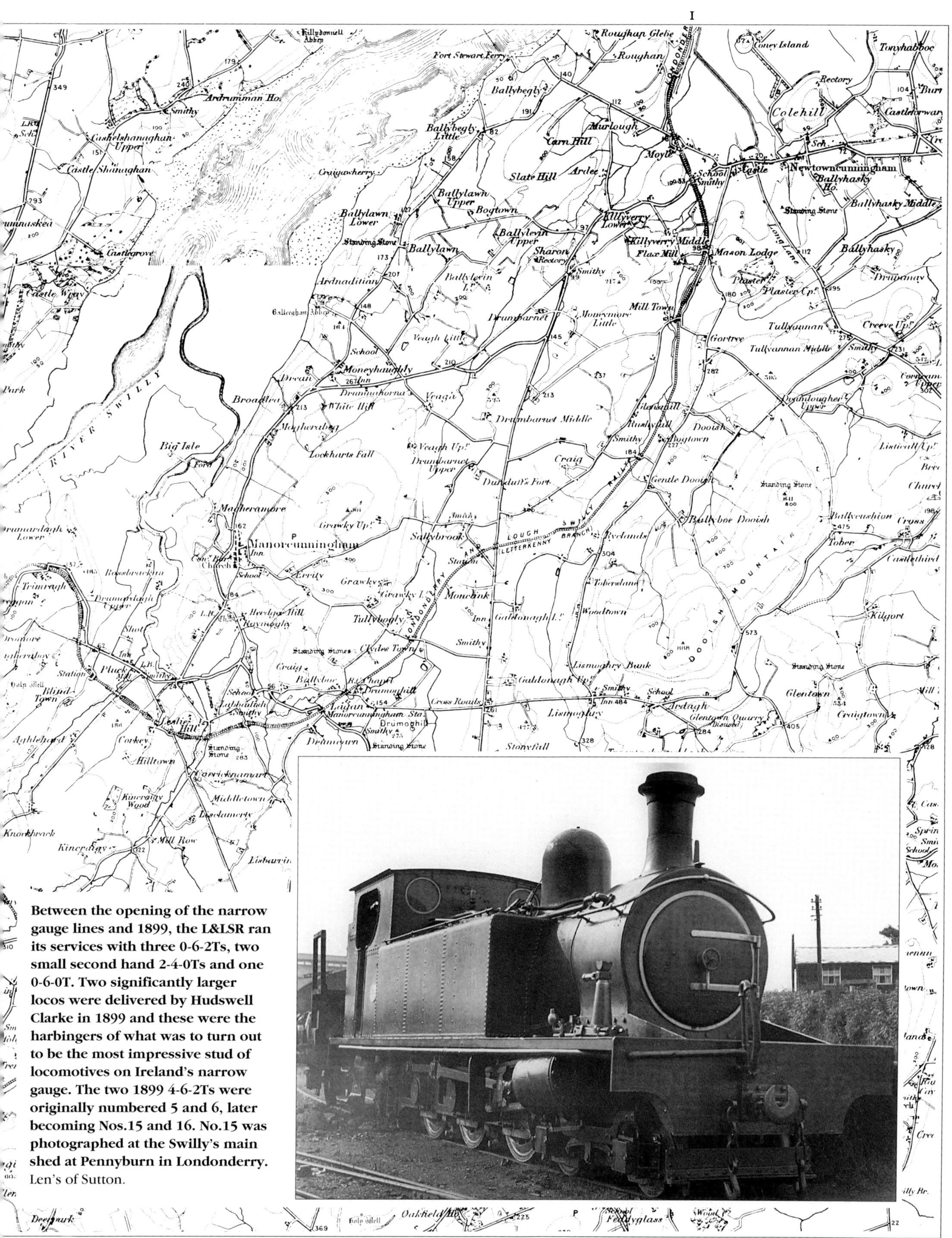

Between the opening of the narrow gauge lines and 1899, the L&LSR ran its services with three 0-6-2Ts, two small second hand 2-4-0Ts and one 0-6-0T. Two significantly larger locos were delivered by Hudswell Clarke in 1899 and these were the harbingers of what was to turn out to be the most impressive stud of locomotives on Ireland's narrow gauge. The two 1899 4-6-2Ts were originally numbered 5 and 6, later becoming Nos.15 and 16. No.15 was photographed at the Swilly's main shed at Pennyburn in Londonderry. Len's of Sutton.

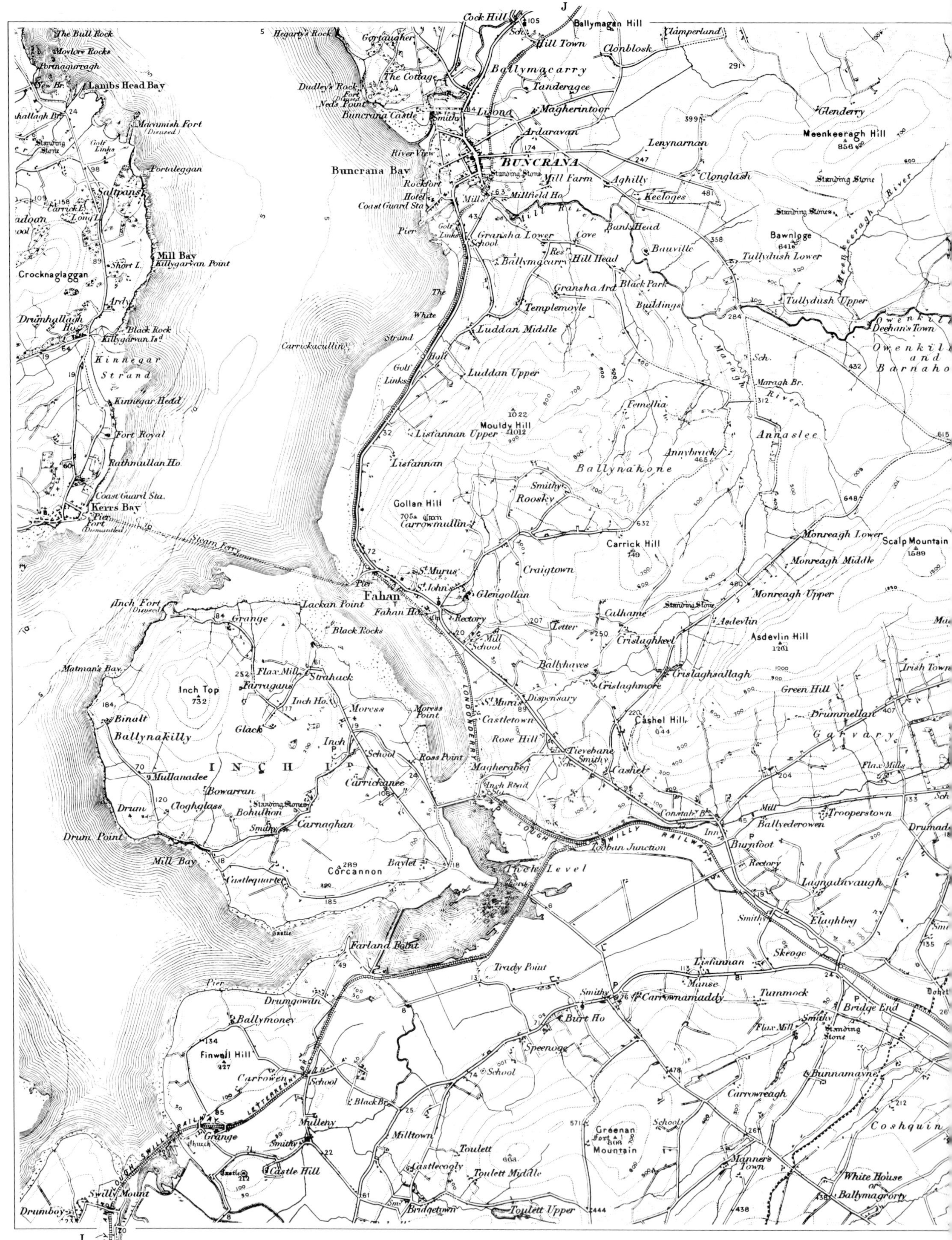
J
I
The Bull Rock
Moylore Rocks
Portnagurragh
New Br.
Lambs Head Bay
Macamish Fort
(Disused)
Golf Links
Portaleggan
Saltpans
Long I.
Mill Bay
Killygarvan Point
Short I.
Crocknaglaggan
Ardy
Drumhallagh Ho.
Black Rock
Killygarvan Is.
Kinnegar Strand
Kinnegar Head
Fort Royal
Rathmullan Ho.
Coast Guard Sta.
Kerrs Bay
Pier
Fort (Dismantled)
Steam Ferry
Hegarty's Rock
Gortaugher
Dudley's Rock
Neds Point
The Cottage
Buncrana Castle
Smithy
Cock Hill
Ballymagan Hill
Hill Town
Clonblosk
Clamperland
Ballymacarry
Tanderagee
Lisfannan
Magherintoor
Ardaravan
Glenderry
Meenkeeragh Hill
Lenynarnan
River View
BUNCRANA
Buncrana Bay
Rockfort
Hotel
Coast Guard Sta.
Standing Stone
Mill Farm
Millfield Ho.
Aghilly
Clonglash
Keeloges
Mill River
Bank Head
Gransha Lower
Cove
Bauville
Bawnloge
Tullydush Lower
Pier
Golf Links
School
Ballymacarry
Hill Head
Gransha Ard
Black Park
Buildings
Tullydush Upper
Meenkeeragh River
Owenkillew
Deehan's Town
Owenkillew and Barnahone
Templemoyle
The White Strand
Luddan Middle
Carrickacullin
Halt
Golf Links
Luddan Upper
Maragh River
Maragh Br.
Femellia
Mouldy Hill
Listannan Upper
Annaslee
Annybrack
Ballynahone
Lisfannan
Smithy
Roosky
Gollan Hill
Carrowmullin
Carrick Hill
Monreagh Lower
Monreagh Middle
Scalp Mountain
Craigtown
Monreagh Upper
Pier
Fahan
St. Murus
St. John's
Glengollan
Fahan Ho.
Rectory
Inch Fort (Disused)
Lackan Point
Grange
Black Rocks
Calhame
Letter
Asdevlin
Asdevlin Hill
Cristaghkeel
Mill School
Matman's Bay
Flax Mill
Strahack
Farragans
Inch Top
Inch Ho.
Ballyhaves
Cristaghmore
Cristaghsallagh
Irish Town
Green Hill
Moress
Moress Point
Dispensary
St. Mura's
Castletown
Binalt
Ballynakilly
Glack
Inch
LONDONDERRY
Cashel Hill
Drummellan
Garvary
Rose Hill
Tievebane
Smithy
Cashel
Flax Mills
INCH ISLAND
School
Ross Point
Magherabeg
Mullanadee
Carrickanee
Bowarran
Inch Road Sta.
Standing Stones
Cloghglass
Bohulhon
Drum
Carnaghan
Constaby. B.
Mill
Ballyederowen
Trooperstown
Drum Point
Smithy
LOUGH SWILLY RAILWAY
Tooban Junction
Inn
Burnfoot
Mill Bay
Corcannon
Baylet
Rectory
Castlequarter
Level
Lagnadavaugh
Castle
Smithy
Elaghbeg
Farland Point
Skeoge
Trady Point
Lisfannan
Manse
Pier
Drumgowan
Smithy
Carrownamaddy
Tunmock
Bridge End
Burt Ho.
Ballymoney
Flax Mill
Smithy
Standing Stone
Speenoge
Finwell Hill
School
Carrowen
School
Bunnamayne
LETTERKENNY
Black Br.
Carrowreagh
LOUGH SWILLY RAILWAY
Grange
Church
Mulleny
Milltown
Greenan Fort Mountain
School
Coshquin
Smithy
Toulett
Castle
Castle Hill
Castlecooly
Toulett Middle
Manners Town
White House or Ballymagrorty
Swilly Mount
Drumboy
Bridgetown
Toulett Upper

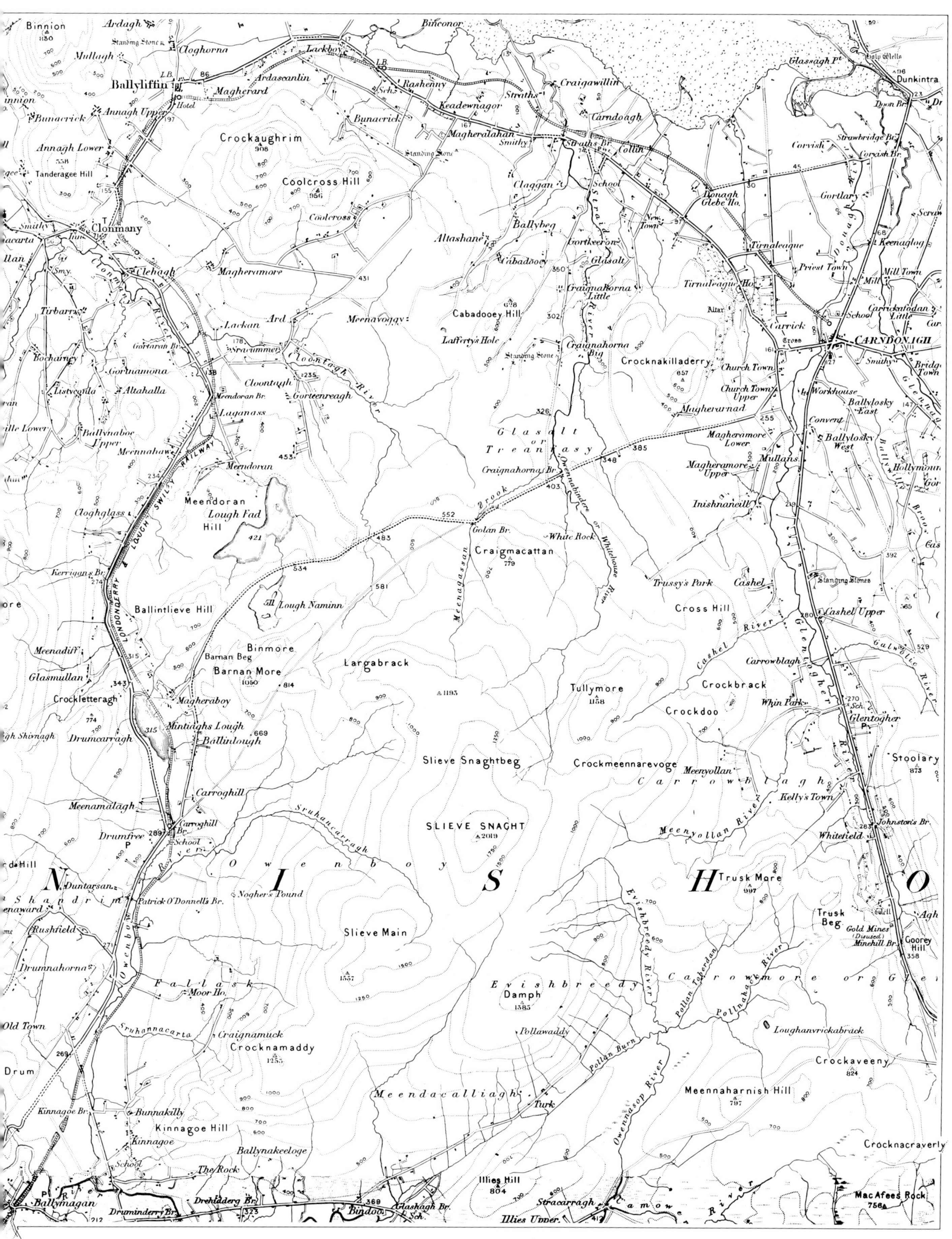
Binnion
Ardagh
Cloghorna
Lackbov
Binconor
Glassagh Pt
Dunkintra
Mullagh
Ballyliffin
Ardascanlin
Magherard
Rasheny
Craigawillin
Straths
Carndoagh
Bunacrick
Annagh Upper
Keadewnagor
Magheralahan
Annagh Lower
Tanderagee Hill
Crockaughrim
Straths Br.
Collin
Corvish
Strawbridge Br.
Corvish Br.
Coolcross Hill
Coolcross
Claggan
School
Donagh Glebe Ho.
Gortlary
Clonmany
Altashane
Ballybeg
Gortkeeran
New Town
Tirnaleague
Keenaglog
Cabadooey
Glasalt
Priest Town
Mill Town
Clehagh
Magheramore
Craignahorna Little
Tirnaleague Ho.
Carrickatodan Little
Tirbarry
Meenavoggy
Cabadooey Hill
Lackan
Ard
Carrick
CARNDONAGH
Lafferty's Hole
Craignahorna Big
Gortaran Br.
Sracummer
Cloontagh River
Crocknakilladerry
Church Town
Smithy
Bridge Town
Gortnamona
Cloontagh
Church Town Upper
Workhouse
Ballylosky East
Listycalla
Altahalla
Meendoran Br.
Gorteenreagh
Magheranad
Convent
Laganass
Glasalt or Treanasy
Magheramore Lower
Ballylosky West
Ballynaboe Upper
Meennahaw
LONDONDERRY & LOUGH SWILLY RAILWAY
Meendoran
Craignahorna Br.
Mullans
Magheramore Upper
Hollymount
Meendoran Lough Fad Hill
Cloghglass
Brook
Inishnancill
Golan Br.
White Rock
Craigmacattan
Kerrigan's Br.
Lough Naminn
Trussy's Park
Cashel
Standing Stones
Ballintlieve Hill
Cross Hill
Cashel Upper
Cashel River
Meenadiff
Binmore
Barnan Beg
Barnan More
Largabrack
Carrowblagh
Glasmullan
Tullymore
Crockbrack
Crockletteragh
Magheraboy
Whin Park
Crockdoo
Glentogher
Mintiaghs Lough
Ballinlough
Drumcarragh
Slieve Snaghtbeg
Crockmeennarevoge
Meenyollan
Stoolary
Carrowblagh
Kelly's Town
Carroghill
Meenamalagh
Carroghill Br.
School
SLIEVE SNAGHT
Meenyollan River
Johnston's Br.
Whitefield
Drumfree
Owenboy
Owenboy River
N
S
H
O
Trusk More
Duntarsan
Shandrim
Patrick O'Donnell's Br.
Nogher's Pound
Evishbreedy River
Trusk Beg
Gold Mines (Disused)
Minehill Br.
Goorey Hill
Rushfield
Slieve Main
Drumnahorna
Pollan Toberdan
Pollnahack River
Carrowmore or Glen
Fallask
Moor Ho.
Evishbreedy
Damph
Old Town
Loughanvrickabrack
Sruhannacarta
Craignamuck
Crocknamaddy
Pollawaddy
Pollan Burn
Crockaveeny
Drum
Meendacalliagh
Turk
Meennaharnish Hill
Owennasop River
Kinnagoe Br.
Bunnakilly
Kinnagoe Hill
Kinnagoe
Crocknacraverly
Ballynakeeloge
School
The Rock
Illies Hill
Mac Afees Rock
Ballymagan
Druminderry Br.
Drehidderg Br.
Bindoo
Glashagh Br.
Stracarragh
Illies Upper
Camowen River

Top left: **Two more Hudswell Clarke 4-6-2Ts were ordered in 1901. Numbered 7 and 8, No.7 seen here at Pennyburn, carried the name *King Edward VII* for a number of years after it had hauled a royal train bearing the monarch in 1903.** Len's of Sutton.

Top right: **No.8, peeping out of the shed at Pennyburn in April 1951, lasted until the end of rail services.** John Edgington.

Left: **Perhaps influenced by the success of the Donegal Railway's 4-6-0Ts, the L&LSR ordered engines of this wheel arrangement for the opening of the Burtonport extension. Numbered 1 to 4, No.1, seen at Pennyburn in August 1930, was withdrawn in 1940. The other three lasted until the railway closed.** H.C.Casserley.

Below: **4-6-0T No.4 in the shed at Pennyburn in April 1951.** John Edgington.

These two pictures of 4-6-0T No.2 at Pennyburn were taken (top) **by H.C.Casserley in 1937 and** (below) **by John Edgington in 1951. In the upper picture No.2 still bears the name of the Letterkenny & Burtonport Extension Railway for which it was built. In the later image she carries the attractive diamond logo and the letters LSR which were used in the railway's last years of operations.**

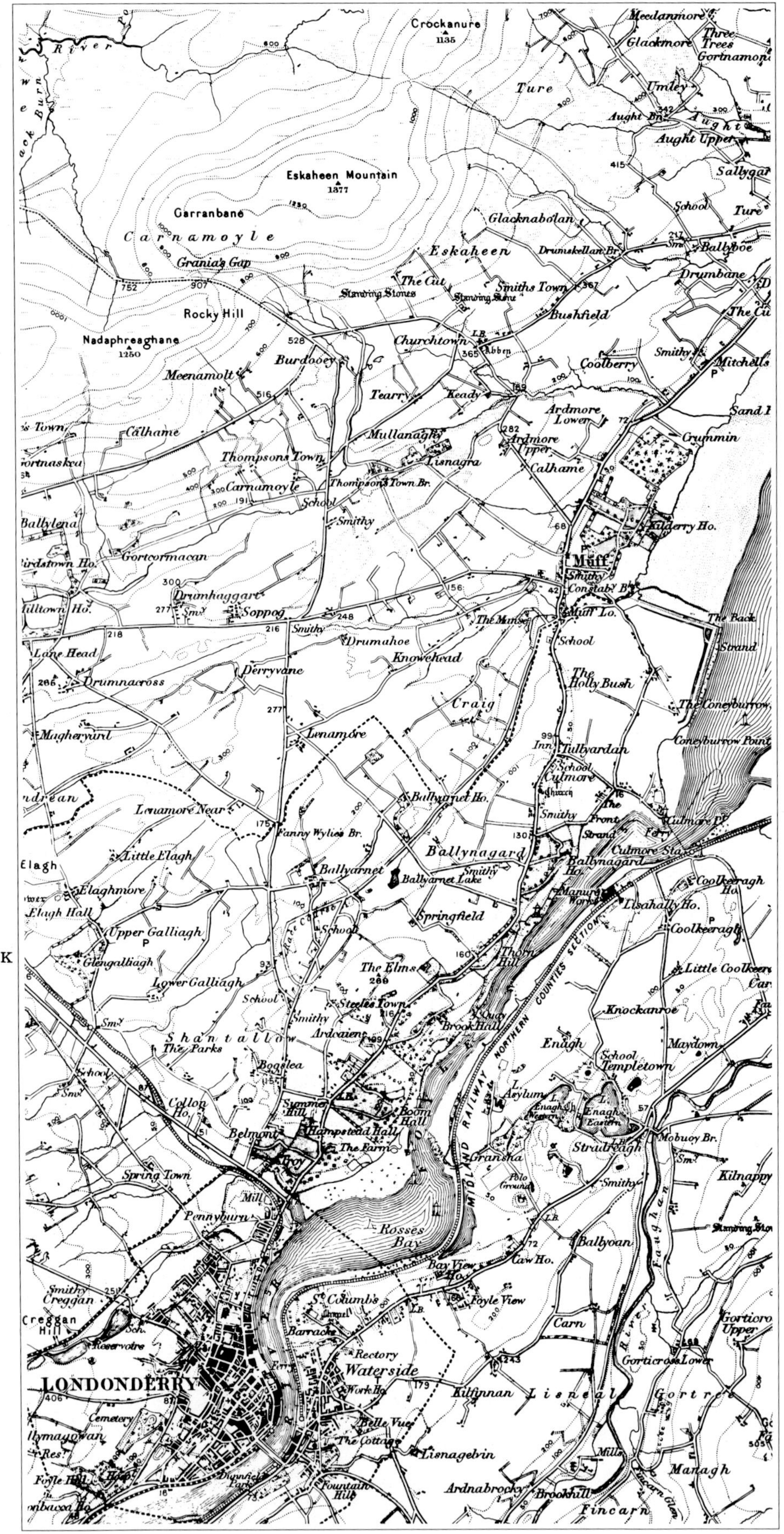

Top: **A further pair of 4-6-2Ts were added to the fleet in 1904. Nos 9 and 10, originally named *Aberfoyle* and *Richmond,* were built by Kerr Stuart. They were smaller and less powerful than the earlier Hudswell Clarke engines. No.9 was photographed at Letterkenny in 1904. Judging by her spotless condition this might well have been one of her inaugural runs. No.9 had a relatively short life, being withdrawn in 1928.** Courtesy of the South Donegal Railway Restoration Society.

Centre: **In 1905 Hudswell Clarke delivered the two engines which, going on for a century later, still stir the imagination in a way no other 3ft gauge engines which ran in Ireland, can. Nos.11 and 12, the only tender engines ever to run on Ireland's narrow gauge and the only 4-8-0 tender engines ever to run in the British Isles, were the right engines for the long haul to Burtonport. More powerful than many contemporary broad gauge locos, No.11 was withdrawn in 1933, apparently worn out by many years of hard work on the extension. No.12 seen here lasted until 1954. She was scrapped just a few years before the preservation of railway artifacts in Ireland became a serious proposition.** Len's of Sutton.

Bottom left: **Nos.13 and 14 were built by Hawthorn Leslie in 1910. These were 4-6-2Ts, more powerful than the earlier locos of this wheel arrangement. No.13, seen at Pennyburn, was withdrawn in 1940.** Len's of Sutton.

Bottom right: **No.14, seen outside the L&LSR shed at Letterkenny on 24th June 1937, lasted until 1943.** H.C.Casserley.

Copyright reserved, Ordnance Survey, Dublin. Reproduced from 1 inch series, sheet nos. 5, 9, 10, 11, 15, 16, 17; revised 1911, 1911, 1911, 1911, 1913, 1913, 1899; published 1913, 1913, 1914, 1913, 1917, 1916, 1902 respectively. Scale 1 inch to 1 mile.

ABERFOYLE

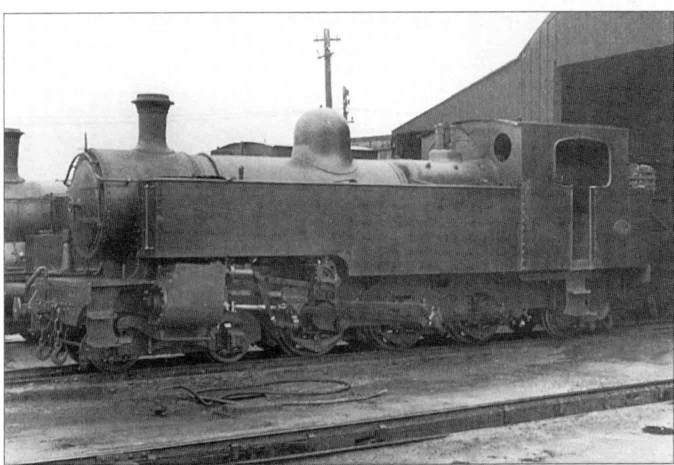

190

Left: **The Swilly added another unique type to its fleet with the last pair of locomotives which it acquired. In 1912 Hudswell Clarke supplied No.5 and 6, the only 4-8-4Ts ever to run in these islands. They can be seen as a tank version of the earlier 4-8-0 tender engines, though more powerful and massive, weighing 51 tons. Both lasted until the end of services. As with No.12, if only they had lasted a few more years one of them would surely have been a candidate for preservation. No.5 pauses on a train at Pennyburn on 6th August 1930** (opposite page, top) **and** (left) **had less than a year left to her when photographed at Pennyburn in April 1953.** H.C.Casserley.

Above, and opposite page bottom: **The Swilly terminus in Derry was not exactly a thing of beauty. Inconveniently situated at some distance from the city centre, its undistinguished exterior gave little hint of the magnificent machines which could be found within, like 4-8-0 No.12, shunting at Londonderry Graving Dock, as the station was known, on 24th June 1937.**

Left: **No.16, the sister engine of No.15 –** ***seen on page*** **57 – was discovered by Henry Casserley, stored out of use in the rather incongruous setting of the end of one of the platforms at the Swilly's Derry terminus, in June 1937. Nos.15 and 16 lasted until 1954 and 1953 respectively.** Both H.C.Casserley.

Left: **In the last year of regular passenger services, No.10 heads a Buncrana train on 19th April 1948.** H.C.Casserley.

Centre left: **On the same day No.15 arrives with a goods from Letterkenny.** H.C.Casserley.

Centre right: **All the clutter usually associated with a railway works is apparent in this 1937 view of the works at Pennyburn.** H.C.Casserley.

Bottom: **In the last month of services on the railway, June 1953, No.15 heads a special train for Buncrana at Graving Dock.** J.H.Price.

Above: **A short distance beyond the terminus were located the railway's main locomotive shed and its workshops. There was also a station here at Pennyburn. In this 1948 view of the shed Nos 10 and 8 are the two locos in the picture.**

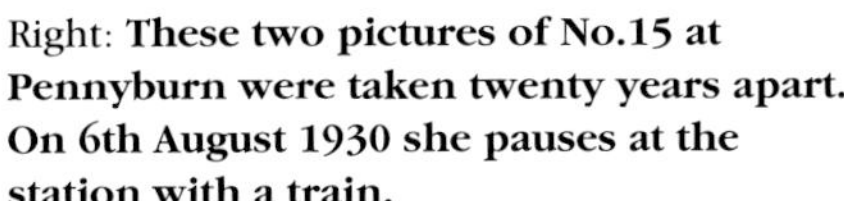

Right: **These two pictures of No.15 at Pennyburn were taken twenty years apart. On 6th August 1930 she pauses at the station with a train.**

Below: **On May 19th 1950, she trundles over the level crossing with a short mixed train.** All H.C.Casserley.

Below: **These two lineside shots were taken near Pennyburn in May 1920. No.12 is near the end of her long journey as she heads the 8.20am from Burtonport towards Derry.**

Below right: **No.7 at the head of the 12.20pm to Buncrana has already lost the name *King Edward VII* which it carried for some years, by this stage in its career.** Both Ken Nunn Collection.

Photographs on the opposite page:

Tooban Junction was a bleak spot some six miles from Derry where the lines to Buncrana and Letterkenny diverged. These pictures from the early 1950s all feature the 4-6-0Ts which were originally built for the L&BER.

Top: **No.2 arrives at the Junction with the Letterkenny goods on 27th June 1953.** D.G.Coakham.

Centre: **No.3 is shunting at Tooban Junction on 28th June 1950. The rails stacked in the foreground had been recovered when the Burtonport extension was lifted.** John Edgington.

Bottom: **These latter day goods trains conveyed a coach in which passengers could travel if they were not in too much of a hurry and did not mind waiting around at intermediate stations while shunting took place.** H.C.Casserley.

Below: **No.10 brings the 1.00pm from Londonderry to Buncrana into Bridgend on 28th June 1950. The train will be subject to an examination by the Customs at this station.** John Edgington.

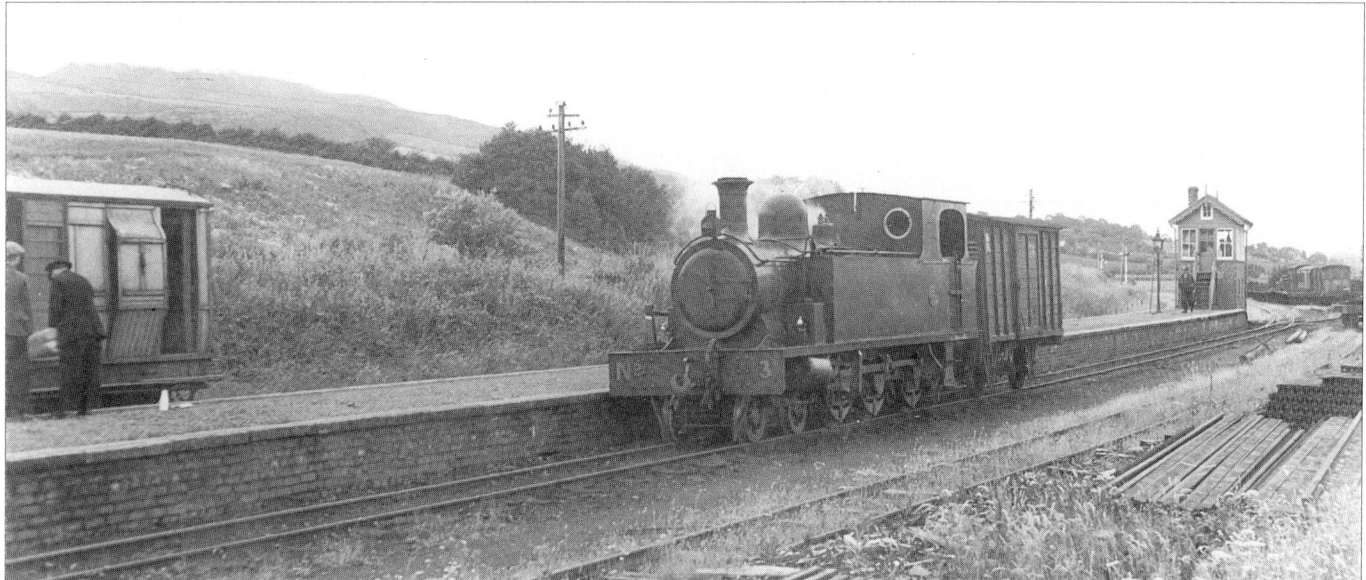
No 3

No 3

SALOON BAR

No 10

Photographs on the opposite page:

Top left: **The L&LSR station at Buncrana was a good deal more distinguished looking than its counterpart in Derry.** H.C.Casserley.

Top right: **This picture of No.4 *Inishowen* at Buncrana was taken in September 1898 before the line was extended to Carndonagh. The engine's original dome was a good deal more elegant than the one it was later supplied with.** Ken Nunn Collection.

Centre: **4-6-2T No.10 has the 5.10pm to Derry on 15th April 1948. One of the L&LSR's buses which had provided a connection, probably from Carndonagh, stands beside the train providing a very convenient road-rail interchange. The company continued to operate bus services for many years after the trains ceased to run.** H.C.Casserley.

Bottom: **No.10 was again at Buncrana on 28th June 1950. Passengers could travel in the brake coach at the head of the goods train in the platform opposite the loco.** John Edgington.

Photographs on this page:

Top: **The railway had about 40 coaches made up of a mixture of bogie and 6-wheel vehicles. Carriages were unheated which must have made for unpleasant journeys, especially on the long haul to Burtonport, in winter. Stock built for the Burtonport line was lettered L&BER and numbered in a separate sequence, as is evidenced by brake-3rd No.9, seen at Letterkenny in June 1937.** H.C.Casserley.

Centre: **Locos, carriages and even goods wagons bought for the extension were lettered L&BER. The Swilly's promiscuous use of these items of rolling stock all over its system was a constant source of aggravation to the Board of Works who had been responsible for the construction and equipping of the L&BER.** H.C.Casserley.

Lower left: **In this line of carriages at Derry in 1937, the vehicle lettered L&LSR, in the centre, is flanked by two L&BER coaches.** H.C.Casserley.

Lower right: **The buffer height of Swilly wagons was some 3 inches lower than those of the CDR. The coupling hooks and vacuum brake pipes were also different. Special conversions allowed the brake pipes to be connected and a batch of wagons acquired for the opening of the CDR's Letterkenny line had special buffers and coupling hooks to enable them to be used with L&LSR vehicles. Unbraked Swilly vehicles were allowed on CDR trains if marshalled at the rear next to the brake van. To get the three wagons pictured here running safely in the one train, could well have posed several operating difficulties for the staff concerned. The saga of different buffer heights and incompatible brake pipes serves to illustrate the strangely distant relationship between Donegals two narrow gauge systems.** H.C.Casserley.

Left: **On the Letterkenny line a goods train stops for water at Newtowncunningham on 20th April 1953.** H.C.Casserley.

Centre: **Further on in the direction of Letterkenny, was the station of Manorcunningham. 4-6-2T No.15 has the Letterkenny goods on 21st July 1952.** D.G.Coakham.

Bottom: **No.12 halts at Letterkenny with a Burtonport train on 24th June 1937.** H.C.Casserley.

Top: **A line up of Swilly buses are parked on the opposite platform as No.3 arrives at Letterkenny with the goods from Derry on 28th June 1950.** D.G.Coakham.

Below: **4-6-0T No.3 poses outside the single road Swilly engine shed at Letterkenny on 23rd June 1937.** H.C.Casserley.

Above left: **The L&LSR favoured an unusual style of single pitched roofs for many of its signal boxes. This was also applied to the wooden hut beside Letterkenny's box. The CDR's station at Letterkenny, which wastefully duplicated virtually all the Swilly's facilities, was located in the area behind the signalbox. No.5, a beautifully proportioned 1899 built 4-6-2T locomotive, displays on her tank side, the diamond shaped logo enclosing the letters LSR, which was carried by the locos in the last years of the railway.** H.C.Casserley.

Above right: **No.15 is shunting wagons into the L&LSR goods shed at Letterkenny on 20th April 1953.** H.C.Casserley.

Left, second down: **No.1 the first of the L&BER 4-6-0Ts, heads a goods train for Burtonport out of Letterkenny on 7th May 1920.** Ken Nunn Collection.

Above right: **Kilmacrenan was the fifth station, 12 miles out from Letterkenny, on the extension.** H.C.Casserley.

Left, third down: **This picture taken from a train to Burtonport gives some indication of the bleak and rocky terrain traversed by the line.** H.C.Casserley.

Left, fourth and fifth down: **The major engineering feature on the Burtonport line was the 380 yards long Owencarrow viaduct. This was the scene of two derailments caused by Atlantic gales blowing trains off the track. The first in 1906 did not cause any fatalities but that on 30th January 1925, when two carriages of a train were blown onto the rocky embankment which formed part of the structure, resulted in the death of four passengers. On the day after the accident one of the big 4-8-4Ts is in attendance with the repair gang.** H.C.Casserley, courtesy George Haire collection.

Henry Casserley travelled the length of the Burtonport line in June 1937 in trains hauled appropriately enough, by the surviving 4-8-0 No.12. I have drawn from his photographic record of these journeys to convey something of this remarkable line.

Top left, right and centre: **No.12 is watered at Creeslough, which gives time for the driver to oil round the engine and to check the tender axleboxes. These pictures show the length of these engines to good effect.**

Bottom right: **Trains to Burtonport were mixed and shunting at stations along the way delayed progress. No.12 is engaged in this activity at Gweedore, in front of the signalbox of distinctively Swilly design.**

Burtonport really was a tiny habitation. It is hard to believe that so much money and effort should have been expended to reach a place of so little consequence. The fish caught by its small fishing fleet was about all it had to offer by way of traffic. Without government money this line would never have been built and without a virtual monopoly of the meagre traffic on offer it could never even approach viability. The Burtonport Extension, driven at great cost through a barren landscape, with the mighty 8-coupled engines hauling its trains, was the Irish narrow gauge at its most magnificent but also its most futile. These pictures were taken by H.C.Casserley at Burtonport in June 1937.

Below: **Back in Derry we take our leave of the Lough Swilly and make a link to Donegal's other narrow gauge system, which is the subject of our next chapter. Londonderry had four railway termini, two on each bank of the River Foyle, which divides the city. On the west bank were situated the Swilly's Graving Dock station and the GNR's Foyle Road terminus. On the other side of the river the NCC line from Belfast terminated at Waterside station and the CDR narrow gauge line from Strabane came into its own station at Victoria Road. The only bridge over the Foyle in the city was the Craigavon bridge and the only way that interchange between Derry's four railway stations could be effected was by means of the mixed gauge track on the bottom deck of the bridge. Locomotives could not venture onto the bridge which was at right angles to the railway lines on both banks. Wagons could be manoeuvred onto the tracks on the bridge by means of the turntables at either end. This 1948 picture shows one of these turntables, the mixed gauge tracks on the bridge and in the distance some wagons on the bridge itself.** H.C.Casserley.

Bottom: **The tracks which served the city's quays on the west bank of the Foyle were owned and operated by the Londonderry Port and Harbour Commissioners. They provided locos to shunt the quayside lines. These were broad gauge but were fitted with drawgear to enable them to haul stock of either gauge. LP&HC No.3 *R.H.Smyth*, built by Avonside in 1928, is seen here, on 24th April 1950, hauling a train of narrow gauge wagons, the first of which belongs to the L&LSR. The two sets of drawgear for the 5ft 3in and 3ft gauges can be clearly seen on the loco's bufferbeam. No.3 was subsequently preserved and is in the care of the Railway Preservation Society of Ireland.** John Edgington.

Chapter Six

THE COUNTY DONEGAL RAILWAYS

THE TITLE of this chapter presents one of those delightful paradoxes for which Ireland is famous. There never was a company called the County Donegal Railway. For sure there was once a West Donegal Railway and for a time there was the Donegal Railway, but the title by which most people refer to what this not too impartial observer believes to have been Ireland's finest narrow gauge system, was an abbreviation of the name of the management committee which ran it from 1906 onwards. The origins of this, the country's most extensive narrow gauge system, like that of its neighbour in Donegal, the L&LSR and the Cork Blackrock & Passage Railway at the other end of the country, lay in a broad gauge line.

As early as 1847 the town of Strabane in County Tyrone had been linked to the city of Derry some 15 miles away by the Londonderry & Enniskillen broad gauge line. Landowners in the neighbouring county of Donegal began to consider linking their area to the L&E. In May 1860 parliamentary authorisation was given to the Finn Valley Railway to build a line from the twin towns of Ballybofey and Stranorlar the 14 miles to Strabane.

The capital of £60,000 proved difficult to raise and a loan of £20,000 was negotiated with the Public Works Loan Commissioners to enable the line to be completed. From its opening in August 1863 the line was worked by the Irish North Western Railway, the successor to the L&E at Strabane and after 1872 by the GNR which was formed in that year by the amalgamation of a number of companies including the INWR. The FVR paid a rental of £375 per annum to share the broad gauge station at Strabane. Though the FVR did not live up to the rather optimistic financial forecasts of its promoters thoughts began to turn to expansion with plans for a line from Stranorlar through Barnesmore Gap to Donegal Town. A separate company, the West Donegal Railway was formed, which was granted powers in July 1879 to construct a 3ft gauge line to Donegal Town. The FVR was heavily involved in the WDR to its own financial detriment. Funds ran out with the line built only as far as Druminin, later known as Lough Eske, 4 miles from Donegal Town. Nevertheless the first narrow gauge locomotives, the three Sharp Stewart 2-4-0Ts, arrived in February 1882 and services to Druminin commenced in April of that year. For the next 12 years Stranorlar station had to play host to two gauges, and by another Irish paradox, so baffling to those unused to them but quite logical to the natives, the broad gauge FVR, whose own line was worked by the GNR, was responsible for working the narrow gauge WDR. The four mile gap to Donegal Town was finally bridged in September 1889. Even then funds did not run to the building of a station there so yet another company called the Donegal Railway Station Company was set up. This concern built the station and leased it to the WDR for £200 per annum. Was this I wonder, an early Irish example of what might today be regarded as creative accounting?

The next extensions of the narrow gauge in Donegal were brought about by the availability of government money under the provisions of the Light Railways (Ireland) Act of 1889. State funding enabled the WDR to extend its line 19 miles from Donegal to the fishing village of Killybegs on the shore of Donegal Bay. The FVR got the cash to continue their line up the valley of the River Finn to Glenties. Logic dictated that the two nominally independent concerns should now merge and that as the future for the railways of Donegal lay with the narrow gauge, the original Finn Valley line should be re-gauged otherwise it would be in the absurd position of operating two short lines on two different gauges. Parliament sanctioned the merger of the FVR and the WDR to form the Donegal Railway Company in June 1892 and in 1893 it authorised the conversion of the Stranorlar to Strabane line to the 3ft gauge. Since it had opened, FVR trains had entered Strabane over the tracks of the L&E and its successors. The legislation of 1893 provided powers for an independent approach to Strabane, a new bridge over the River Mourne and a separate narrow gauge station adjacent to that of the GNR. The FVR line was re-gauged over a weekend in July 1894 and with the opening of the Killybegs line in August 1893 and that to Glenties in June 1895, the DR now had a route mileage of 75.

The expansion of the system continued right through the first decade of the twentieth century. For some time there had been, within the DR, a hankering for a narrow gauge line to Londonderry. Much of the freight for County Donegal, especially coal, came through the port of Derry, a 3ft gauge line to the city would overcome the problems of trans-shipment of goods between the gauges at Strabane. The GNR naturally objected to the scheme on the grounds that it would duplicate their existing line.

Despite these complaints the Donegal Railway Act of 1896 authorised both the line to Londonderry and a branch, at the other end of the system, from Donegal to Ballyshannon. The Derry line was tackled first. It followed the eastern side of the River Foyle and terminated at Victoria Road not far from the B&NCR Waterside station.

With the opening of this line in August 1900 all four of Londonderry's termini were now in place and with appropriate symmetry there was one each of both the broad and narrow gauge species on either side of the River Foyle which divides the city.

Collectors of Irish paradoxes may already have noted that the Donegal Railway route to Derry studiously avoided the County Donegal side of the Foyle where the GNR line ran, making its way to the city by progressing through the counties of Tyrone and Londonderry.

Though authorised in 1896 neither the Derry nor the Ballyshannon lines received any funding under the Railways (Ireland) Act of that year. Neither of the districts served by the two lines were deemed to be sufficiently impoverished to benefit from the public funding provided for in the legislation. It took a long time to raise the capital to build the Ballyshannon line which was not opened until September 1905. The two new lines brought the extent of the system up to 105½ miles. It was at this point that a new era began to dawn for the railways of Donegal when a new and powerful player emerged on the scene.

In 1903 the English Midland Railway bought the Belfast & Northern Counties Railway. Keen to expand its Irish interests, shortly after this, the MR offered to purchase the DR. The GNR was alarmed at this intrusion into its fiefdom and protested at the proposal. Eventually an agreement was reached between the two companies to jointly purchase the DR and parliamentary approval was given for this on 1st May 1906.

The railway was to be managed by a joint committee made up of three appointees from both the MR and the GNR. One odd consequence of this takeover was that the DR line from Strabane to Derry became the sole property of the Midland though it continued to be worked by the CDRJC. This new management structure guided the railway throughout the rest of its existence and indeed continued in being up to 1971 to run the road services which continued after the closure of the railway in 1959.

One final line remained to be added to the CDR (as we may call it from this point on) network and that was the section from Strabane to Letterkenny. It may be recalled that the first plan of the promoters of the Letterkenny Railway in the 1860s – *see page 50* – was a line from the town eastwards in the direction of the River Foyle and not towards Tooban Junction as was built eventually. A variant of this scheme was revived in 1902 for a line from Strabane through Lifford, Raphoe and Convoy, to Letterkenny. Parliamentary approval was given to the Strabane & Letterkenny Railway in 1904. Nominally this was an independent company but most of the capital was provided by the GNR and the MR and it was worked from the start by the CDRJC. The opening of this line in 1909 brought the route mileage of the CDR up to 124½ making it by some way the largest narrow gauge system in Ireland.

A brief history of CDR motive power can be divided into two phases. Though its last steam locomotive was purchased in 1912 the steam fleet was well maintained and used on goods and excursion traffic up to the end of rail services. However, parallel to steam traction, from the 1930s onwards the CDR became a pioneer of the use of diesel railcars for passenger services and the development of this form of traction is of equal interest and importance to the steam locomotives. What is noticeable about the CDR is that both forms of traction were used for the activities to which they were best suited and were operated in harmony. The usual story of precipitous dieselisation making steam prematurely redundant certainly does not apply to this railway.

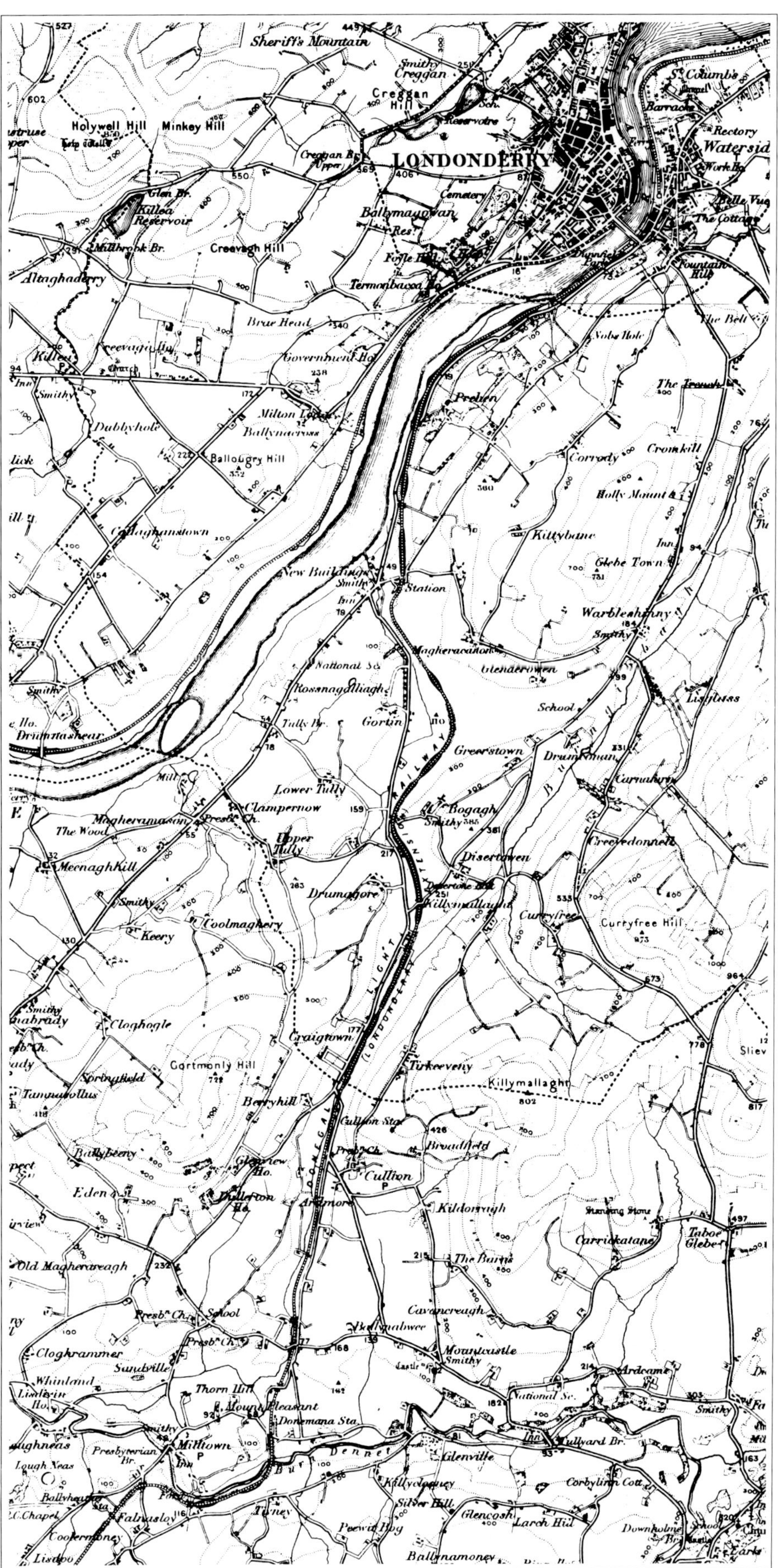

Copyright reserved, Ordnance Survey, Dublin. Reproduced from 1 inch series, sheet nos. 11, 15, 16, 17, 23, 24, 25, 31, 32; revised 1911, 1913, 1913, 1899, 1899, 1913, 1913, 1913, 1899; published 1913, 1917, 1916, 1902, 1901, 1916, 1915, 1917, 1901 respectively. Scale 1 inch to 1 mile.

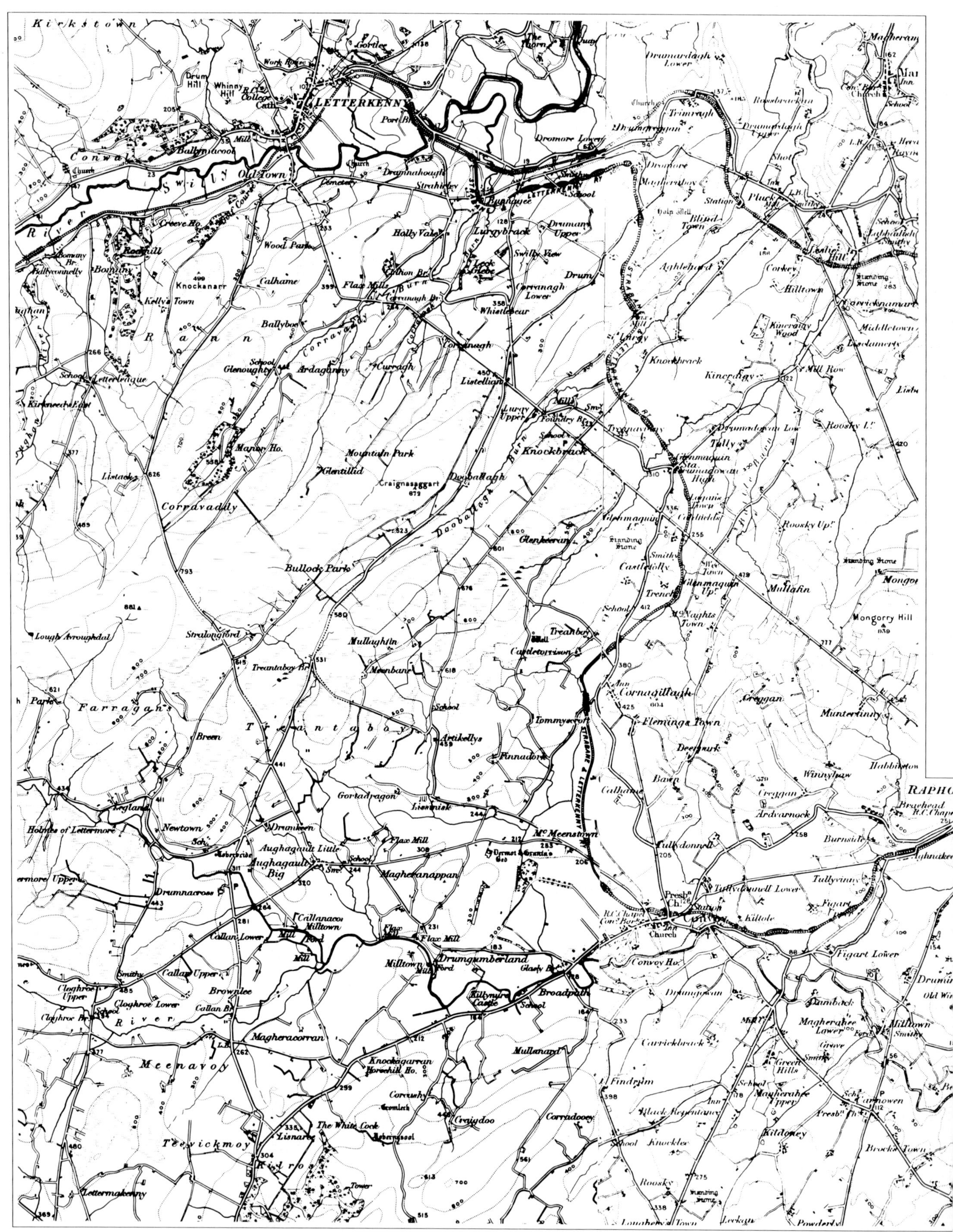
Kirkstown
Letterkenny
Work House
Gortlee
Drum Hill
Whinny Hill
R.C. College
Cath.
Ballymacool
Conwal
Church
Swilly
Old Town
River
Dromore Lower
Drumnahough
Cemetery
Strahitfey
Bunnagee
School
Creeve Ho.
Rockhill
Bomany Br.
Ballyconnelly
Bomany
Knockanarr
Kelly's Town
Wood Park
Holly Vale
Lurgybrack
Druman Upper
Calhame
Flax Mills
Corravaddy
Corranagh Br.
Corranagh Lower
Whistlebear
Drum
Swilly View
Ballyboe
Raan
Glenoughty
Ardagunny
Curragh
Listellian
Letterlague
Manor Ho.
Mountain Park
Glentillid
Craignasaggart
Doobaragh
Knockbrack
Listack
Corravaddy
Glenkeeran
Bullock Park
Lough Avoughdal
Stralongford
Mullaghtin
Treantaboy Br.
Meenbane
Treanboy
Castletorrison
School
Farragans
Treantaboy
Artikellys
Tommyscroft
Finnadork
Breen
Gortadragon
Lisminisk
Mc Meenstown
Leglands
Newtown
Drumkeen
Aughagault Little
Aughagault Big
Flax Mill
Magheranappan
Drumnacross
Callanacor
Milltown
Callan Lower
Mill
Ford
Flax Mill
Drumgumberland
Milltown
Callan Upper
Cloghroe Upper
Cloghroe Lower
Brownlee
Callan Br.
Cloghroe Br.
River
Killynure Castle
Broadpath
Magheracorran
Meenavoy
Knockagarran
Horsehill Ho.
Mullanard
Corcushy
Cromlech
Craigdoo
The White Cock
Lisnarick
Corradooey
Teevickmoy
Lettermakenny
Tower
Drumardagh Lower
Trimragh
Drumagreggan
Rossbracken
Drumardagh Upper
Dromore
Station
Plack
Blind Town
Aghlehard
Corkey
Hilltown
Leslie Hill
Carricknamart
Kinercany Wood
Middletown
Knockbrack
Kincraigy
Mill Row
Roosky Lr.
Tully
Glenmaquin Sta.
Glenmaquin Lr.
Standing Stone
Castletolly
Trench
Glenmaquin Upr.
Mullafin
Mongorry Hill
Roosky Upr.
Cornagillagh
Flemings Town
Creggan
Muntertinny
Deerpark
Winnyhaw
Bawn
Calhame
Ardvarnock
Creggan
Tullydonnell
Tullyrannell Lower
Tullyvinny
Burnside
Raphoe
Braehead
R.C. Chapel
Presbn. Ch.
Station
Kiltole
Church
Convoy Ho.
Drumgowan
Figart Lower
Dunback
Magherahee Lower
Milltown
Carrickbrack
Green Hills
Grove
Findrum
Magherahee Upper
Carnowen
Black Repentance
Knocklee
Kildoney
Brocks Town
Roosky
Standing Stone
Loughery's Town
Leckan
Powderly
Stranorlar & Letterkenny Ry.

The first narrow gauge locomotives were the three Sharp Stewart 2-4-0Ts supplied to the WDR. The last of these, No.1 *Alice,* survived until 1926. All Donegal locomotives were given class numbers from the first 2-4-0Ts which logically became class 1, to the last 2-6-4Ts of class 5A. To work the extensions built in the mid 1890s six 4-6-0Ts were ordered from Neilson in 1893. These were the first locomotives of this wheel arrangement supplied to an Irish narrow gauge railway and not dissimilar engines were later acquired by the L&LSR for the L&BER and the West Clare Railway. The last of the Donegal class 2 4-6-0Ts was scrapped in 1937. The next new engines, the two which made up class 3, were unusual and quite interesting. No.10 *Sir James* and No.11 *Hercules* were the only examples of the 4-4-4T wheel arrangement to run on the Irish narrow gauge. Built by Neilson Reid in 1902, they had driving wheels of 4ft in diameter and were designed with the Derry line in mind. Passengers from Strabane to Londonderry now had a choice of routes and the narrow gauge line had to offer a reasonably quick journey time to compete with the broad gauge trains of the GNR. It was this requirement which probably led to the reversion to 4-coupled engines whose larger driving wheels would have given them a reasonable turn of speed. By the standards of the Irish narrow gauge the two 4-4-4Ts did not last very long, both being scrapped in 1933.

The rest of the CDR steam fleet was built between 1904 and 1912 by Nasmyth Wilson of Manchester. The first four engines which arrived in 1904, were the only Baltic or 4-6-4Ts to run on the Irish narrow gauge. One of these, originally No.14 renumbered 11 in 1937, *Erne,* remained in use up to the end of the CDR by which time it was the last 4-6-4T remaining in the British Isles. The remaining CDR engines were all 2-6-4Ts divided into two classes – 5 and 5A. Three class 5 engines arrived in 1907, two more in 1908 and the class 5A 2-6-4Ts, built to an improved design, came in 1912. The main differences between the two classes were that the 5As were built with superheaters whereas the other 2-6-4Ts had to wait until the 1920s to have them fitted and the later engines also had greater water capacity, their larger tanks making them easily identifiable from the earlier locomotives.

All the 2-6-4Ts were renumbered and renamed during their careers. In the photographic section I have used the numbers and names they carried on the date the photographs were taken. To avoid confusion the changes of identity were as follows:

Class	Original name and number	Date changed	Later name and number
5	16 *Donegal*	1937	4 *Meenglas*
5	17 *Glenties*	1937	5 *Drumboe*
5	18 *Killybegs*	1937	6 *Columbkille*
5	19 *Letterkenny*	1937	7 *Finn*
5	20 *Raphoe*	1937	8 *Foyle*
5A	21 *Ballyshannon*	1928	1 *Alice*
5A	2A *Strabane*	1928	2 *Blanche*
5A	3A *Stranolar*	1928	3 *Lydia*

The class 5 engines took the names of the withdrawn class 2 4-6-0Ts, the 5As took those of the old WDR 2-4-0Ts.

The first internal combustion engined vehicle to come to the CDR appeared as early as 1906. This was a four wheeled inspection car built by Allday and Onions in Birmingham. It saw only occasional use until the 1926 coal strike when it was pressed into service for the carriage of mails. Its success in this capacity got the CDR manager Henry Forbes thinking about developing larger vehicles for passenger services. The first two railcars were acquired second hand in 1926 from the Derwent Valley Light Railway in Yorkshire. These petrol engined vehicles were regauged and put to work and lasted until 1934. Several other petrol engined railcars were built or bought up to 1930 when railcar No.7 appeared. This was the first diesel engined railcar in the British Isles. Powered by a Gardner engine, as were all subsequent CDR railcars, No.7 and its twin No.8 had a pair of wheels at the front and a driving bogie at the rear. To put these railcars in context they came only two years after the GSR took delivery of their Clayton steam railcars and at a time when the London & North Eastern Railway was still fiddling around with Sentinel steam railcars.

Two more petrol engined railcars were built in 1933 before the appearance in 1934 of the first vehicle from Walkers of Wigan, who were to be associated with the construction of the rest of the CDR railcars. This firm developed a type of railcar with a powered bogie articulated from the passenger accommodation. The first of these vehicles to come to Ireland was actually supplied to the Clogher Valley Railway in 1932 though on the closure of that line in 1942 it was bought by the CDR, becoming No.10 in the fleet. The CDR's first Walker railcar was No.12 dating from 1934. Between then and 1951 it was joined by another 8 railcars (this

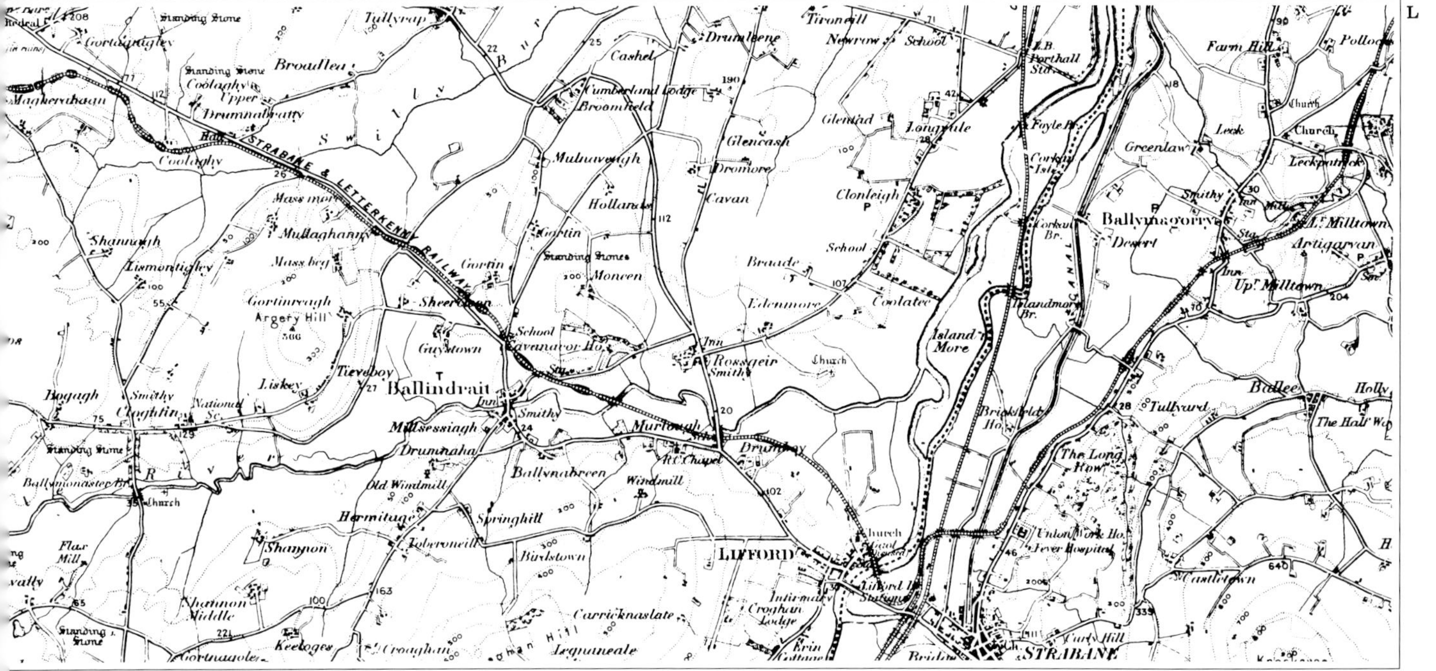

M

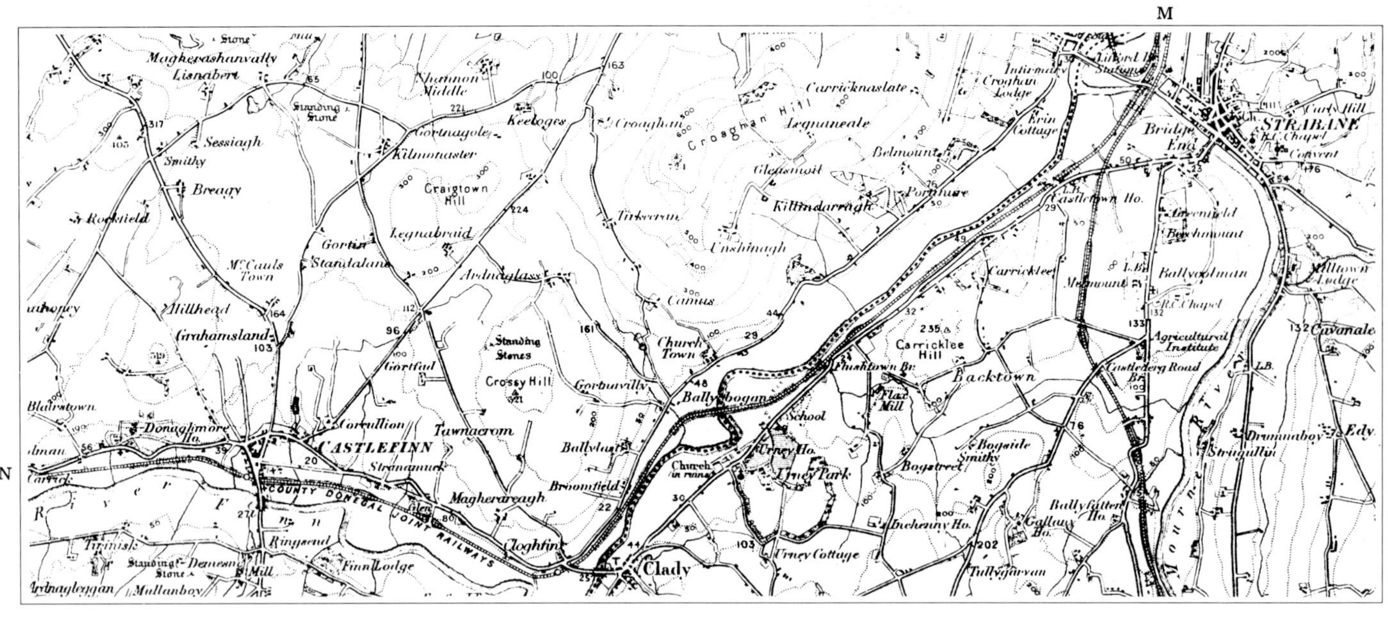

Magherashanvally
Lisnabert
Sessiagh
Smithy
Breagy
Rockfield
Gortnagole
Kilmonaster
Craigtown Hill
Legnabraid
Gortin
Standalane
McCauls Town
Millhead
Grahamsland
Ardnaglass
Standing Stones
Crossy Hill
Gortfad
Blairstown
Donaghmore Ho.
CASTLEFINN
Corcullion
Tawnacrom
Stranamurk
Maghereragh
Broomfield
Cloghfin
Ringsend
Finn Lodge
Mullanboy
Ardnagleggan
COUNTY DONEGAL JOINT RAILWAYS
Shannon Middle
Keeloges
Carricknaslate
Croaghan Hill
Legnaneale
Belmount
Gleamoil
Killindarragh
Portnure
Unshinagh
Camus
Church Town
Ballyshogan
Clady
Urney Ho.
Urney Park
Urney Cottage
School
Flax Mill
Carricklee Hill
Rushtown Br.
Backtown
Bogside
Smithy
Bogstreet
Bucheny Ho.
Tullyarvan
Ballyfatten Ho.
Gallany Ho.
Strabane Station
Croghan Lodge
Erin Cottage
Castletown Ho.
Carricklee
Greenfield
Beechmount
Ballycolman
R.C. Chapel
Agricultural Institute
Castlederg Road Br.
Drumnaboy
Straghullin
Bridge End
STRABANE
Convent
Milltown Lodge
Cavanale
Edy

N

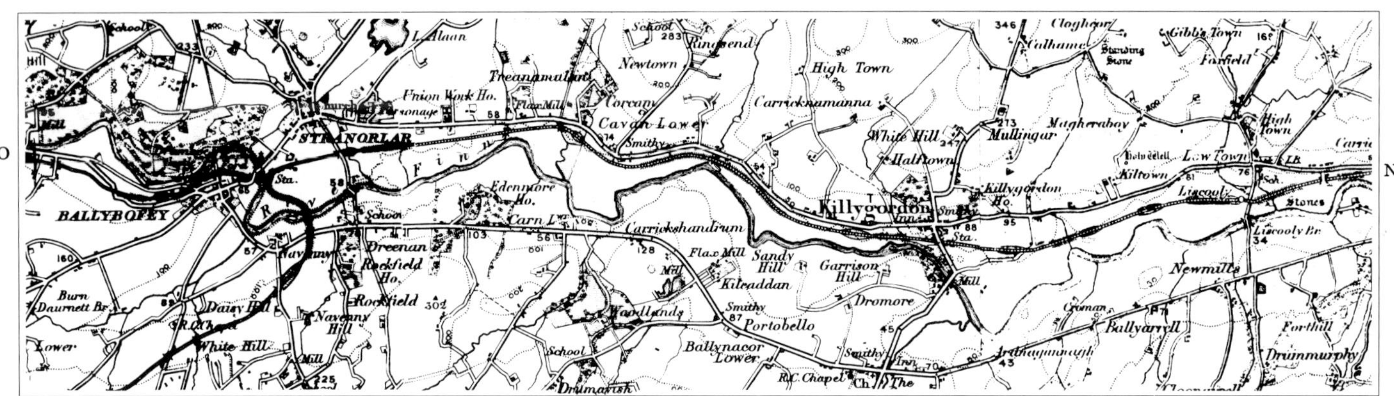

School
Hill
Mill
BALLYBOFEY
STRANORLAR
Union Work Ho.
Parsonage
Sta.
Dreenan
Rockfield Ho.
Rockfield
Navenny
Navenny Hill
Daisy Hill
White Hill
Burn
Lower
Treanamullin
Corcam
Cavan Lower
Smithy
Edenmore Ho.
Carn L.
Carrickshandrum
Flax Mill
Sandy Hill
Kilcaddan
Garrison Hill
Dromore
Woodlands
Portobello
Ballynacor Lower
R.C. Chapel
Drumarish
School
Ringsend
Newtown
High Town
Carricknamanna
White Hill
Halftown
Mullingar
Magheraboy
Killygordon
Killygordon Ho.
Sta.
Cloghcor
Calhame
Standing Stone
Gibbs Town
Fairfield
High Town
Belvedere
Low Town
Kiltown
Liscooly
Liscooly Br.
Stones
Newmills
Ardnagannagh
Cronan
Ballyarrell
Forthill
Drumnurphy

O N

P

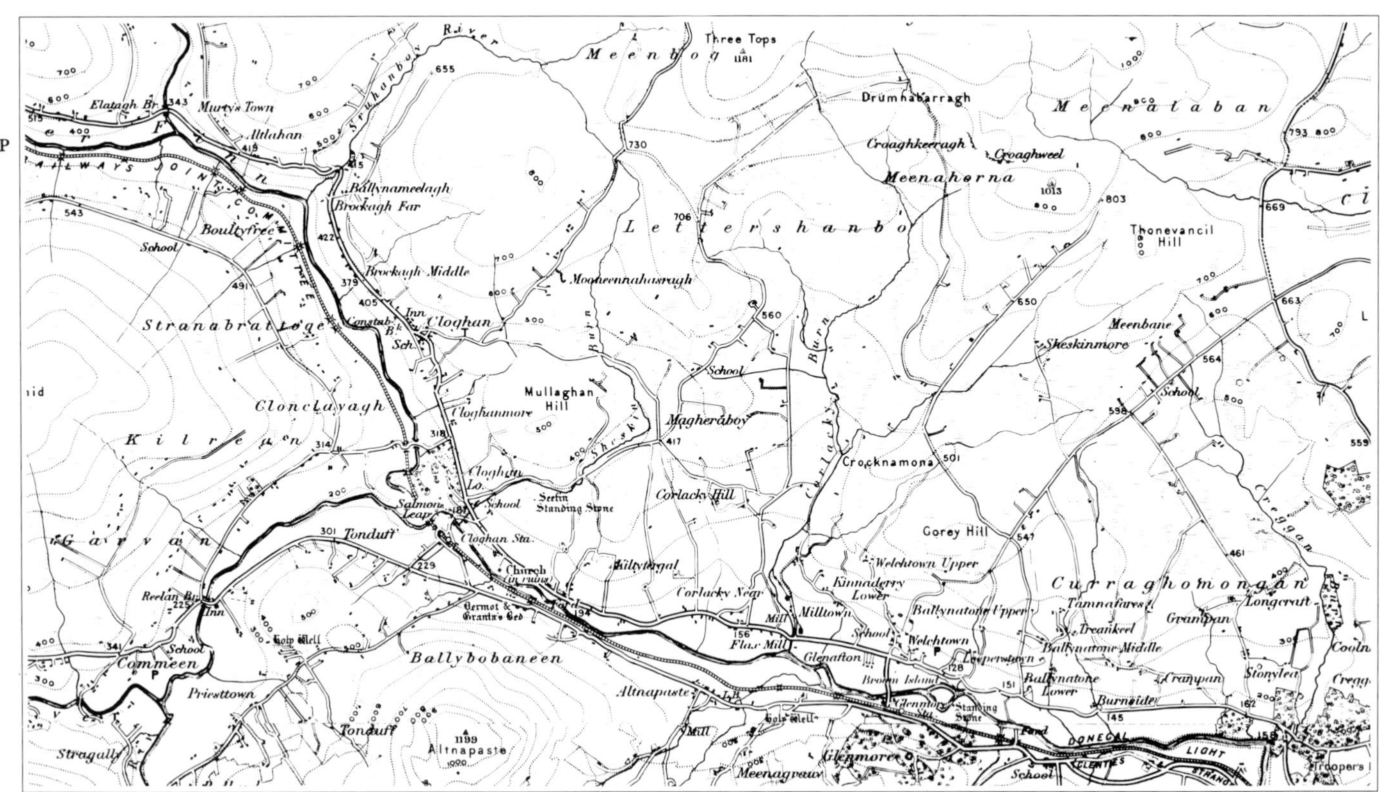

River
Meenbog
Three Tops
Elatagh Br.
Murty's Town
Altlahan
Ballynameelagh
Brockagh Far
Boultyfree
School
Brockagh Middle
Stranabrat Lodge
Cloghan
Inn
Sch.
Cloncláyagh
Kilrean
Cloghanmore
Mullaghan Hill
Cloghan Lo.
Salmon Leap
School
Cloghan Sta.
Church in ruins
Tonduff
Garvan
Reelan Br.
Inn
Commeen
Priesttown
Stragally
Holy Well
Ballybobaneen
Altnapaste
Tonduff
Letter shanbo
Mooneennahasragh
Magheraboy
Corlacky Hill
Killygordon
Corlacky Near
Seefin Standing Stone
Drumnabarragh
Meenataban
Craaghkeeragh
Croaghweel
Meenahorna
Thonevancil Hill
Sheskinmore
Meenbane
School
Crocknamona
Gorey Hill
Welchtown Upper
Kinnaderry Lower
Milltown
Flax Mill
Glenafton
School
Welchtown
Ballynatone Upper
Tamnafiarsi
Treankeel
Ballynatone Middle
Ballynatone Lower
Curraghomongan
Longcraft
Granaghan
Cranpan
Stonylea
Cooln
Burnside
Brown Island
Glenmore Sta.
Standing Stone
Glenmore
Meenagrauv
School
DONEGAL LIGHT
Troopers

O

includes the ex-CVR vehicle). These railcars had bodies of various sizes and seating capacities built by the GNR at Dundalk works. The design reached its final development with Nos.19 and 20 delivered in 1950 and 1951 respectively. The railcars supplied to the WCR section of CIE were very similar to this pair which were sold to the Isle of Man Railway on the closure of the CDR where they are still to be seen.

The CDR railcars provided an economical method of running the railway's passenger service. Their capacity could be extended by their ability to haul a variety of trailers and vans and they could stop at convenient places between stations, like level crossings, to pick up passengers. The early adoption of diesel railcars undoubtedly prolonged the life of the CDR and its pioneering work in the development of this form of traction should not be forgotten.

Secure in the bosom of the GNR and the MR (later the LMS) and because of it straying into Northern Ireland, safe from the grey paint brushes of the GSR, the CDR was in a stronger position than most other Irish narrow gauge concerns. Its traffic seems to have been less badly affected by partition than that of the L&LSR and there was continuity in its management. From 1910 until his death in 1943 the CDR manager was Henry Forbes who was succeeded by Bernard Curran from then until 1966. There is no denying that Forbes was a dynamic and forceful personality who must be credited with the development of the railcars, but the CDR's historian Dr Edward Patterson has suggested that if he had spent more time securing capital investment from the relatively affluent owning companies and devoted less of his energies to an incessant drive to achieve economies, then the railway might have been in a stronger position to fight the onslaught of competition that came from road transport, especially after the Second World War.

Because of the remoteness of much of County Donegal and the condition of its roads, the railway was not badly hit by road competition until the late 1940s. Profits generated by the war years had been put aside and were used to meet later losses. The first line to close was that to Glenties which lost its regular services in 1947. With the nationalisation of the railways of Britain in 1948 the LMS stake in the CDR passed to the London Midland Region of British Railways. The Strabane to Derry line, which had been the sole property of the MR and subsequently the LMS, passed to the Ulster Transport Authority in 1948 when that unloved organisation took over the former LMS/NCC lines in the province. The CDR

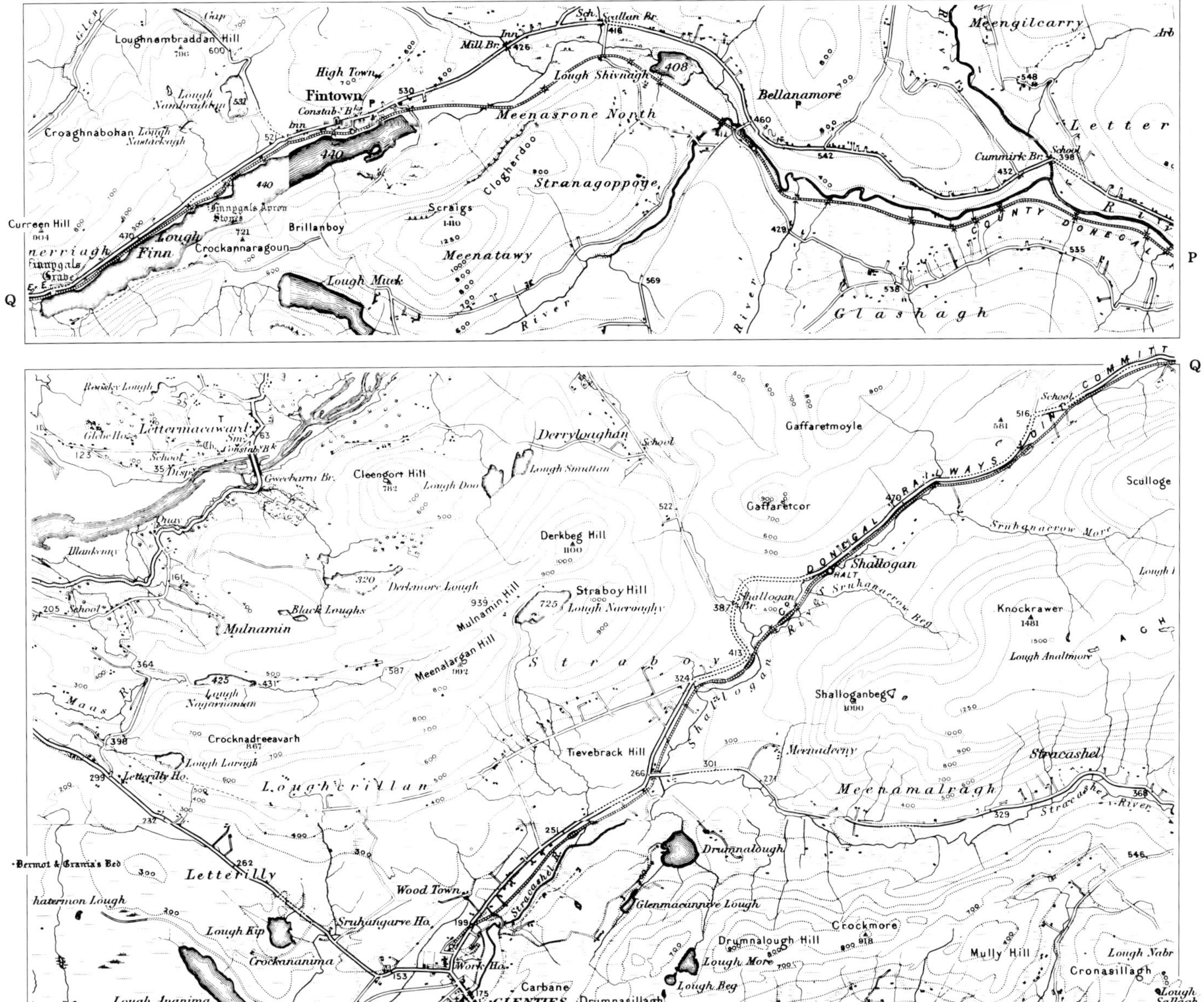

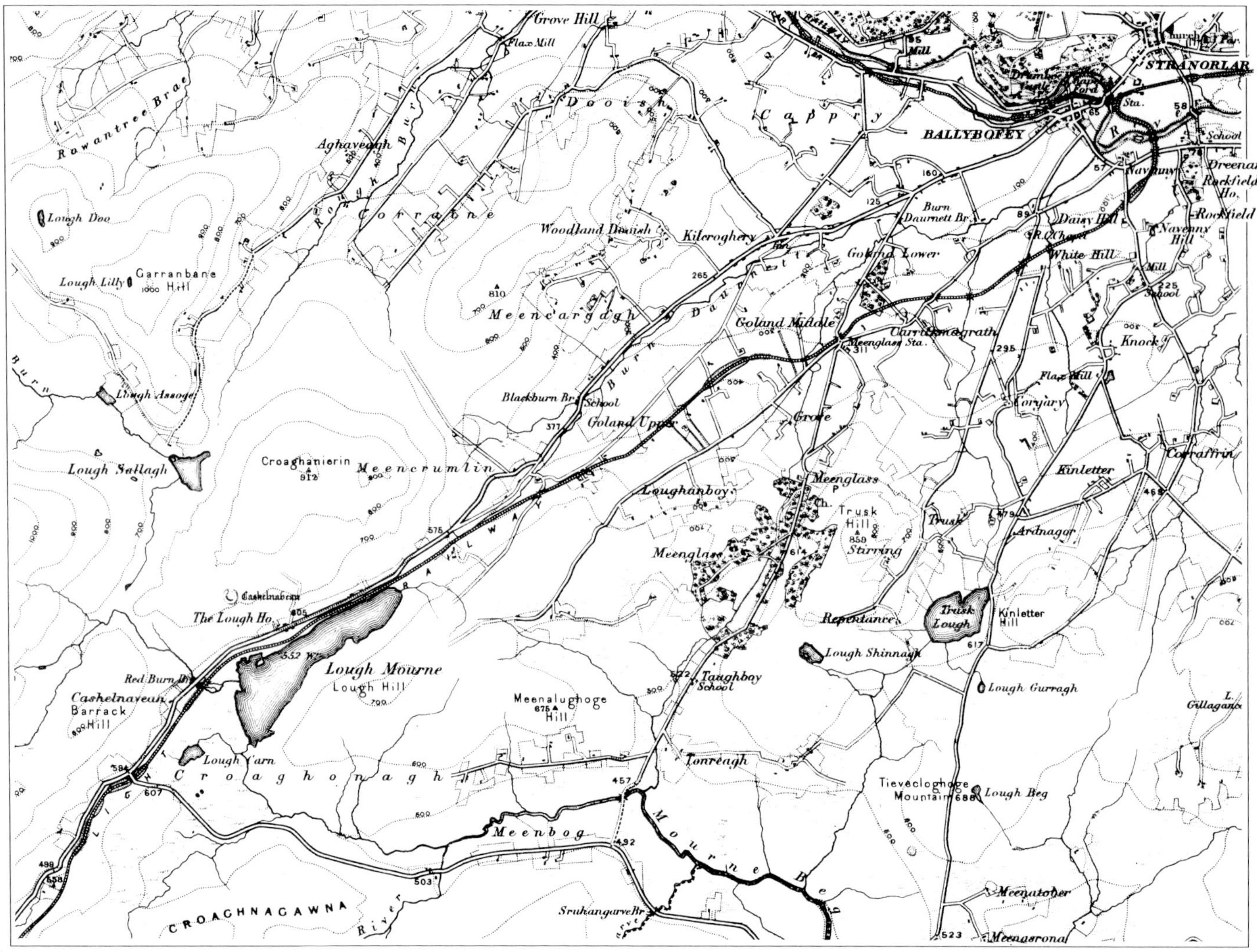

Grove Hill
Flax Mill
STRANORLAR
N
BALLYBOFEY
Sta.
School
Dreenan
Rockfield Ho.
Rockfield
Navenny
Navenny Hill
Dooish
Cappry
Aghaveagh
Rawantree Brae
Rough Burn
Corraghe
Lough Doo
Garranbane Hill
Lough Lilly
Woodland Dooish
Kilcroghery
Burn Daurnett Br.
Daisy Hill
R.C. Chapel
Goland Lower
White Hill
Meencargagh
Burn Daurnett
Goland Middle
Meenglass Sta.
Carricknagrath
Knock
Lough Assoge
Blackburn Br.
School
Goland Upper
Grove
Flax Mill
Corgary
Corraffrin
Lough Sallagh
Croaghanierin
Meencrumlin
Kinletter
Meenglass
Loughanboy
Trusk Hill
Stirring
Trusk
Ardnagor
Meenglass
RAILWAY
Cashelnaheaw
The Lough Ho.
Repentance
Trusk Lough
Kinletter Hill
Lough Shinnagh
Red Burn Br.
Lough Mourne
Lough Hill
Taughboy
School
Lough Gurragh
Cashelnaveau Barrack Hill
Meenaluphoge Hill
Gillagan
Lough Carn
Croaghonagh
Tonreagh
Tieveclogh Mountain
Lough Beg
Meenbog
Mourne Beg
Meenatober
Srukangarve Br.
River
CROACHNAGAWNA
Meenasrona
R

Faiafannan
Drumagny
Stranenen
Lugnawley
Tullinscullan
Cunlin Lough
DONEGAL RAILWAYS JOINT
Ardara Rd. Sta.
Five Points
Gilbertstown Lough
Drumrainy Hill
Drummeenanagh Hill
Inver Sta.
Tullaghacullion
Calhame Lough
Lisavaddy
Drumsippeen
The Commons Br.
The Lough Head
Croaghlin
Cashelbane Hill
Calhame
Bloody Br.
Tonnegee Hill
Drumadart
Coolshangan
Ford
Carricknagore
Sch.
Drumnakilly
Drumnakilew Br.
Inver
Clover
Aighan
Crocknakilew
Carn More Hill
Mill
Milltown Hotel
Bruckless
Bracklagh
Keelogs
Little Craig
Inver Bar
Coast Guard Sta.
KILLYBEGS
White Ho.
Killybegs Harbour
Binroe Hill
Ballyloughan
Bruckless Bruckless Cott.
Bruckless Harb.
Quay
Darney
Ballymagowan
Kilmacreddan Ho.
Port
Quay
Rock o' the Port
Buncronan Port
Castle Pt.
Industrial School
Rough Point
Binroe
Green Isd.
Darney Pt.
Flat Rock
Killaghtee
Smithy
School
Belville
Dunkineely
Bunlacky Br.
Whillins
Scar Point
Spamount
COUNTY DONEGAL RAILWAYS JOINT COMMITTEE
Church
Standing Stones
Buncronan
Croughlin
Carntullagh
Black Rock
Sentry Hill
The Scar
Creevins
Roshin
Rashenny Pt.
Port Roshin
Richies Bay
Dreelans
Illannanuan
Mc. Swyne's Bay
Castle Pt.
Castle Murray
Inver Bay
Rotten Isd.
Ballyboe Cott.
Cavan Point
Lack Islands
Raneely Port
Tullyvoo
Carntullagh Head
Kiln Port
Riggyheugh
Raneely

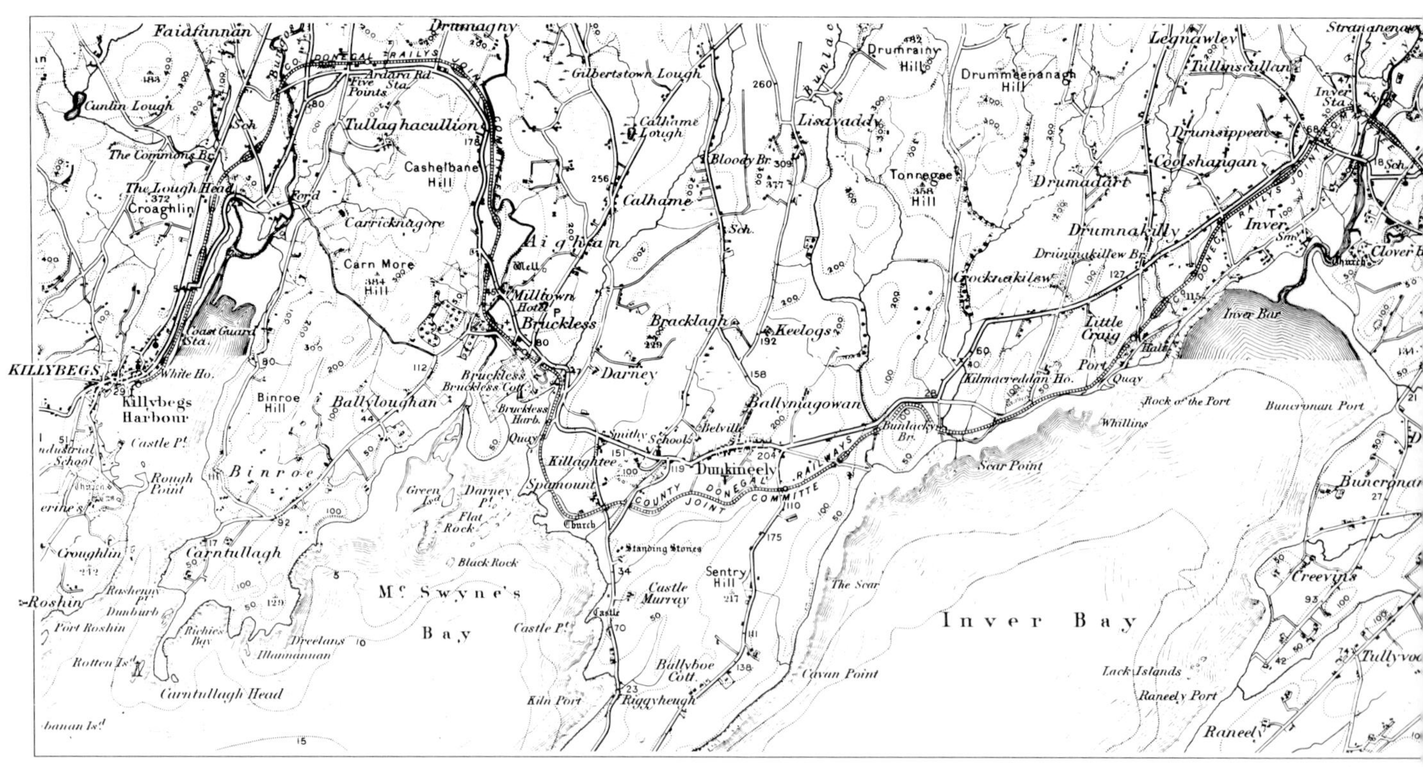

R

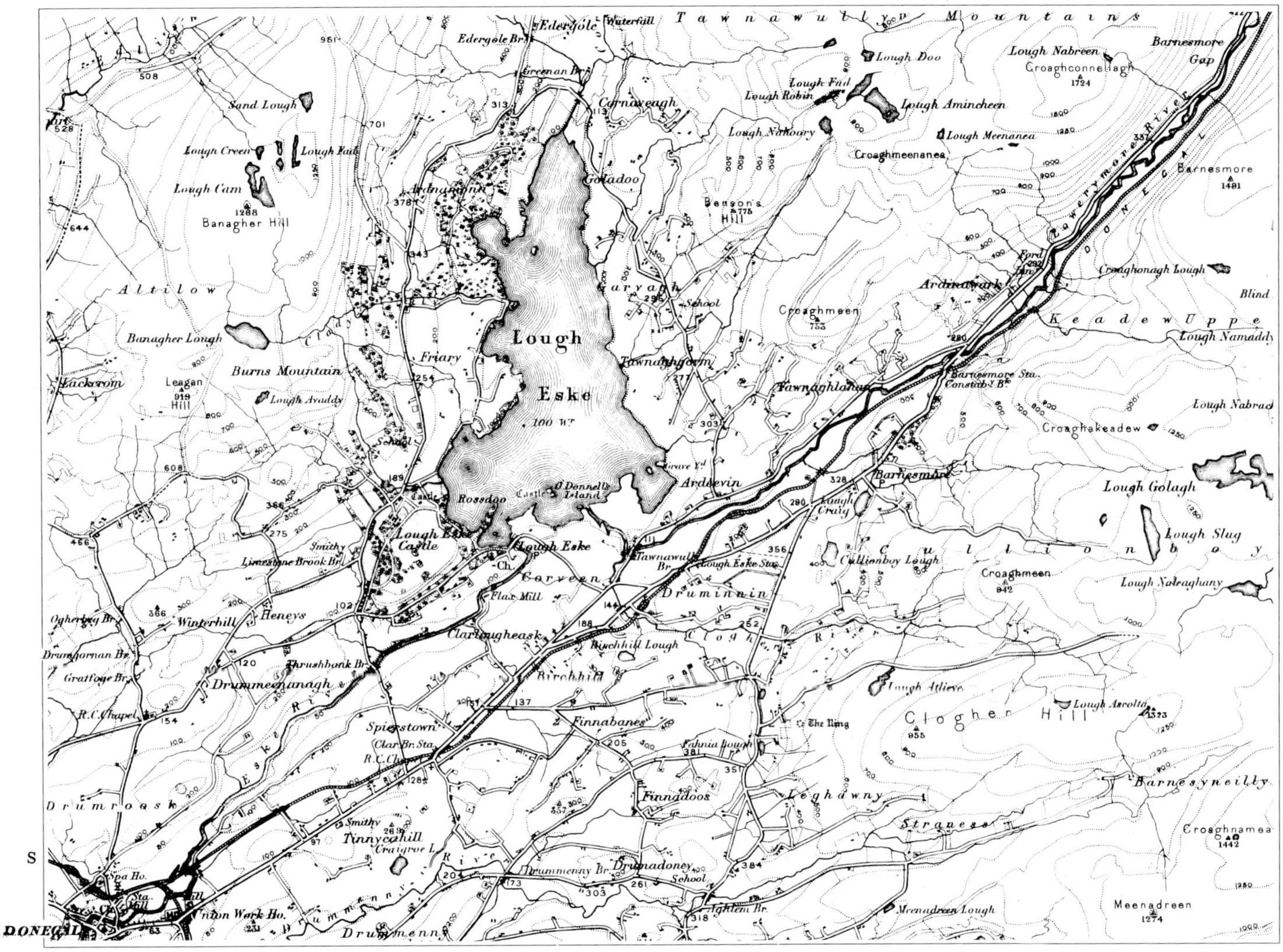

S

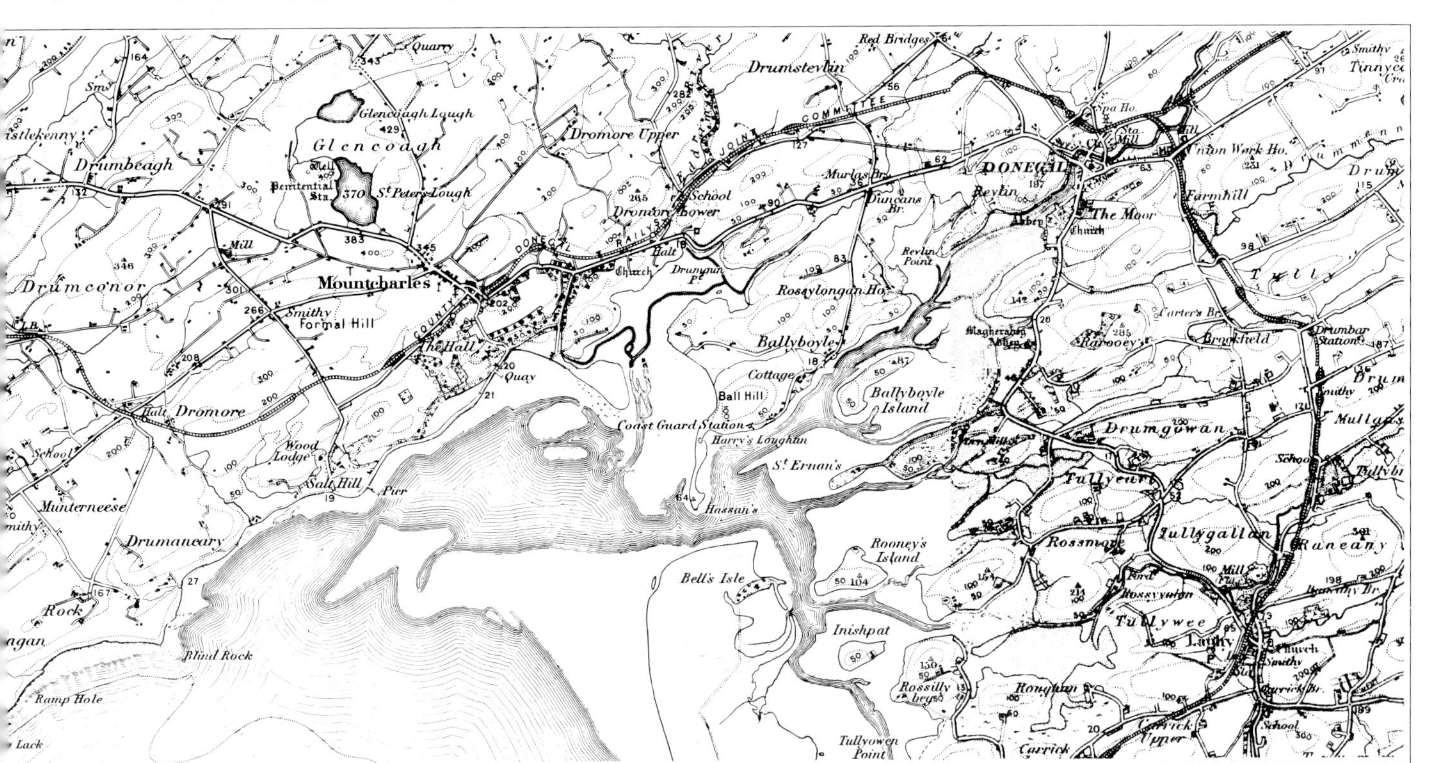
Drumstevlin
Red Bridges
Glencoagh Lough
Glencoagh
Dromore Upper
Drumbeagh
St Peters Lough
Penitential Sta.
DONEGAL
Reylin
The Moor
Abbey
Farmhill
Drumconor
Mountcharles
Formal Hill
The Hall
Quay
Rossylongan Ho.
Ballyboyle
Ballyboyle Island
Ball Hill
Coast Guard Station
Harry's Loughan
St Ernan's
Drumgowan
Tullycurry
Dromore
Wood Lodge
Salt Hill
Pier
Munterneese
Drumaneary
Hassan's
Rooney's Island
Tullygallan
Raneany
Rossmore
Bell's Isle
Inishpat
Rossylongan
Tullywee
Laghy
Blind Rock
Ramp Hole
Rossilly Island
Rongham
Carrick Upper
Carrick
Tullyowen Point
Drumbar Station
Brookfield
Mullagh
Lack

R

R

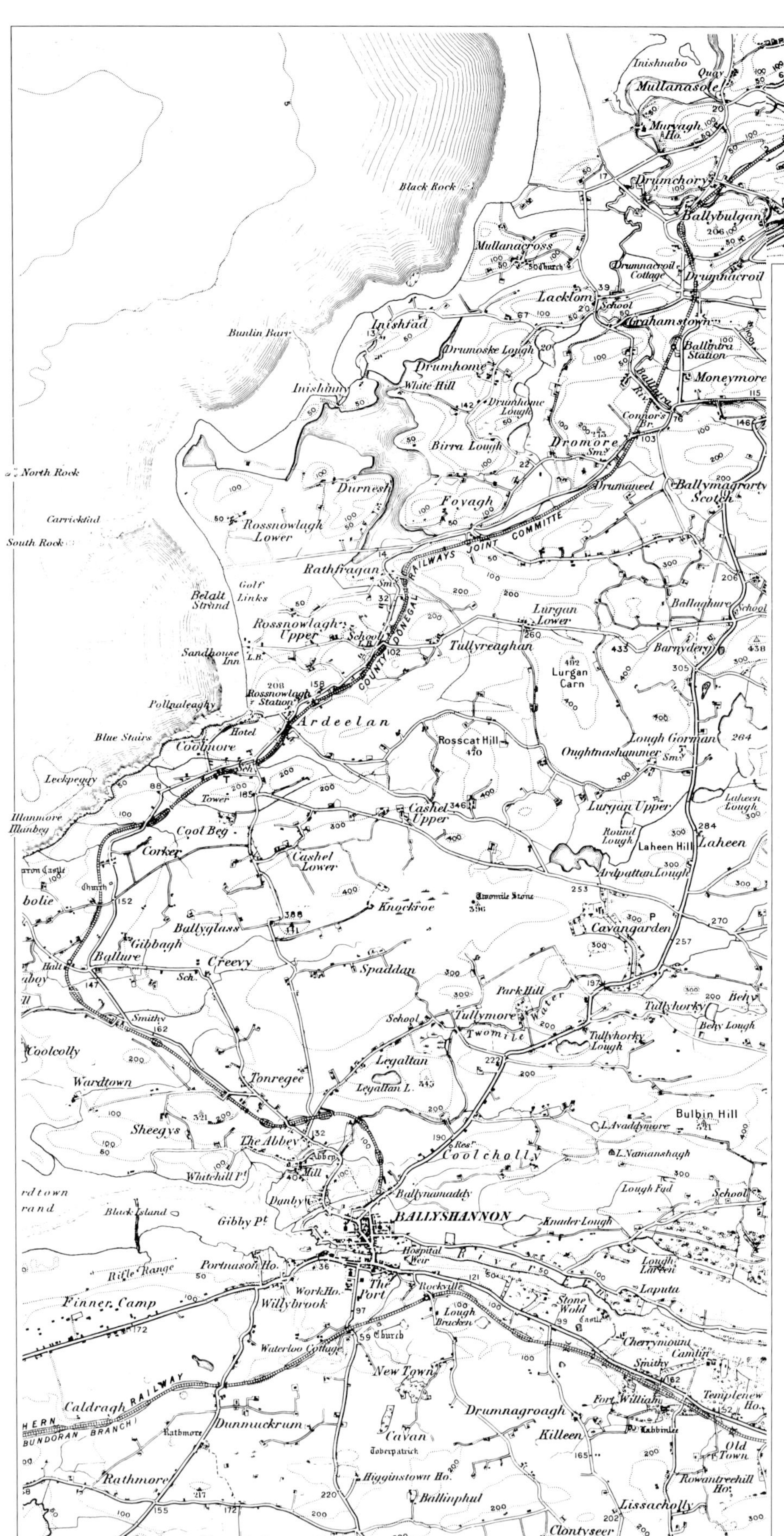

continued to work the line until December 1954 when regular services were suspended. The rest of the system lasted another five years. Though losses grew and traffic declined there was no slipping of standards. Steam locomotives continued to be used on freight trains whilst the railcars maintained the passenger services. The CDR's fleet of passenger coaches had been retained and were used for excursion traffic up to the end. The CDR's rail services finally succumbed on the last day of 1959. Road freight and buses continued to be operated up to 1971 when they were taken over by CIE thus severing a link with the past.

As a footnote to the CDR it must be remarked that by Irish standards quite a lot of the railway's rolling stock has survived. On the closure of the system, locomotive No.2 *Blanche,* railcar No.10, a directors' saloon and the unique diesel loco No.11 *Phoenix* were all saved by Belfast Transport Museum. In addition to these a considerable amount of other equipment, including four locomotives, was bought by Dr Ralph Cox, an American who planned to build a private railway in his own country. Cox's purchases were assembled at Strabane where they stayed for many years. It appears that the cost of shipping the stock to the USA had proved to be prohibitive. This little Irish narrow gauge version of Woodham's famous Barry scrapyard was eventually cleared by a preservation group, and even though in a dreadful state by the time they were rescued, as Barry has shown, where there is a hulk there is still the potential for life. A total of four CDR steam locomotives still exist though sadly the unique 4-6-4T *Erne,* part of Dr. Cox's purchases was cut up in 1967.

Preservation groups are active in Northern Ireland and in Donegal itself. A 3ft gauge line is being built from the site of the GNR's Foyle Road station in Derry on which ex-CDR stock is operated and the South Donegal Railway Restoration Society is working to rebuild part of the CDR mainline from Ballybofey, through Barnesmore Gap towards Donegal Town. Who knows, those of us too young to remember the old CDR may yet see a red liveried 2-6-4T working hard on the climb through the Gap, its exhaust echoing through the hills of Donegal once again.

Right: **Our photographic coverage of the CDR begins at the railway's terminus in Derry. The branch from Victoria Road to Strabane was the property of the MR and later the LMS/NCC, the Joint Committee were paid to work it. On 24th April 1951 4-6-4T No.11 *Erne* is at the head of a train for Strabane.** John Edgington.

Below: **In this June 1953 view, 2-6-4T No.8 *Foyle,* which was scrapped in 1955, is the engine on duty. The covered ramp that led from the street to the station can be seen to the right. The tank wagons were used to convey fuel oil from Derry to Killybegs, were it was used by the fishing fleet. When the railway closed this traffic was conveyed in CDR road tankers.** J.H.Price.

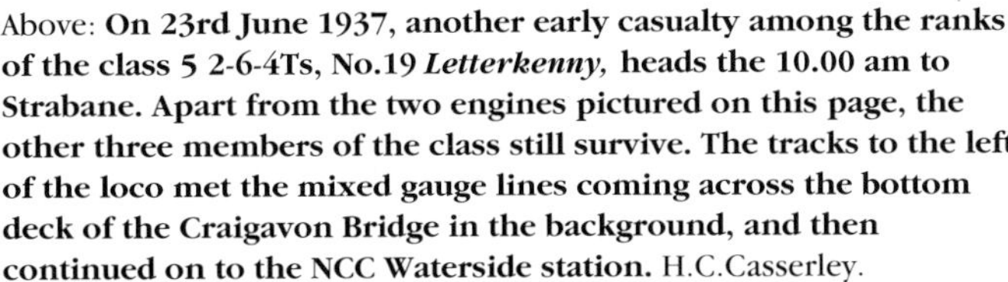

Above: **On 23rd June 1937, another early casualty among the ranks of the class 5 2-6-4Ts, No.19 *Letterkenny,* heads the 10.00 am to Strabane. Apart from the two engines pictured on this page, the other three members of the class still survive. The tracks to the left of the loco met the mixed gauge lines coming across the bottom deck of the Craigavon Bridge in the background, and then continued on to the NCC Waterside station.** H.C.Casserley.

Above: **In a picture, which to judge from the livery of the carriage, was taken in the 1920s or early 1930s, 4-6-4T No.13 *Owenea,* an engine scrapped in 1952, stands outside Victoria Road. On the opposite bank of the river may be observed GNR stock at the terminus of its line from Belfast. Today a 3ft gauge line and preserved CDR vehicles run along part of the old GNR trackbed on the opposite side of the river to where they were originally to be found.** Len's of Sutton.

Top: **Baltic tank No.9 *Eske* leaves Derry with the 10.15am mixed train for Strabane.** Drew Donaldson, courtesy W.T.Scott.

Centre left: **Donemana was the scene of a bad accident on the evening of 7th September 1913 when a driver, somewhat the worse for drink, took his train headed by No.19 *Letterkenny* into the loop at the station at excess speed. One passenger was killed and another seriously injured.** D.Fitzgerald collection.

Centre right: **2-6-4T No.1 *Alice* at Cullion, one of the intermediate stations on the Strabane to Derry line, recorded in 1954, the year the branch closed.** Drew Donaldson, courtesy W.T.Scott.

Left: **A typical mixed Derry line train headed by 2-6-4T No.2 *Blanche,* approaches Strabane. The train is the 1.45pm from Londonderry on 20th April 1948.** H.C.Casserley.

Top left and right: **The first narrow gauge locomotives were a trio of 2-4-0Ts, built by Sharp Stewart in 1881, which maintained the service unaided until 1893. They were named after relations of Lord Lifford who played a prominent part in promoting the WDR. The most notable difference between the maker's photograph of *Blanche* and the later picture of *Alice* is the metal plate wedged on top of the tank at the cab end. Extra supplies of coal were carried on top of the firebox and the plate was to stop them falling onto the track. No.2 *Blanche* was scrapped in 1909 whilst No.1 *Alice*, after a sojourn on the CB&P at the behest of the Railway Executive, from 1918 to 1922, lasted until 1926.**
Both George Haire collection.

Right, second down: **The six class 2 locomotives were the first 4-6-0Ts to run on the Irish narrow gauge. Built by Neilson they were successful machines though somewhat restricted by their low coal and water capacity. To overcome the fuel problem coal was heaped on top of the firebox, as is apparent in this view of No.8 *Foyle* shunting at Stranorlar. This engine and its sister No.4 *Meenglas* were the last survivors of the class, lasting until 1937.**
Len's of Sutton.

Right, third down: **The two class 3 engines, No.10 *Sir James* and No.11 *Hercules,* built by Neilson Reid in 1902, were the only 4-4-4Ts ever to run in Ireland on the 3ft gauge. They had 4ft drivers and were designed to be able to run fast on the recently opened line to Derry in order to compete with the GNR's trains. Both the 4-4-4Ts were withdrawn in 1933.**
George Haire collection.

Right: **Near the end of its career No.10 *Sir James* was photographed at Donegal Town on 6th August 1930.** H.C.Casserley.

Top: **Following the withdrawal of the last of the 4-6-0Ts in 1937, only three classes of steam locomotive remained in use until the end of railway services. The quartet of 4-6-4 or Baltic tanks were built by Nasmyth Wilson in 1904. This firm was to build all subsequent Donegal locomotives. Named after rivers, No.14 *Erne* lasted as long as 1967 when she was cut up at Stranorlar. In this picture No.15 *Mourne,* scrapped in 1952, is at Stranorlar on 7th August 1930.** H.C.Casserley.

Centre left: **The Baltic tanks were followed in 1907 by the first three class 5 2-6-4Ts. The CDR was the only Irish narrow gauge line to make use of locomotives of this wheel arrangement. By benign coincidence the first three delivered have all survived, No.6 *Columbkille* seen here is now at the Foyle Valley Railway centre in Derry.** Len's of Sutton.

Bottom left: **The three class 5A engines built in 1912 had been conceived as being similar to the earlier 2-6-4Ts but with greater water capacity. In fact they were quite sophisticated engines by the standard of the Irish narrow gauge, being fitted from new with superheaters, mechanical lubricators and even speed recorders. To accommodate the additional water required, the tanks were extended almost up as far as the chimney, as can be seen in this broadside view of No.2 *Blanche.* In 1928 these locomotives took the names and numbers of the original WDR trio of locomotives.**

Top right: **The CDR's pioneering work in the development of railcars began with this modest vehicle seen here at Stranorlar. No.1 had been supplied in 1906 as an inspection car with an open body. Rebuilt in 1920 with the 10-seater body, it proved its worth in the course of the coal strike in 1926.** Len's of Sutton.

Below: **In 1949 No.1 was rebuilt again with a larger engine. It is seen in its new form at Stranorlar in May 1950.** H.C.Casserley.

Bottom left: **This is what CDR railcars No.2 and 3 looked like when they were in service with the standard gauge Derwent Valley Light Railway in Yorkshire.** D.Fitzgerald collection.

Bottom right: **No.2 was rebuilt from one of the DVLR vehicles. The body was set much lower to accommodate the CDR's platforms but a surprising amount of bodywork detail is retained. Though they only lasted eight years, these cars were a significant advance on the first railcar, having 17-seat bodies powered by 22hp petrol engines.** Courtesy South Donegal Railway Restoration Society.

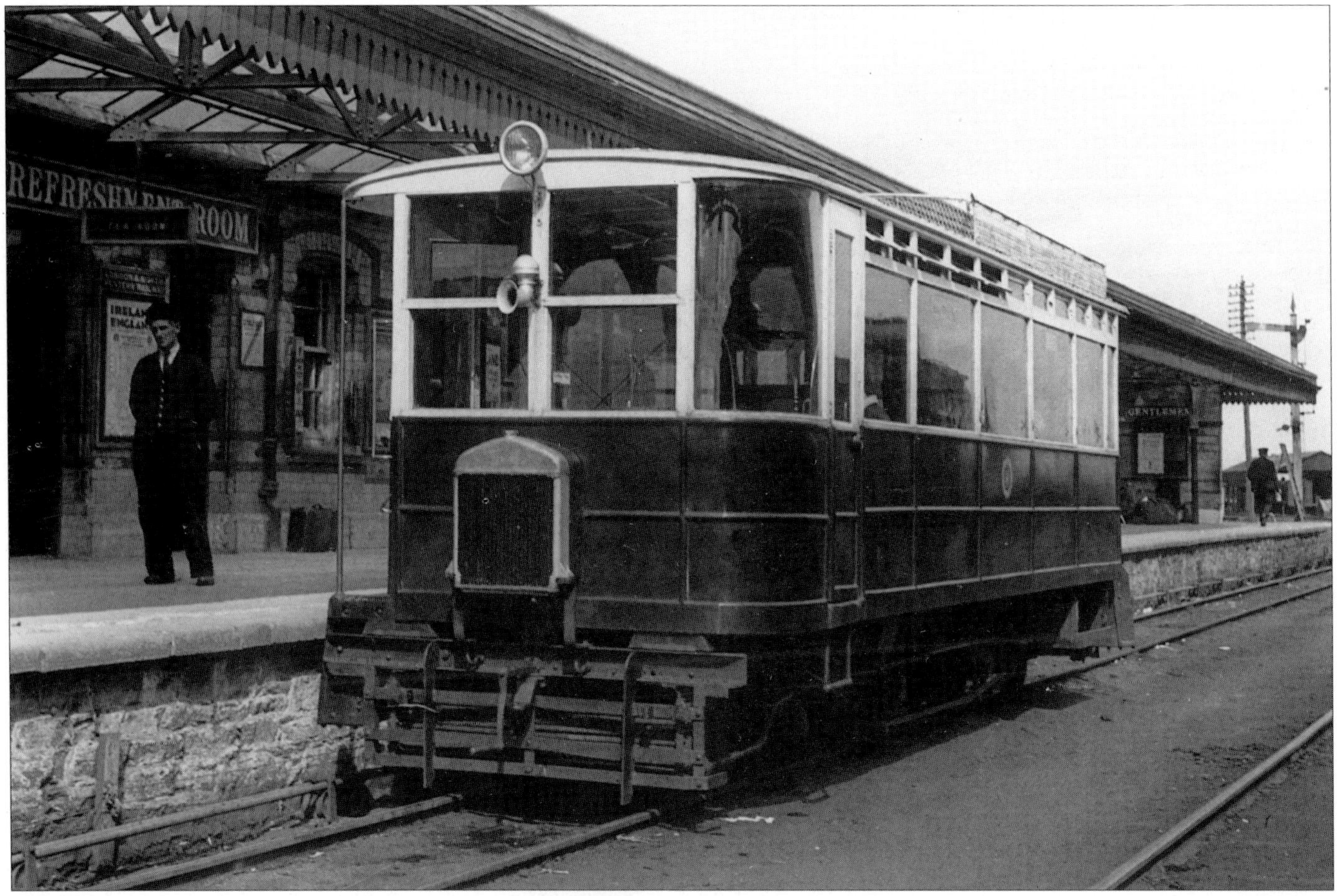
REFRESHMENT ROOM
GENTLEMEN

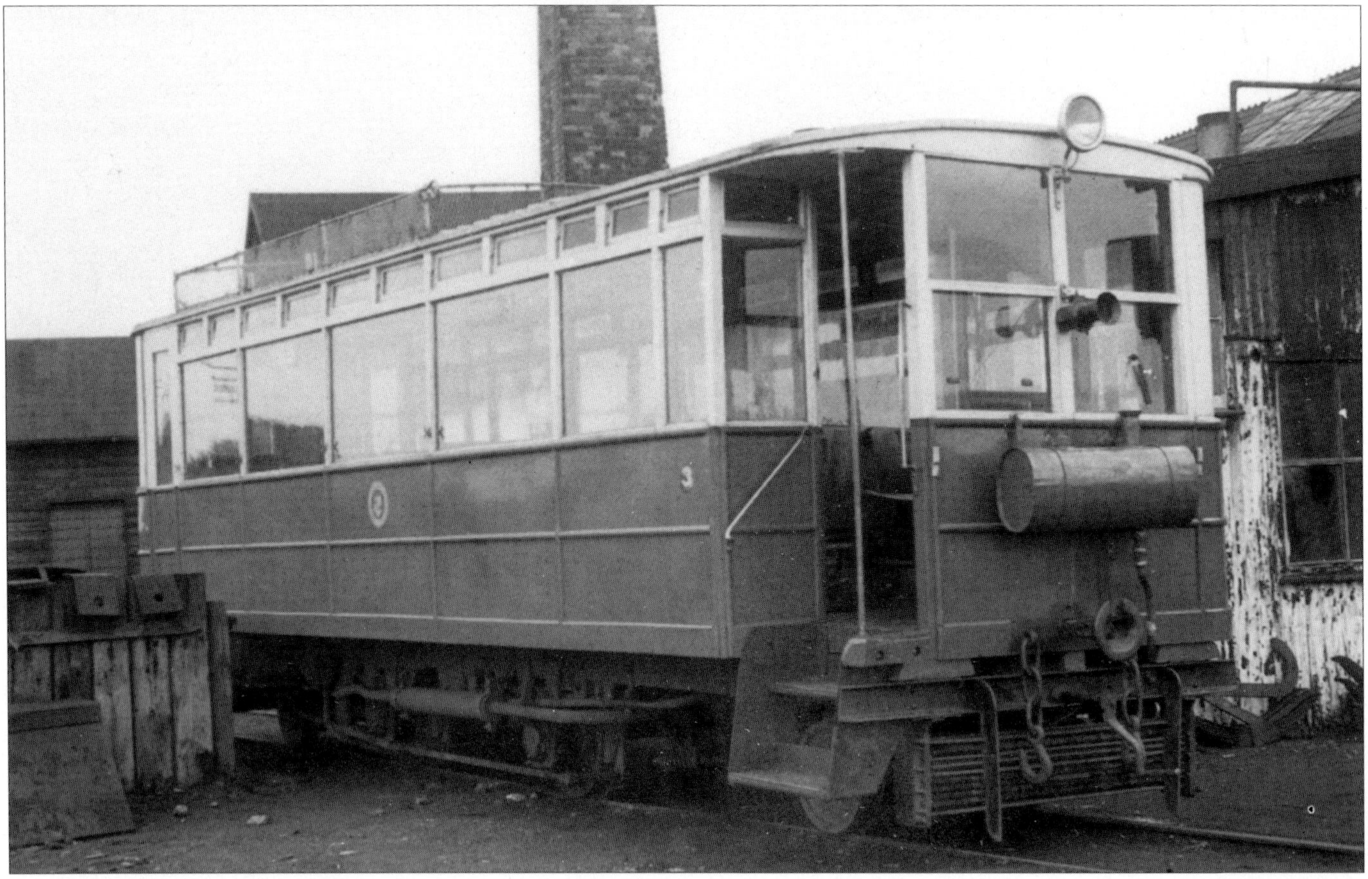
3

Opposite page: **The ex-DVLR railcars were replaced in 1934 by a new No.2, based on a chassis obtained from the recently defunct C&VBT and a new No.3 seen here. This was an eight wheel Drewry railcar bought from the closed Dublin & Blessington Steam Tramway and converted to the 3ft gauge at Stranorlar. This had a 40-seat body and was the only Donegal railcar that could be driven from either end. It was converted to an unpowered trailer in 1944 and finished up in Belfast Transport Museum. No.3,** top, **is seen at Strabane, and** bottom **at Stranorlar in June 1937.** Len's of Sutton (top), H.C.Casserley (bottom).

This page, top right: **Railcar No.4 was constructed at the GNR's Dundalk works in 1928 and lasted until 1947. It combined a Ford 36hp engine and chassis with a 21 seat body built by the Strabane coachbuilders, O'Dohertys.** Courtesy South Donegal Railway Restoration Society.

Bottom: **The railcars were becoming larger and more sophisticated. This is apparent from this picture of Railcar No.6 and trailer No.5. The former was a 1930 collaboration between the GNR and O'Dohertys of Strabane. It had a 32hp Reo engine which drove the rear bogie. The railcar could seat 32 passengers. The four wheel trailer attached to it here was another product of O'Dohertys.**

Centre right: **This picture of the inside of No.6 shows a bus type layout of seats. The secret of the CDR railcars' success is displayed at the front of the vehicle. Their ability to stop at level crossings, farm gates or anywhere that was convenient for their passengers gave them a flexibility that the steam train could not match. The notice on the back of the seats reads: 'Please do not spit on the floor'.** Both photographs courtesy of the Deputy Keeper of the Records, Public Records Office of Northern Ireland.

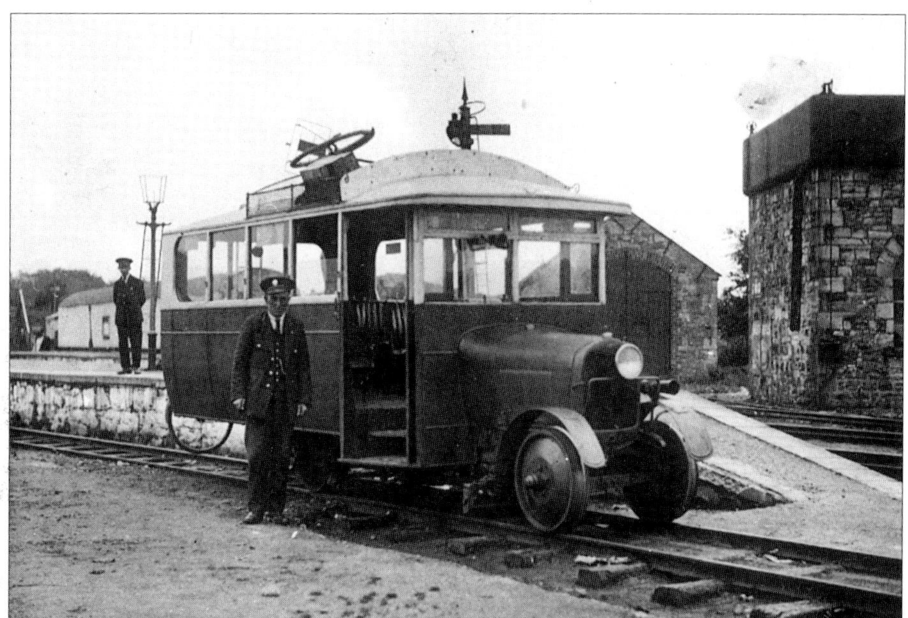

Photographs on the opposite page:

Top left: **Railcar No.7 was a vehicle of considerable historical significance as it was the first diesel railcar to run in regular service in the British Isles. Another joint GNR/O'Doherty production, No7, built in 1930, had a 32-seat body and was powered by a Gardner diesel engine. Seen here at Stranorlar in 1948, it was withdrawn the following year.** H.C.Casserley.

Centre: **No.8 was identical to the first diesel railcar. It was put in service in 1931 and was also withdrawn in 1949. In original condition it is on the turntable at Strabane in the 1930s,** Len's of Sutton.

Top right: **No.8 at the same location near the end of its career on 20th April 1948.** H.C.Casserley.

Bottom: **Railcars 9 and 10 display Henry Forbes' 'waste not want not' attitude to the full. In 1930 the CDR acquired four Reo buses second hand from the GNR. A few years on Donegal's poor roads reduced them to wrecks but Forbes had the two in the best condition converted to railcars. They had 20-seat bodies and were powered by 36hp petrol engines. No.10 was destroyed in an accidental fire in 1939 but No.9, seen here in the shops at Stranorlar, lasted until 1949.** George Haire collection.

Photographs on this page:

Below: **In 1934 the CDR took delivery of Railcar 12 which was to set the pattern for the rest of the fleet. This was the first CDR railcar supplied by the firm of Walkers of Wigan. It combined Walkers' diesel engined power bogie and a body built by the GNR at Dundalk. Two years previously a similar vehicle had been supplied to the CVR and its success there was obviously not lost on Henry Forbes who sat on that line's Committee of Management. No.12 is on the turntable at Donegal Town, on 29th June 1950.** John Edgington.

Bottom: **On the closure of the CVR, that line's pioneering Walker articulated railcar was bought by the CDR. It became No.10 in the CDR fleet. It retained its 28-seat body, making it the smallest of the diesel railcars. On the closure of the CDR it was preserved in Belfast Transport Museum. Photographed at Stranorlar on 24th April 1951.** John Edgington.

Below: **A rare view of a fitter working on the bogie of No.12 at Stranorlar.** Courtesy South Donegal Railway Restoration Society.

Above: **Some of the later Walker articulated railcars are seen here. No.16 was built in 1936 at a cost of £2,408. This car and several others often ran with their engine covers open to allow nature to give their engine's cooling system a bit of assistance. No.16 is seen here at Stranorlar on 29th June 1950.** John Edgington.

Below: **Nos.17 and 18 were built respectively in 1938 and 1940 and had the greatest capacity of all the railcars with bodies that could seat 43 persons. No.17 was destroyed in a collision in 1949, but No.18, seen here in ex-works condition at Stranorlar in June 1950, has been preserved.** John Edgington.

Right: **The ultimate development of the CDR railcar came with the delivery of Nos.19 and 20 in 1950 and 1951 respectively. The later CIE railcars for the West Clare were of the same design as Nos.19 and 20, which can still be seen on the Isle of Man, as they were bought by the IOMR on the closure of the CDR in 1959. No.19 was at Killybegs in June 1953 forming a special train for the Light Railway Transport League.** J.H.Price.

Centre right: **Strabane was the hub of the CDR with lines to Londonderry and Letterkenny in addition to the original Finn Valley line to Stranorlar and beyond. CDR trains used an island platform connected to the adjacent GNR station by a covered footbridge. Railcar No.16, coach 30 and one of the light red painted vans which were hauled by the railcars form the 11.20 train to Letterkenny on 31st May 1957.** F.W.Shuttleworth.

Bottom: **No set of pictures of Strabane is complete without the inclusion of one of the CDR's only diesel locomotive, No.11 *Phoenix,* which was usually to be found shunting there. We first encountered her as a steam tractor on the CVR. Acquired by the CDR and rebuilt with a Gardner engine similar to those used on the railcars, No.11 was preserved in Belfast Transport Museum when the CDR closed.** F.W.Shuttleworth.

Above: **On the other side of the CDR platform, No.2 *Blanche* heads an excursion train in the 1950s. The coach furthermost from the engine is one of the three corridor coaches built by the LMS/NCC for the boat trains between Ballymena and Larne. These were bought by the CDR in 1951.** Len's of Sutton.

Below: **A road by-passing the town has obliterated all traces of Strabane's stations. Nothing remains to remind one that this was once a busy railway junction where scenes such as these were once commonplace.** Len's of Sutton.

Right and centre: **Before we head up the Finn Valley line, our last glimpses of Strabane station reveal Railcar No.20 on the 4.50pm service to Letterkenny on 3rd April 1956, and earlier in the day 2-6-4T No.1 *Alice* on the Letterkenny goods.** Both W.A.C. Smith.

Below: **Relatively few Irish locomotives have escaped the scrapman, so it is pleasing to report that both the engines in this picture are still in existence. In the foreground is CDR No.5 *Drumboe,* whilst in the distance, with a GNR train for Omagh and Belfast, is GNR S class 4-4-0 No.171 *Slieve Gullion.*** Len's of Sutton.

Top: **On the Finn Valley line a short freight rattles over the Urney Bridge, near Clady, the major engineering feature on the line.** Drew Donaldson, courtesy of W.T.Scott.

Left: **The first few miles of the CDR had been in County Tyrone. Castlefinn, the first station in County Donegal, was where the southern Irish Customs examined trains, following the partition of Ireland. No.8 *Foyle* heads the 1.05pm Donegal to Derry train at Castlefinn on 23rd June 1937.** H.C.Casserley.

Bottom: **On 20th April 1948, No.5 *Drumboe,* on the 12.45 Stranorlar to Strabane, has the road. The table on the opposite platform was used by customs officials to examine passengers' luggage. Smuggling became a new industry in the border counties following partition and reached a peak during the Second World War, when northerners headed south in droves to stock up on provisions rationed in the United Kingdom, but freely available in neutral Southern Ireland.** H.C.Casserley.

Top: **The last of the CDR 4-6-0Ts were Nos 9 *Columbkille* and No.8 *Foyle.* Here, the latter is shunting at Stranorlar in the 1930s.** Len's of Sutton.

Above: **Steam days at Stranorlar in the 1930s. 4-6-4T No.14 *Erne* heads the 9.58am mixed train to Strabane on 7th August 1930. The coach livery used by the CDR before the railcar livery of red and cream was introduced to the carriage fleet from the late 1930s onwards, has been described to me, as chocolate brown.** H.C.Casserley.

Right: **A lovely portrait of No.14 *Erne,* on a train for the Donegal Town line.** Len's of Sutton.

Left: **The branch to Glenties, which opened in June 1895, made a junction with the line to Donegal actually in the station at Stranorlar. Immediately beyond the end of the main platform which had been extended to accommodate Glenties trains, the branch crossed the River Finn on a fine girder bridge. Two very different types of motive power are seen here on Glenties services. On 8th May 1920, 4-6-0T No.9 *Columbkille* arrives at the platform with the 4.50pm from Glenties. The lines to the left passing Stranorlar West cabin are for Donegal Town.** Ken Nunn collection.

Below: **Diesel railcar No.8 rumbles across the bridge with the 10.50am from Glenties on 23rd June 1937.** H.C.Casserley.

Left: **Inside Stranorlar shed on 29th June 1950 were 2-6-4Ts No.5 *Drumboe* and No.2 *Blanche*.** John Edgington.

Below: **The points which had controlled entry to the Glenties line are seen in the foreground in front of Railcar No.20.** J.H.Price.

Above: **Railcar 10 has just passed Stranorlar East cabin with a train from Strabane on 20th April 1948.** H.C.Casserley.

Right: **No.11 *Phoenix*, usually associated with Strabane, has risked a trip up to Stranorlar in June 1950.** John Edgington.

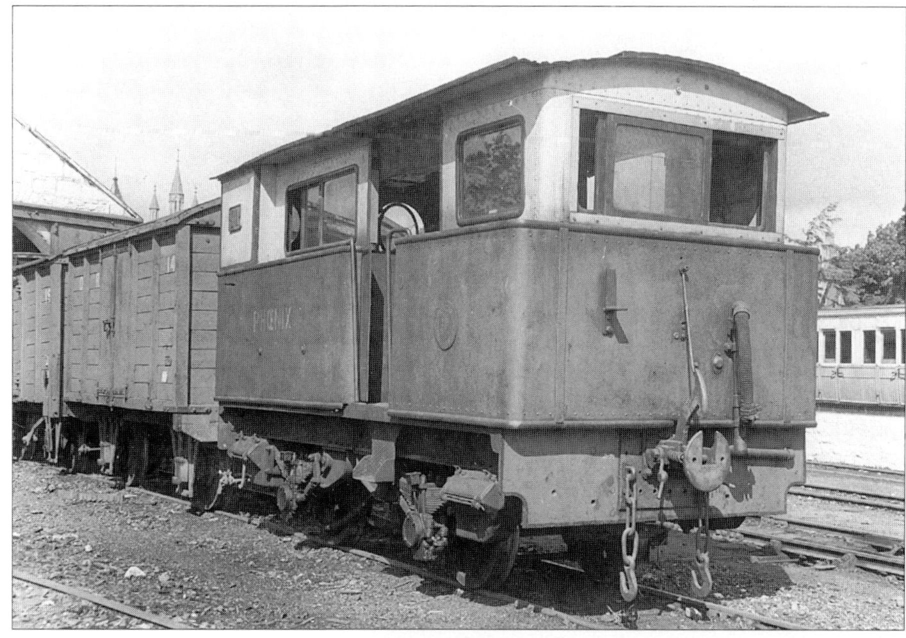

Below: **On 31st May 1957 Railcar No.12 is at Stranorlar's main platform, with a train from Donegal Town. By this time the former Glenties branch had been closed and lifted and a carriage is parked on the stub that remained, leading off the main line at the end of the platform.** F.W.Shuttleworth.

Left: **Lough Eske, then called Druminin, had been the original terminus of the WDR for some years in the 1880s when funds ran out before the line could be completed to Donegal Town. On 20th May 1924, 4-6-4T No.13 *Owenea* pauses with the 10.10 train from Derry to Killybegs. In the 1922 timetable this train had taken 4 hours and 5 minutes to cover the 65 mile journey, an epic of near Lough Swilly proportions.** Ken Nunn collection.

Below: **The three railcars in the picture are on three separate workings. No.12, nearest the camera, has come from Strabane. No.15, behind, has arrived from Ballyshannon, whilst No.16, on the other track was working a service from Killybegs. Donegal Town station was a busy place on the morning of 30th May 1957.** F.W.Shuttleworth.

Opposite page, bottom: **Railcar No.15 pauses at Rossnowlagh on the Ballyshannon branch in May 1957.** F.W.Shuttleworth.

Right: **By the 1950s it was rare to see two engines at Ballyshannon. Class 5 2-6-4T No.6 *Columbkille* and No.4 *Meenglas* had brought a 'Hills of Donegal' excursion into the station. This was a tour which originated on the GNR. The passengers travelled to Strabane where they changed to the narrow gauge for the run to Ballyshannon. They were then escorted from the CDR station, to that of the GNR, over a mile away on the other side of the town. As the engines were being serviced the excursionists were trudging through the streets of Ballyshannon on their way to the next stage of their journey along the GNR branch to the seaside at Bundoran.** Drew Donaldson, courtesy of W.T.Scott.

Above: **The opening of the 3ft gauge line to Ballyshannon on 2nd September 1905, gave the town its second station. The GNR station, on its line to Bundoran, was some distance away to the south of the town. Railcar No.12 has arrived at Ballyshannon on the 2.12pm from Donegal on 21st April 1953.** John Edgington.

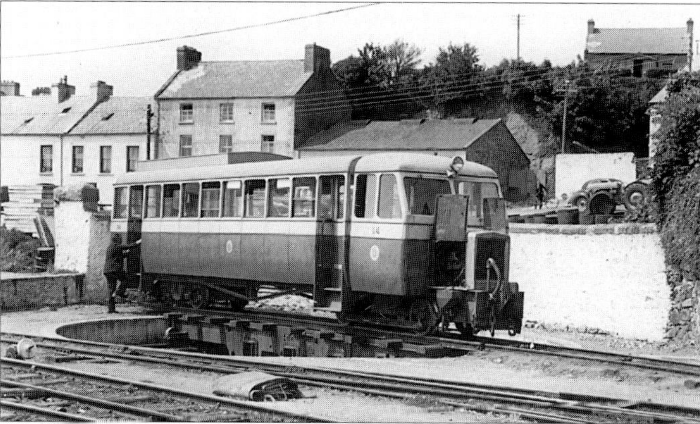

Top left: **Dunkineely was 12 miles from Donegal on the line to Killybegs. Railcar No.12 was on duty with the 1.37pm from Donegal on 21st April 1953.** H.C.Casserley.

Top right: **The turntable at Killybegs was constructed in the 1950s from the frames of withdrawn 2-6-4T No.19 *Letterkenny*.** F.W.Shuttleworth.

Above centre: **Killybegs station, located beside the sea, was one of the most attractive on the CDR. The overall roof was provided to protect the passengers from the worst of the Atlantic weather. This view dates from the summer of 1957.** W.T.Scott.
Below: **Inside Killybegs station.** J.H.Price.

Right: **Photographs of Irish narrow gauge lines under construction are rare but several exist of the S&L as it came so late in the day. The main contractor was Robert McAlpine and Sons, and one of their engines, the Hudswell Clarke built 0-4-0 saddle tank *Isabella* and a steam excavator are seen here at the works near Convoy.** Courtesy of the Deputy Keeper of the Records, Public Record Office of Northern Ireland.

Photographs on the opposite page:

Top: **The Strabane and Letterkenny Railway was not only the last part of the County Donegal system to be built, but the last common carrier narrow gauge line to be opened in Ireland. Leaving Strabane the line curved sharply away from the joint station and the existing Finn Valley line.** Len's of Sutton.

Centre left: **4-6-4T No.14 *Erne* heads a freight from Letterkenny towards Strabane.** Len's of Sutton.

Centre right: **When the CDR ended its rail services in 1959 a fleet of six P class Leyland buses were hired from CIE to operate passenger services on the former rail routes. Until the road bridge over the Foyle at Lifford could be strengthened the CDR built a temporary road over the railway bridge between Strabane and Lifford which had formerly carried the trains to Letterkenny. One of the P class buses is taken on a test drive across the new road.** Joe Curran collection.

Bottom: **Railcar No.20 pauses at Raphoe with the 11.20am service from Strabane to Letterkenny on 20th April 1953.** H.C.Casserley.

ZJ5954

RAPHOE

Left: **We have seen the Swilly shed at Letterkenny in the previous chapter; this is the CDR version. A point of interest is that both the locomotive and the railcar in the picture carry the number 16.** H.C.Casserley.

Centre left: **Railcar 18 was photographed at Letterkenny not long after it had been built in 1940. Its luggage trailer is not dissimilar to those hauled by broad gauge railcars on the GNR.** Courtesy Joe Curran.

Centre right: **2-6-4T No.6 *Columbkille* prepares to take the Strabane goods out of Letterkenny on 31st May 1957.** F.W.Shuttleworth.

Bottom: **The CDR station had a fine canopy on its island platform which was not unlike that at the Victoria Road station in Londonderry.** F.W.Shuttleworth.

Above: **From the beginnings of the railcar fleet a variety of unpowered trailers were utilised to increase the capacity of the railcars. No.13 was originally a powered railcar itself on the Dublin & Blessington Steam Tramway but in the ten years from 1934 in which it ran on the CDR, it was always used as a trailer. It was photographed at Stranorlar in June 1937.** H.C.Casserley.

Above: **No.5 was specially built as a trailer by O'Dohertys of Strabane on a chassis supplied by Knutsford Motors. It could seat 29 passengers and lasted until the end of rail services.** F.W.Shuttleworth.

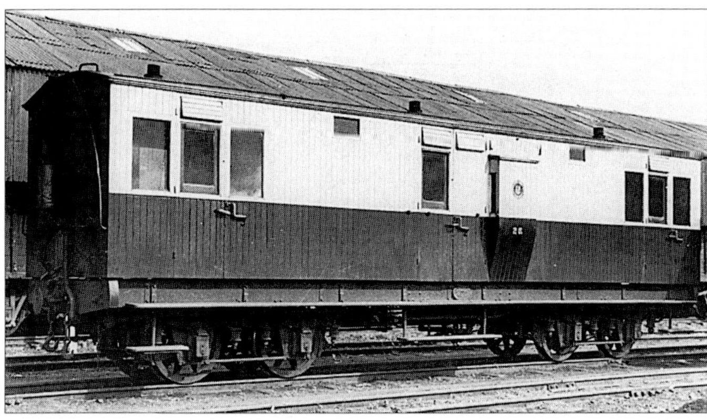

Left: **Bogie passenger brake van No.28, later preserved by the SDR Restoration Society, was built by Oldbury in 1893. There was a third class compartment seating ten passengers on either side of the guard's area. These vehicles were used on both passenger and freight trains. On the latter they provided accommodation for the Guard. The CDR wagons were vacuum braked, so heavy ballasted brake vans were not required.** D.Fitzgerald collection.

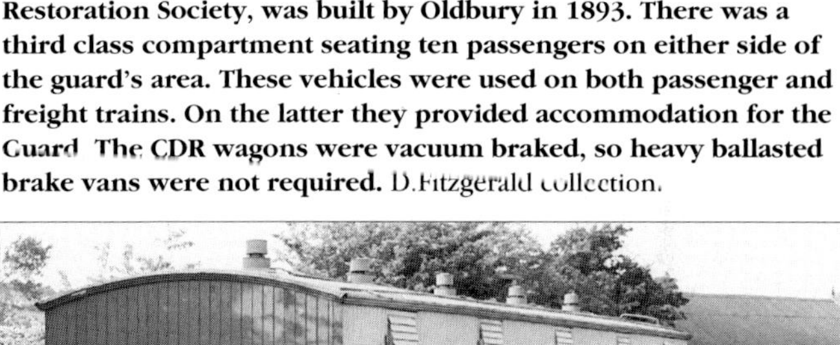

Right and bottom: **Nos.14 and 16 were part of an order for 11 bogie coaches given by the DR to Oldburys to be supplied for the re-gauging of the Finn Valley line and the other extensions to the system. No.14, recorded at Stranorlar in 1957 by F.W.Shuttleworth, has survived into preservation on the Foyle Valley Railway in Derry. No.16, photographed by John Edgington, was not so fortunate, being sold for scrap in 1961.**

Top left: **The original WDR passenger stock consisted of ten 6-wheelers built by the Railway Carriage and Wagon Company. Of these the only surviving example is No.1, the Directors' Saloon, pictured here at Stranorlar in 1937, which was preserved by Belfast Transport Museum.** H.C.Casserley.

Left, second from top: **Coach No.30 was built by Oldburys in 1901. It was one of a batch of six thirds purchased at that time. Unusually for the CDR the vehicle has an internal corridor.** John Edgington.

Below: **These pictures of CDR freight trains are included to show how varied the make up of such trains were. No.19 *Letterkenny* enters Strabane before the last war.** George Haire collection.

Bottom: **No.11 *Erne* is nearing Strabane on the Finn Valley line with a mixed freight. The red and cream liveried brake van can just be discerned at the back of the train.** Len's of Sutton.

Top left: **Over 100 wagons were built between 1881 and 1893. Many of these were still in service in the 1950s. No.13 was one of the first batch of forty supplied by Oldbury in 1882 to the WDR. Covered wagon No.57 came from the same maker in 1893.** F.W.Shuttleworth.

Top right: **Representing the wagons acquired by the CDR from the CVR and the C&VBT is No.228. This ex-C&VBT vehicle is noticeably smaller than the CDR wagons on either side of it.** H.C.Casserley.

Above right: **This picture shows another trans-ship wagon, No.155, carrying the body of No.252.** George Haire collection.

Centre left: **The CDR devised an ingenious system to tackle the problem of transferring goods from one gauge to the other. A number of wagons were fitted with rollers which enabled loads such as stone and coal to be moved onto broad gauge wagons which had compatible fittings. The transfers took place by using the mixed gauge turntable at Strabane. The upright bars at the end of wagon No.252 folded down to enable the load to be moved on or off the narrow gauge chassis.** George Haire collection.

Bottom right: **1893 built wagon No.108 carries one of the containers, which when sealed by Customs, could be used to take goods from County Donegal, through Northern Ireland, to the rest of the Irish Republic.** George Haire Collection.

Chapter Seven

THE BESSBROOK & NEWRY TRAMWAY

PASSENGERS speeding from Belfast to Dublin on today's comfortable expresses run by Northern Ireland Railways and Irish Railways, might just notice, as their train glides over the mighty Craigmore viaduct, north of the mainline station opened in 1984 to serve Newry, a track that looks like any other country lane passing along the valley below. What today's traveller may not know is that this is in fact the trackbed of one of the first electric tramways to run in the British Isles.

The growing and spinning of flax was for many years one of the major industries in Ulster. Some of the first mills in the province were established at Bessbrook in County Armagh where there was a plentiful supply of water to power the machinery. In 1846 these mills were taken over and expanded by the Richardson family, and though a model village was built for the workers at Bessbrook, many of the employees came from the nearby town of Newry. To facilitate these workers, to convey coal and flax up to the mills from the port of Newry and to expedite the movement of the cloth produced in the mills a tramway was mooted in the early 1880s. The first sod was cut on 8th September 1883, though oddly enough this ceremony took place quite some time before the line was officially incorporated on 26th May 1884. It had been decided from the outset that the line would be worked by electricity and construction was entrusted to Dr Edward Hopkinson, a pioneer of electric traction. The line was inspected by Major General Hutchinson of the Board of Trade, who was kept busy in Ireland in the years following the passing of the Tramways Act of 1883. The line opened in October and was worked by the contractor Dr Hopkinson for six months before being handed over to the owning company in April 1886.

Power for the line was produced by hydro-electric generators located at Milvale near Bessbrook. Power collection at 245 volts DC, was from a third rail located between the running rails except for one short section of overhead where the tracks crossed the Newry to Bessbrook road. For this stretch of about 50 yards bow collectors had to be used. The line was just over three miles in length and was built to the 3ft gauge. From its terminus in Newry, adjacent to the Edward Street station of the GNR, the tramway rose steadily on an average gradient of 1 in 86 which steepened to 1 in 50 in places. The Bessbrook terminus was outside the mill.

The original passenger stock consisted of two motor cars and one trailer, all bogie vehicles, supplied by Ashbury. Two more motor cars and a trailer were built by Hurst, Neilson in 1921 and two additional trailers were acquired from the Dublin & Lucan, following that line's closure in 1925. One interesting aspect of the tramway's operations was its handling of freight traffic. The line had 27 4-wheeled goods vehicles with flangeless wheels. These wagons were kept on the track by the simple expedient of an extra rail laid along each side of the running rails at a slightly lower level. The flangeless wheels allowed the wagons to be hauled on the road as well as on the tramway and made for great ease of transhipment thus overcoming one of the main drawbacks of railways for the movement of freight. Perhaps this simple idea should be revived and tried on standard gauge railways today, though it would need some development as the maximum permitted speed was 10mph and the goods vehicles were usually conveyed sandwiched between a power car and a trailer.

Despite this innovative approach to the conveyance of freight, the spread of buses and lorries after the Second World War made the Bessbrook & Newry Tramway another victim of road competition and the last tram ran on 10th January 1948. It had provided an early and successful demonstration of the potential of electric traction and it had served its district faithfully for over sixty years.

Copyright reserved, Ordnance Survey, Dublin. Reproduced from 1 inch series, sheet nos. 59, 60; revised 1900, 1900; published 1901, 1902 respectively. Scale 1 inch to 1 mile.

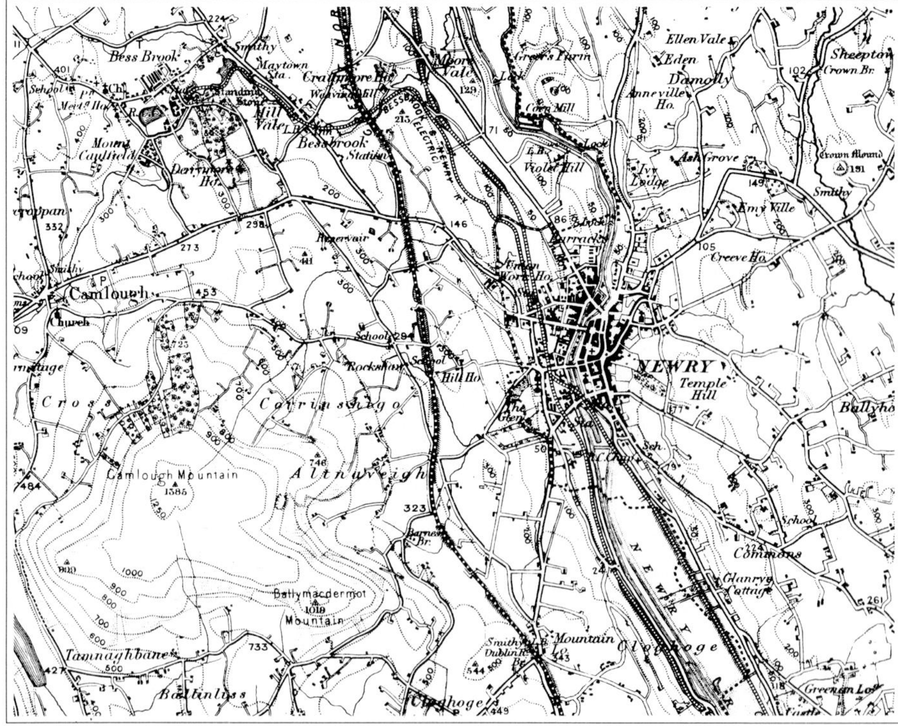

Top right: **Tramcar No.1 stands at the platform at Bessbrook in June 1932. This was the second No.1 on the line, replacing the original 1885 car in 1921. It was built by Hurst, Nelson and Company of Motherwell.** H.C.Casserley.

Centre right: **The car shed at Bessbrook was beside the passenger platform and both were adjacent to the mill, part of which can be seen in the background. The five rails which this line used can be seen in the foreground. The two outer rails were for the flangeless goods vehicles, the pair inside these were the conventional running rails for the tramcars whilst the rail in the centre is the conductor rail from which the tramcars drew their electricity.** H.C.Casserley.

Below: **Two of the flangeless goods wagons, a covered van and a two plank open are seen here, off the rails.** Courtesy Railway Magazine.

Bottom: **This early picture of the tramway, dating from the 1880s, shows the original tramcar No.1, built by Ashbury in 1885, on the road crossing at Millvale – the only place on the line where the overhead collectors of the trams were required.** Ulster Folk and Transport Museum.

Chapter Eight

THE CASTLEDERG & VICTORIA BRIDGE TRAMWAY

IN 1852 the Londonderry & Enniskillen broad gauge line reached the little hamlet of Victoria Bridge in County Tyrone, named logically after the adjacent 1840s built bridge over the River Mourne. A station was opened to serve as a railhead for the surrounding district including the small town of Castlederg, some seven miles distant. Though Castlederg had a population of less than 1,000, it was the market town for quite a large part of west Tyrone and adjoining districts in County Donegal. Complaints about the condition of the road between Castlederg and Victoria Bridge and the charges imposed by carters working on it, mixed no doubt with a degree of civic pride in the town, led to moves to establish a railway. First thoughts were for a broad gauge line from Victoria Bridge, perhaps going on beyond Castlederg in the direction of Donegal Town. However, a more realistic plan was put forward at a meeting in Castlederg in August 1881 for a 3ft gauge tramway from the town to meet the broad gauge at Victoria Bridge.

As first promoted the line was called the Victoria Bridge & Castlederg but by the time its Act was passed its name had been changed to the Castlederg & Victoria Bridge Tramway Company. It was also the first line in the north of Ireland to seek a baronial guarantee. Of the £20,000 required for the construction of the line the Grand Jury of County Tyrone undertook to guarantee £13,000 at 5% for 35 years from the opening of the line. For this the Grand Jury had the privilege of appointing one director.

Interestingly, provision was made in the C&VBT's Act, for guarantees which might be paid out in bad years, to be repaid if the line later prospered and showed a surplus after all expenses and dividends had been covered. I have found no evidence that this ever happened even though, by the modest standards of the Irish narrow gauge, the C&VBT was relatively prosperous for at least part of its existence.

The C&VBT was authorised just before the passing of the Tramways Act of 1883. This attempted to encourage the building of lines such as this. Baronial guarantees had existed long before the passing of this Act, but had the Castlederg line's Act been delayed and if it had been promoted under the provisions of the Tramways Act, the ratepayers of west Tyrone would have benefited from the government assistance available under the new provisions. Major Marindin of the Board of Trade inspected and approved the line in July 1883 and it opened shortly afterwards. The course of the tramway followed the road for most of its length and there were halts at Spamount, Crew – not to be confused with a somewhat larger station with a similar name in Cheshire, and Fyfin. These had sidings but no passing loops. The first half year saw the carriage of what strikes me as the very large number of 16,000 passengers. These had had to cram into the four 4-wheeled carriages that had been acquired for the line's opening.

The first two locos were Kitson 0-4-0T tram engines. They had enclosed motions and condensers to comply with the stiff Board of Trade regulations of the period. A third, similar but slightly more powerful locomotive, was supplied in 1891. Because of a sharp gradient on the approach to the GNR station at Victoria Bridge and the possibility of narrow gauge vehicles breaking away and fouling the broad gauge line, the Board of Trade insisted that the C&VBT fitted continuous brakes to their rolling stock. At considerable expense the little tramway installed the Westinghouse brake, becoming the first line in Ireland to do so. In the light of the Armagh disaster a few years later, the Board of Trade might have been better employed in forcing the GNR to fit continuous brakes. Three further locomotives completed the C&VBT's loco fleet. In 1904 Hudswell Clarke supplied a 2-6-0T and a 0-4-4T in 1912 as replacements for two of the original Kitson tram engines, by then life expired. The railway's final acquisition was a 2-4-0T bought in 1928 from the LMS/NCC narrow gauge lines. As will be seen from the photo section, this Beyer Peacock built engine was very similar to those supplied by that manufacturer to the Isle of Man Railway, some of which are still in service to this day on the island. One final item of rolling stock worth noting was a railcar built on the cheap at Castlederg in 1925 to the designs of the Locomotive Superintendent George Pollard. This seated 24 passengers and was powered by a 20 hp Fordson paraffin engine. It had controls at both ends and was an early example of one man operation with the driver issuing the tickets.

The C&VBT provided a service which usually consisted of three trains daily with an additional service on Fridays and on Fair days in Castlederg. This pattern of service was noted when the line opened and again in 1922. No trains ran on Sundays. Financially speaking the line was less of a disaster zone than some of the small Irish narrow gauge lines, but it could not be described as consistently profitable. Any out of course expenditure could plunge the line into the red and wipe out its modest profits. The tramway had a good war, paying a dividend of 5% in two of the years during which the conflict raged but nemesis was round the corner as it had to face the full rigour of road competition in the 1920s. Regular deficits began to appear in the accounts from 1925 onwards.

In 1932, its last year of operation, expenditure outpaced receipts by £1,026 and the cumulative debt had risen to £4,662. Traffic receipts for 1932 amounted to only £2,166, a decline of some £611 on the previous year and less than half the line's total debt. The tramway was insolvent, whether it could have carried on was rendered academic by the strike which paralysed the railways of Northern Ireland from 31st January to 7th April 1933. This was taken as an opportunity to discontinue the service. A last board meeting was held on 30th September 1933 at which the line's General Manager was appointed as its liquidator. A steam engine left Castlederg for the last time on 27th July 1934 to haul the rolling stock to Victoria Bridge for auction. Some wagons and a loco were bought by the CVR and the remains of the railcar went to the CDR where it was revived as Railcar No.2. Thus was the C&VBT an early victim of the growing attrition which motor vehicles were inflicting on Ireland's 3ft gauge railways.

Copyright reserved, Ordnance Survey, Dublin. Reproduced from 1 inch series, sheet no.25; revised 1913; published 1915. Scale 1 inch to 1 mile.

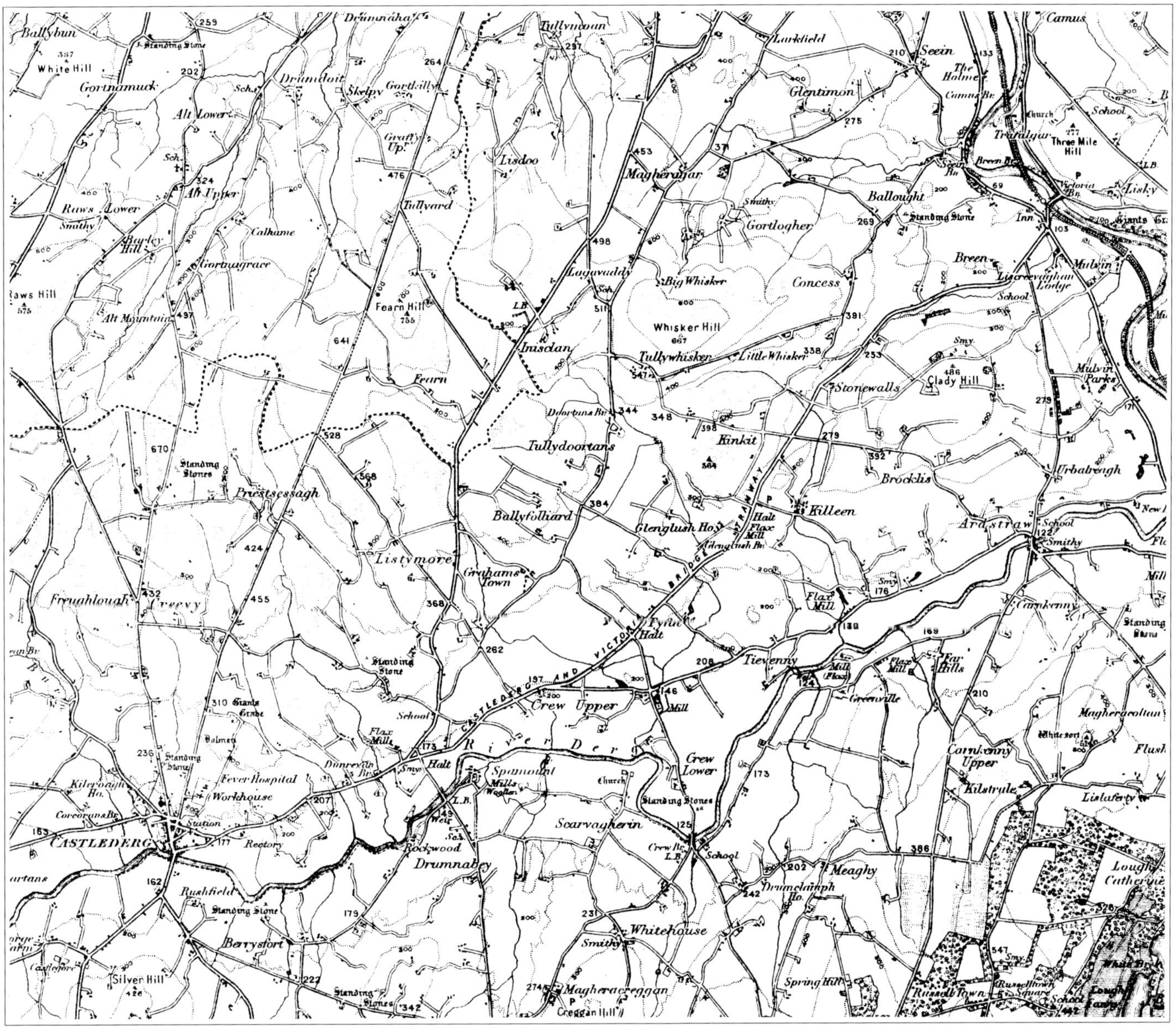

The first two locos bought by the C&VBT were Kitson 0-4-0T tramway engines. No.1 *Mourne* and No.2 *Derg* were named after local rivers and were the only C&VBT locos to be named. Available for the opening of the line in July 1884, they had been withdrawn by 1914. They were joined in 1891 by No.3, another Kitson tramway type, but to an improved design. The first two locos had been totally enclosed but a relaxation of the regulations governing roadside tramways meant that No.3, seen here at Castlederg in May 1924, looked more like a conventional locomotive, being only partially sheeted over. Two odd features of No.3 are worth noting. The cylinders and valve chests were above the frames and to give the crew access to these when the engine was in motion a door was provided, opened by a carriage handle, on the left hand side of the cab. No.3 lasted until 1928 when it was scrapped. Ken Nunn collection.

Above: **This is the other side of No.5 showing the wheels and motion with the Westinghouse pump at the front. No.5 was photographed at Castlederg on 7th August 1930.** H.C.Casserley.

Top left and right: **In 1904 a new engine, much larger than the existing Kitsons, was obtained. This was No.4, a 2-6-0T built by Hudswell Clarke at a cost of £1,600. No.4 weighed 25½ tons, had a boiler pressure of 160 lbs per sq. in. and driving wheels of 3ft 1in in diameter. As these pictures show, C&VBT locomotives had their motions shielded on one side only. This was because they were never turned and always ran with the chimney facing Castlederg. The view of the unprotected side of No.4** (H.C.Casserley) **also shows the Westinghouse brake pump. Westinghouse continuous air brakes had been in use on the tramway since 1886 at the insistence of the Board of Trade.** Len's of Sutton.

Bottom: **In 1912, to replace one of the original Kitson locomotives, a new engine was purchased, a Hudswell Clarke 0-4-4T. This wheel arrangement was chosen as it was felt that it could negotiate the sharp curves on the tramway more easily and with less wear on the track, than the six-coupled No.4. The new engine had less adhesion than the earlier machine. Perhaps this is why it needed the two rather inelegant sandboxes, mounted on the boiler, on either side of the dome.** Len's of Sutton.

Right: **Just one other steam locomotive graced the metals of the C&VT and a most interesting one it was. The line's financial position was already on the decline in 1928 when it became necessary to replace the 1891 built No.3. A new engine was out of the question so the company purchased an old 1877 built 2-4-0T from the NCC. This engine had been supplied by Beyer Peacock to the Ballymena & Larne Railway as their No.4. It became No.64 when the B&NCR took over the B&L and was finally renumbered 105 in 1897. The design of this locomotive was almost identical to those supplied in the 1870s by Beyer Peacock to the Isle of Man Railway, a number of which are still in service on the island. See *Rails in the Isle of Man, A Colour Celebration;* Midland Publishing 1993. Even though the wheels, cylinder and motion have been boxed in, in typical C&VBT fashion, the elegance of the design, so long associated with the Isle of Man, is clear to see.** H.C.Casserley.

Right: **No.5 arrives at Castlederg on 6th August 1930, on a train from Victoria Bridge while No.4 stands outside the shed and workshops to the left of the picture.** H.C.Casserley.

Bottom: **On 7th August 1930 the crew of No.5 pose beside their engine which has just brought a mixed train up from Victoria Bridge.** H.C.Casserley.

Left: **This view was taken at one of the intermediate stopping places, Spamount. The ex-NCC engine poses with some of the tramway's staff and two of the locals in a picture that seems to have been published to commemorate the ending of services on the line.** Michael Pollard collection.

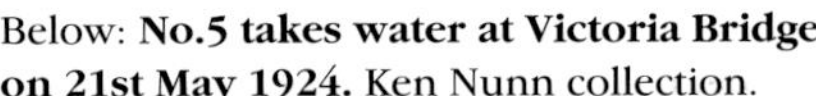

Below: **No.5 takes water at Victoria Bridge on 21st May 1924.** Ken Nunn collection.

Above centre: **No.5 pauses at Spamount in this undated view. It will be noted that the passenger coach at the rear of the train has its wheels protected by skirts, similar to those used on the locos.** Michael Pollard collection.

Above: **No.4 with a cattle train for Victoria Bridge, passing No.5 near Crew. The sight of two engines in steam on the tramway was an unusual one. The reason for this was probably a fair at Castlederg. For decades the conveyance of cattle was an important source of traffic for both broad and narrow gauge railways throughout Ireland.** H.C.Casserley.

Above: **Henry Casserley photographed the remains of the tramway's home made railcar lurking in the undergrowth at Castlederg in August 1930. This had been designed by the line's Locomotive Superintendent George Pollard. The railcar could seat 24 people and was powered by a 20hp Fordson paraffin engine. It had a four wheel chassis with the wheels running on SKF roller bearings. In the three years it was in service it ran 30,000 miles. In 1930 its engine was sold to a saw mill and when the tramway closed the remains of the vehicle were snapped up by Henry Forbes on behalf of the CDR. The chassis was fitted with a Reo petrol engine and a new 30-seat body in 1934. It ran as a railcar until 1944 and afterwards as an unpowered trailer until the closure of the system in 1959.**

Appendix A

THE NARROW GAUGE IN INDUSTRY

ULSTER was the most heavily industrialised of the four Irish provinces. It is not surprising therefore that narrow gauge railways played their part in the industrial life of the province. With the generous assistance of the historian of those minor lines, Walter McGrath, we have compiled this brief selection of some of the more interesting industrial narrow gauge systems which could be found in various parts of Ulster in days gone by.

THE UPPERLANDS HORSE RAILWAY
County Derry

One of the most famous stretches of railway in Ireland was the Fintona branch in County Tyrone, which was operated by a horse tram. Much less well known was a small narrow gauge line in the same province, which lasted longer than the Fintona branch. The two parts of a large linen factory at Upperlands in County Derry, were joined by about ¼ mile of narrow gauge track. Finished cloth was conveyed on bogies, from the part of the factory where it was made to the examining room where it was checked for flaws. These pictures (top right and above) **taken in the summer of 1958, show the line in its sylvan setting, and its motive power called *Fanny*.** Walter McGrath.

THE BRITISH ALUMINIUM COMPANY
Larne, County Antrim.

Above: **From 1900 to 1960 the British Aluminium Company had a plant at Larne Harbour. There was a 3ft gauge railway connecting the works to the harbour and this was used to move both minerals and coal. The line was worked by three diminutive Peckett 0-4-0Ts. This picture of No.1 at rest outside its engine shed, and those on the next page were taken by Desmond Coakham in 1951. No.1 was later preserved and can be seen at work on the Shane's Castle Railway in County Antrim.**

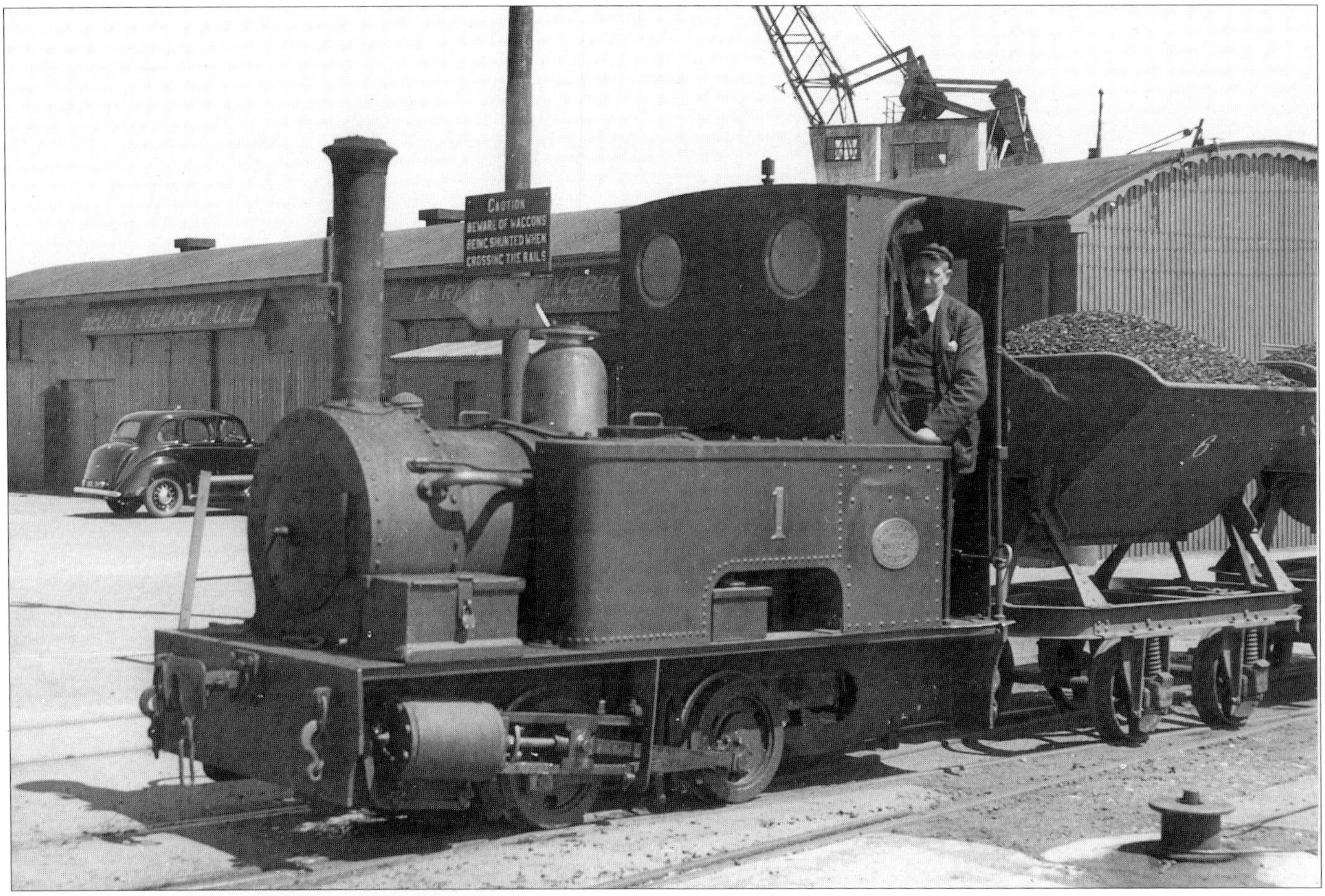

Top: **Shunting on the quays at Larne.**

Above: **Propelling wagons into the works.**

THE CARNLOUGH LIMESTONE COMPANY

As described in chapter two, the origins of the Irish narrow gauge grew out of the need to exploit the mineral wealth of the glens of Antrim. Close to the location of the first 3ft gauge lines, a fascinating industrial railway system was developed in the 1850s, to move limestone, quarried in the hills above Carnlough, to the harbour, for onward transportation by sea. A system of railways with inclines worked by cables and winding engines was built to bring the limestone down to the coast. These lines were constructed to a gauge of 4ft 8½in, which of course in Irish terms is narrow gauge! In the 1890s a new quarry was developed about 2 miles from the mill where the limestone was processed. A railway was built to connect the new quarry to the mill. This had a gauge of 3ft 6ins. The Carnlough Company certainly liked to do things differently; their standard gauge was narrower than that used in the rest of Ireland and their narrow gauge was broader than the Irish standard.

Top right: **Wagons are brought down from the upper quarries. They will go into a head-shunt on the left and then be taken along the tracks leading off the picture on the right, down another incline to the mill.**

Centre right: **This is the mill where limestone was ground. Tracks on the right are 4ft 8½ins, those to the left are mixed gauge.**

Bottom: **At Carnlough Harbour there was a triangular layout of mixed 4ft 8½in and 3ft 6in gauge tracks.** All photos D.G.Coakham.

THE ANNAGHMORE TURF RAILWAY

The exploitation of Ireland's peat bogs is normally associated with the south of the country. There was however a remarkable bog railway to be found in County Armagh near the shores of Lough Neagh. The Irish Peat Development Company began to produce peat, mainly for agricultural and horticultural purposes, from about 1907 onwards. A 3ft gauge railway was constructed which had about 8 miles of track, over which, from 1907 until the 1950s, worked the only 3ft gauge electrical locomotives (as opposed to tramcars) in Ireland. The two locomotives were built in Belfast and it must be said that they looked like garden sheds on wheels. They propelled rather than pulled their wagons, which was also unusual. The trolley pole was located at the side of the locomotive and not in the centre as is the usual arrangement. The overhead was at the side of the track supported on wooden poles. The company had its own generating station whose boilers were naturally fired by turf. In the 1950s electrical haulage was phased out and two diesels took over. The railway ceased operations in the 1960s but in 1988 part of the line was reopened to form an attraction at the Peatlands Country Park which was developed in the area and the two original diesels, which had survived, have been restored and are now used to haul visitors through the park – *see page 124.*

Top: **In 1953 one of the electrical locomotives propels a train of peat into the factory at Maghery where it was milled. Note the unusual position of the trolley pole.** Walter McGrath collection.

Centre left: **At one point the railway traversed this long low viaduct where it ran alongside a public road. This scene was recorded in September 1954.** Walter McGrath collection.

Bottom: **One of the diesels was a Planet and the other was this German built Schoema, seen crossing over a road on one of the several ungated crossings on the line.** Walter McGrath.

Appendix B

THE NARROW GAUGE REVIVED

THE CLOSURE of the CDR at the end of 1959 was not quite the end of the narrow gauge in Ulster. Bord na Mona continued to operate a 2ft gauge system near Glenties in County Donegal – *see page 119* of *Irish Railways in Colour*, Midland Publishing, 1992 – and in recent years the 3ft gauge has seen a modest revival in the province, though in a form very different from that pictured in the preceding chapters. We conclude our story of the narrow gauge in Ulster with these views of the narrow gauge today, making its contribution to the leisure and tourist industry.

Above: **The Shane's Castle Railway runs through the estate of Lord O'Neill near Antrim. In May 1977 No.1, the Peckett 0-4-0T which we previously saw on pages 117 and 118, working for British Aluminium at Larne, is at the line's Shane's Castle terminus near the shores of Lough Neagh.** Richard Whitford.

Below: **The other steam locomotive which is a regular performer on the line is the former Board na Mona 0-4-0T No.3. All three of these locos, built by Andrew Barclay in 1949, have been preserved. Is this some sort of record for a complete class to have survived?** Richard Whitford.

Shane's Castle is on the north eastern shore of Lough Neagh, the biggest freshwater lake in the British Isles. On the opposite south western shore of the lake can be found the Peatlands Country Park which now covers the district where the Irish Peat Development Company once operated their unique electrically powered industrial railway system – ***see page 122.*** **Part of the narrow gauge line has been revived and the original diesel locomotives have been restored to convey visitors through the park. In August 1990 the German built Schoema diesel locomotive brings a train into the line's terminus after a trip through the park.** Richard Whitford.

The narrow gauge is stirring from its slumbers in the north west of Ireland as well. On the site of the old GNR broad gauge station at Foyle Road in Londonderry, a fine museum building has been built and 3ft gauge track is being laid on part of the former GNR trackbed out from the city. Various items of CDR rolling stock are to be seen or are in the course of restoration. Railcar No.12 stands at the platform on 6th April 1991. The CDR station in Derry was located on the opposite bank of the River Foyle to where the narrow gauge revival in the city is taking place. Plans exist to extend the line over the county boundary and into County Donegal itself. Thanks to the EC it will no longer be necessary to have Customs officials stopping and examining the trains as was the case in the heyday of the narrow gauge in County Donegal.
Des McGlynn.

In County Donegal itself, an ambitious project is under way to rebuild one of the most scenic stretches of the old CDR – that which ran through Barnesmore Gap between Stranorlar and Donegal Town. The South Donegal Railway Restoration Society is working hard to raise the necessary funding from Irish government and EC sources for the rebuilding of the line which would be a major tourist attraction for the region if it came to fruition. In our picture 2-6-4T No.5 ***Drumboe*** **is unloaded at the society's base in Ballybofey. She bears the scars of many years of neglect, lying derelict at Strabane but I am sure that many readers of this book will have travelled behind former British Railways locos which were rescued from Barry scrapyard in similar or worse condition. Steam engines are made of stern stuff and I very much look forward to the day when she steams once again.**
South Donegal Railway Restoration Society.

SELECT BIBLIOGRAPHY

The Ballycastle Railway: E.M.Patterson; David & Charles.

The Ballymena Lines: E.M.Patterson; David & Charles, 1968.

The County Donegal Railways: E.M.Patterson; David & Charles, 1969.

Encyclopaedia of Narrow Gauge Railways of Britain and Ireland: Thomas Middlemass; Patrick Stephens Limited, 1991.

The Giant's Causeway Tramway: J.R.McGuigan; Oakwood Press, 1964.

In the Days of the Clogher Valley: Jack Johnston; Friar's Bush Press, Belfast.

The Irish Narrow Gauge Railway: J.D.C.A.Prideaux; David & Charles.

Irish Steam: O.S.Nock; David & Charles.

Light and Narrow Gauge Locomotives: Light Railway Handbook No.8, R.W.Kidner; Oakwood Press, 1949.

The Londonderry and Lough Swilly Railway: J.I.C.Boyd; Bradford Barton.

The Lough Swilly Railway: E.M.Patterson; David & Charles.

The Narrow Gauge Railways of Ireland: Light Railway Handbook No.4, 3rd edn. R.W.Kidner; Oakwood Press, 1949.

The Portstewart Tramway: J.R.L.Currie; Oakwood Press.

Some Industrial Railways of Ireland: Walter McGrath; Walter McGrath, 1959.

Journal of the Irish Railway Record Society, Spring 1956, D.B.McNeill: *The Clogher Valley Railway.*

Journal of the Irish Railway Record Society, Autumn 1959, A.T.Newham: *The Castlederg & Victoria Bridge Tramway.*

The Railway Magazine – Vol.86, No.515, May 1940: *The Bessbrook & Newry Tramway.*

Immediately south of Strabane station the CDR and the GNR crossed the River Mourne on two separate bridges. Up to the change of gauge in 1894, the Finn Valley Railway and latterly the Donegal Railway, had shared the GNR bridge which can be seen on the left of the picture. To coincide with the change of gauge a new bridge and narrow gauge station in Strabane were built. Railcar No.20 enters Strabane by a MR/NCC somersault signal. W.A.C.Smith.

INDEX

Numbers in *italic* refer to illustrations. Only one illustration is given for each entry in the index though in many cases, several photographs of the same geographical location or locomotive are to be found in the book.

As the last train of the day is captured pulling away from Ballycastle station by Henry Casserley on 18th April 1948, and rattles off over the viaduct to make its main line connection at Ballymoney, just over 16 miles away, perhaps this is an appropriate place to offer some final reflections on the Irish narrow gauge.

At the end of the twentieth century, when personal transportation is so dominated by the private car and the railways have largely abdicated freight haulage to the juggernaut, it is difficult to appreciate how important these lines were to the communities they served in their heyday. The closest you can come to experiencing something of what the Irish narrow gauge lines must have been like in the British Isles today, is probably the steam railway on the Isle of Man. From the perspective of a railway enthusiast the trip from Douglas to Port Erin is an absolute delight, though to those whose experience of travel by rail is mainly restricted to air conditioned stock running on continuously welded rail, the journey comes as a bit of a shock to the system. Travel on the Isle of Man is slow, noisy and on track which has probably seen better days, the ride is lively. One is left with a healthy respect for those who ventured from Londonderry to Burtonport or Tynan to Maguiresbridge. Lengthy journeys on the 3ft gauge were not for the faint hearted – or perhaps we have become *effete* as the century progressed?

It takes some effort to put ourselves in the position of the promoters of the narrow gauge lines built in the last century. They saw these thin ribbons of steel as the means to improve and develop the districts they served and even to make some money as well, though it must be emphasized that profitability was an aspiration rather than a reality for most of the railways dealt with in this book and its companion volume.

When their only competition was the horse and cart, labour was cheap and they had a virtual monopoly of the often meagre traffic in the districts they served, the narrow gauge lines were secure. However, once the bus and the lorry, and in later years the private car, began to make inroads into their traffic, many of the 3ft gauge lines were quickly in trouble.

The narrow gauge railway was a late nineteenth century solution to the problem of extending the benefits of railway communications to remote districts where the traffic likely to have been on offer would not have justified the construction costs of a standard gauge railway. That there were more districts in Ireland answering this description than in the rest of the kingdom and that there were some government incentives in the form of grants and loans, was the reason for popularity of the narrow gauge on that island.

With the revolution brought about in the world of transport in the years following the Great War by the spread of the internal combustion engine, what is remarkable is not that a few of the 3ft gauge lines in Ulster closed in the 1920s and 1930s, but that some of them survived into the second half of the century.

The era of the narrow gauge as portrayed in these pages is now history. We are fortunate that the photographers have recorded much from those years, so that we can relive through these pictures, not just the locomotives, the operations and the atmosphere of the narrow gauge lines, but that a glimpse of the social history of the communities they served may also be revealed.